Creating Spaces of Freedom

Culture in Defiance

Creating Spaces of Freedom examines three alternative spaces of freedom: exile, margins and mass attention – in other words, giving ground, going underground and taking up the challenge in the public arena. Both written and visual essays illustrate these distinct spaces. By appearing independently of each other, text and images should be read separately.

Edited by
Els van der Plas
Malu Halasa
Marlous Willemsen

Saqi Books, London
Prince Claus Fund Library, The Hague

2002

Editors: Els van der Plas, Malu Halasa, Marlous Willemsen
Image and Final Editing: Els van der Plas, Malu Halasa
Design: irmaboom@xs4all.nl, assistant Sanne Beeren
Assistant Editors: Nupu Chaudhuri, James Westcott
Copy Editors: Jo Glanville, Louise Gray
Translators: Nahed El Gamal, Jaime Flórez, Doris Hefti, Nina McPherson, Shirin Shenassa, Hazel Wachters, Amelia White, Veronique Whittall

Published by the Prince Claus Fund, the Netherlands and
Saqi Books, Lebanon / United Kingdom
Printed in the Netherlands
British Library Cataloguing-in Publication Data
A catalogue record for this book is available from the British Library

ISBN 0 86356 736 3

This edition is first published in 2002

Prince Claus Fund
Hoge Nieuwstraat 30
2514 EL The Hague
The Netherlands
www. princeclausfund.nl

Saqi Books
26 Westbourne Grove
London W2 5RH
England
www.saqibooks.com

Prince Claus
Fund Library

Saqi
Books

Wole Soyinka gave a speech on the occasion of the launch of *Creating Spaces of Freedom*, ICA London, 5 February 2002

Demonstration, Tiananmen Square, The People's Republic of China (PRC), 1989

In a bulldozer shovel, workers in the Chinese capital of Beijing wave placards and shout slogans in front of the Forbidden City in Tiananmen Square on 25 May 1989. The next day, the last ten buses protecting the hunger strikers were taken away, even though student demonstrators voted to continue the hunger strike against martial law. A new emblem was needed. The ten-metre high, plaster-made Goddess of Democracy statue was unveiled in the square on 30 May. In secret transcripts leaked from China, one of Deng Xiaoping's advisers called the statue 'neither human nor demon'. The reaction of retired General Wang Zhen was 'Give [the students] no mercy!' Photo: Catherine Henriette/ANP

Contents Images

Contents Text

Els van der Plas, Malu Halasa, Marlous Willemsen

'A Delirium That Rises from a World of Mud'[1]: Creating Spaces of Freedom

The Indonesian artist Heri Dono writes in his monograph: 'People find it difficult to confront and express the truth and the reality of their lives. Fear is the disease which prevents them from saying what they want to say. The word of truth cannot always run in a straight course but, like the *kris* [Javanese knife], has a wavering edge. Some people have to use a coded, slang language, or write graffiti as the only means by which authority and government can be criticised.' In 1995, he was given a retrospective exhibition in London, which was accompanied by this monograph, a small, engaging book containing Dono's own images and texts. These texts led the Indonesian government to threaten to ban Dono from the land of his birth, if the book were to become more widely available. (He was staying in London at the time.) The London Institute for New International Arts (INIVA), the book's publishers, decided not to distribute it, which enabled Dono to return home. He had to wait until 1998 when, partly due to the student uprisings, Suharto finally stood down and Dono could put the book back in circulation. In 1998, Dono was presented with a Prince Claus Award for his work and for promoting political debate through his art. He is one of the many in this book who have created a space for cultural freedom for both themselves and others. *Creating Spaces of Freedom* focuses attention on these places, which provide cultural refuge and which in times of oppression offer opportunities for freedom of speech and thought.

Duong Thu Huong, the Vietnamese author of *Paradise of the Blind* (written in 1988) and *A Novel Without a Name* (smuggled out of Vietnam in 1991) explains in her keynote essay for this book, 'Freedom: An Imaginary Space for the Survival of Writing', that she has had to learn how to be free; free – despite the oppression she was subjected to in prison, despite her country's regime and her powerlessness to oppose it. 'Freedom is in the mind,' writes Duong, which is why she is able to feel free.

This is the complete opposite of Janis Joplin's lyrics, 'Freedom's just another word for nothing left to lose'; a cry for help from a desperate pop singer trapped by uncertainty and drugs, who, as a young woman in a so-called 'tolerant' western society, feels hemmed in and threatened in a very different way. Over 30 years later in 1999, on the other side of the pop world, the Algerian-French band Gnawa Diffusion sings, 'I would like to be an armchair in a hair salon for ladies/ so that the bottoms of these beautiful souls/ would crush against my pride ...'; lyrics that proved too liberal for Algeria. However, these scandalous words still manage to reach the youth of Algiers through illegally imported tapes.

The fourteen essays in *Creating Spaces of Freedom* aim to illuminate the various nuances of the concept of freedom, in relation to a physical or spiritual space in which people may operate: exile, the margins and mass attention. Structured along these lines, the anthology is especially concerned with cultural spaces that have been found or created by writers and artists, which also

Demonstration, Tiananmen Square, PRC, 1989

When six military convoys entered Beijing, city inhabitants shouted at the soldiers, 'You are Chinese. So are we. Go home and leave Beijing!' Some people sat in front of the convoys to stop them from moving. The first group of 500 soldiers managed to get as far as the Beijing Hotel across from Tiananmen Square. The next day more than 100 tanks occupied the square, although four had been stopped for twenty minutes by a lone protester. On June 4, Chinese troops crushed the demonstrations, killing hundreds. Snipers from the 27th Army division shot people in the head and in the heart.

Photo: Catherine Henriette/ANP

Taliban, Afghanistan, 1996

When Afghanistan's Taliban movement to create a pure Muslim state began in 1996, the ban on 'morally corrupting' media was crucial. Local journalists criticising the movement had families tortured or issued with death threats. Many have since fled to neighbouring countries for safety. Afghanistan's television station was shut down and access to foreign media through satellite dishes was banned. Television sets, books and video and audio tapes were taken from private homes and destroyed in public. Above, ruined cassettes, a testament to culture lovers, hang from a powerline. Photo: Hugo Philpott/AFP offer a refuge for other seekers of freedom without immediately putting them in danger. Just as there are no borders between these spaces, analyses also overlap. *Creating Spaces of Freedom* surveys the creation of alternatives through which suppressed art can seek refuge in order to continue the passing on of its message. The book also focuses on 'locations of freedom', where the weed can outgrow any danger of extinction, and it is these different types of freedom-creating strategies that offer opportunities and, more importantly, hope.

Public space is the obvious area that attracts the most attention. Here, critics are able to make their stand in the public arena. They aim at broad, often international exposure and challenge their opponents openly, while being protected by the large numbers who witness the message. The Qatari satellite channel Al-Jazeera broadcasts all over the Arab world. As the only news organisation operating in Kabul in the aftermath of the 11 September 2001 terrorists attacks in New York City, it assumed a new importance, in some places notoriety. Al-Jazeera uses mass media to create a space for anyone who needs one. 'To present a view we must also present the other view,' explains the channel's managing director. Al-Jazeera does just this. Egyptian social analyst Ahmed Abdalla researches the unique space of freedom realised by Al-Jazeera.

'Freedom comes, like control, in many guises,' writes the Indian multimedia expert Kiran Karnik in his essay, which explores the power and impotence of another public arena: the internet. Almost universally accessible, the internet seems to be creating a new world without borders. But the freedom of the internet also provides oppressors – such as neo-Nazis and pornographers – with the means to spread their messages and images via the worldwide web. The government in Germany began a campaign to try to remove neo-Nazis from the internet, while oppressive regimes elsewhere are trying to deny artists and writers access. Neither are sinecures. Paradoxically, it was the American army who designed the net because military defence needed a network that was independent and difficult to trace. This virtual space, which is used by millions, cannot be controlled and censured through traditional methods. The internet is therefore the ultimate form of individual freedom for everyone who has access to a computer and a telephone.

Individuals can also enjoy relative safety in the mass adoration of their fans, such as the pop idols in bands like Junoon in Pakistan and Molotov in Mexico. Both are described in this anthology respectively by the Pakistani journalist and democracy campaigner Arif Azad and the Mexican poet and writer Carmen Boullosa. Due to their popularity, these pop heroes are often able to sing what they want and perform their music freely. However, huge popularity does not always offer sufficient protection: the 26-year-old Raï singer Cheb Hasni was shot dead on the way to a football match in Algeria. If the murderers intended to initiate a decline in the popularity of Raï music through this act, it backfired. Raï became more popular than ever before. However, because of the complex political situation surrounding the music, Raï musicians are sometimes forced to nestle in the margins of society.

The huge popularity of the critical Colombian comic Jaime Garzón, who promulgated humorous analyses of politics, drugs and the relationship between them, also appeared to allow him more freedom than others. His assassination sent a shock wave through the Colombian nation. Garzón's funeral thus became a radical political statement against corruption and crime.

As luck would have it, major media coverage sometimes offers protection. It can also be used to communicate difficult and forbidden messages. Soap operas in some countries carry messages about taboos. The Brazilian soaps make controversial subjects like homosexuality, adultery and AIDS accessible to millions. Laura Graziela Gomez discusses this media form in her essay 'The Case of Brazilian *Telenovelas*'.

There are governments who will not tolerate any form of opposition, and there are courageous people who steadfastly uphold the counter-current. In a moving, personal letter to the editors of this book, Duong Thu Huong writes, 'My existence is an act of defiance against this regime. For a long time they have wanted to crush me. They may lock me up again at any time. And I myself am ready to go to prison any day. I am sure of this. It is my fate and my choice. If my name were not yet on the list of those protected by Amnesty, I think I would now be in another place.' In her essay, she explains how freedom has been one of the most misused words in literary history. For her, freedom is something fragile and precarious, something special. For most westerners, she writes, it is as normal as a streetlamp.

The Cuban physicist and writer Ernesto Ortiz Hernández describes the freedom of light through the symbol of the *vitral* [vitrail], a stained glass window. In this he refers to the subtitle of the magazine *'Vitral, La Libertad de la Luz'* – the liberating light radiated by the magazine *Vitral* across the Cuban intellectual landscape. Under the protection of the Roman Catholic Church, *Vitral* operates from the margins of a totalitarian state. Using the intellectual and cultural talents with which Cuba is so generously endowed, the journal tries to be both of good quality and critical. A brave activity from the margins on the part of both the protector and the editors, *Vitral* is made up of 'hundreds of collaborators who dare to be free and are fully aware of, and some are suffering from, the consequences of expressing and writing different ideas, according to their conscience ... They take responsibility for their opinions ... They are citizens who exercise their right not to live a lie,' writes Hernández.

Reinaldo Arenas was another Cuban who dared to err on the side of truth. He thwarted the censors, smuggled his novels abroad and, through his actions, told the familiar story of cultural repression. Story-tellers have always held a special place in central and south America, where novelist and academic Edmundo Paz-Soldán examines the impact of 'an eclectic new generation' of fiction writers, born in the Sixties, 'who engage literarily with problematic and controversial issues affecting Latin American societies.' Their works suggest a reality contrary to that which some governments and revolutionary movements have maintained by force, and one that has been propped up by other, more accepted, 'official' writers.

To escape the lies, some choose the relative freedom of exile, like the Nigerian writer Wole Soyinka. 'When and where is exile?' he asks himself in his essay on the subject. Is every writer or artist not in a permanent state of exile, 'lifting, shattering and confronting barriers of control and repression'? And is exile not a different experience for everyone? Where some desperately immerse themselves in the unhappiness of their forced exile (as in the case of the South African writer Arthur Nortje), others consciously choose another country (such as the Nigerian author Ben Okri).

Like Soyinka, many artists leave their restrictive environments and move to cities beyond the reach of their oppressors. They move to 'external cultural capitals', such as London for the Pakistanis or Cairo for the Sudanese who have fled their country's civil war. According to the journalist Ahmed Al-Mukarram, engagement in cultural activities – from publishing to painting and film-making – remind the Sudanese of a vibrant, multiethnic homeland that has been decimated by the fundamentalist government in Khartoum. From Cairo, exiled artists and writers continue to exert influence on the situation in their country of birth, until they go home.

In 1995, the Algerian comedian Mohamed Fellag moved to Paris, where he has made humour a platform for the discussion of Algerian taboos relating to colonisation and post-colonial problems of corruption. To his audiences in France and Algeria, his tapes and texts come as a great relief. He has described humour as a form of freedom: 'Laughing where it hurts. That's my way of

Jaime Garzón, Bogota, Colombia, 1999

In the capital city of Bogota, Colombians pay their respects to the best-loved comic Jaime Garzón who was murdered by two gunmen on a motorcycle. Garzón 'had a deep sense of justice and was, by nature, a blabbermouth ... He did imitations of politicians and prominent people in his programmes. [A] court jester, [he] said what other Colombians thought, but didn't dare to say.' Mourners hold flags with the words, 'No Mas' [No More] – a call for an end to the country's long-running civil conflict. Garzón was buried on 20 August 1999. Authorities blame right-wing death squads for his murder, a charge denied by the paramilitary gangs. (Ineke Holtwijk, *De Volkskrant*, 20 August 1999) Photo: AP

Demonstration, Bogota, Colombia, 1999

On 24 October 1999, thousands of Colombians marched through the streets of Bogota in support of the peace talks which began in the Colombian city of La Uribe. People hoped that the talks would end the civil conflict that has left more than 120,000 people dead since 1964. Comic Jaime Garzón was killed, probably because he supported the talks. Earlier in the year, he 'brought together a number of influential people to try to quickly settle a peace agreement between the government and the ELN, the second largest guerrilla group in Colombia. After that, Garzón began to receive threatening telephone calls.' (Ineke Holtwijk, *De Volkskrant*, 21 August 1999) Photo: Valerie Berta/ANP combating the evils which eat away at my country: poverty, censorship, taboos, intolerance, machismo, hatred of love, fatalism ... if I weren't laughing myself along with the audience, I would feel like suicide.' Fellag has contributed his performance on censorship to *Creating Spaces of Freedom*.

Humour is an excellent form of resistance that offers catharsis, itself a form of freedom. Rich Eisendorf and Jens Robinson elaborate on this topic in relation to the function and role of cartoons in certain countries in the world. The series of cartoons printed in this book speak volumes. 'Shoot the guy, he is against our democratic elections' by Jens' father, the activist editorial cartoonist Jerry Robinson, from the Seventies, is one of many devastatingly simple comic complaints against injustice.

Humour shares these functions of resistance, as well as catharsis, with literature and the arts. Throughout the book, subtle, courageous, humorous, beautiful and impressive forms of art are presented which seek out the borders of freedom, or rather, find the free borders. For example, the multimedia art of the Indian artist Nalini Malani, which raises the partition of India and Pakistan as a subject for discussion; the sexually candid novel *Lolita* by the Russian author Vladimir Nabokov; the lyrics of the Nigerian musician Fela Kuti and the American singer Madonna; Salman Rushdie's famous and infamous book *The Satanic Verses*; and the work of the Colombian artist, Fernando Arias, which is made using cocaine and blood as an indictment against the Colombian government: all these works are illustrated and accompanied by a brief description. Besides being strong works of art, all these are bearers of a message; a message that people often cannot keep to themselves. They have to share it, because they can't do otherwise.

South African writer and judge Albie Sachs encapsulates this fearless will to communicate. Surviving a car bomb in Maputo, Mozambique, in 1988, seemed to strengthen him in his battle for equality and justice. He retained his integrity and continues to write and say what he thinks. He has even gone so far as to forgive the man who attacked him. Forgiveness also creates a space; it takes away the hate and the energy consumed by hate. His keynote speech at the ceremony for the 1999 Prince Claus Awards, within the framework of 'Creating Spaces for Freedom', addressed the role of art and artists in providing the possibility of an answer: 'Artists and non-artist alike, we will most comfortably and creatively fill the spaces life allots us if we do so as we are, and not as someone tells us we ought to be, and if we do so, we must do so with the pride and serenity that can only come from calm and peaceful self-affirmation.' The work by the artists collected in this book only confirms Sachs' optimism. The artists express their views of the political, religious, social and cultural circumstances, in which they live and work. In some parts of the world, their frank observations are occasionally met with social exclusion, cultural resistance or, at worst, state oppression. In response, they seek refuge, often within their imaginations and artistic endeavours, and in the process they create and inhabit spaces of freedom.

Or, as Frantz Fanon writes in *The Wretched of the Earth* in 1961: 'Literally, it is the people who freely create a summit for themselves, and not the summit that tolerates the people.'

This is also what Duong Thu Huong maintains in her essay. Freedom is in the mind, that is where it will make you free.

1. Duong Thu Huong, 'Freedom: An Imaginary Space for the Survival of Writing', the keynote essay in *Creating Spaces of Freedom*

Duong Thu Huong

Freedom: An Imaginary Space for the Survival of Writing

If freedom is the first flame of all revolutionary fires, it is also the flood that drowns them out. Of all human aspirations, none rallies crowds like the yearning for freedom. From Spartacus to Gandhi, the human struggle for the right to live – in all forms of opposition, and in the most diverse spheres – echoes forth from the chant of freedom. In its echo, we can see the dense, swirling dust of the long road of history, we can see the face of a weary, tormented, anxious, frightened, restless, angry, frenzied, cruel humanity that in the end disappears into the deserted twilight.

> No aspiration costs us so dearly.
> No challenge is more ruthless.
> We both desire and fear it.

Perhaps you will say I am repeating old clichés? No doubt. For the west, freedom is a given, as banal as a streetlamp or a signpost at a nearby corner that no one pays attention to any more. But I am talking about a delirium that rises from a world of mud. A place where freedom is still a dream in broad daylight. A dream that haunts us, refuses to let go. Allow me here to repeat the call of freedom that still echoes in famished souls.

For us, the Vietnamese, freedom, like our existence, has its own history. Freedom has not always stood at our side, a fellow-traveller. The seeds of freedom are sown everywhere, but they are not sown evenly or identically in every place; here, they give birth to dense forests, there, to stubby bushes or clambering vines. For certain peoples, it runs in the very blood of men and women. For others, it passes like a fleeting rain through a grey, oppressive sky.

Is freedom not one of the elements of civilisation, of national character? Even if it is not, we must search the histories of various peoples for the standard of revolt and liberty that is the *sine qua non* of the dignity of man and the nature of states. In any society, artists and writers are the first to feel the need for freedom. It is not without reason that art and literature have three godmothers: Freedom, Luxury, Leisure.

This is obvious in civilised countries. But the sun of civilisation only illuminates a third of the lands of our planet; the remaining two-thirds are still shrouded in darkness and shadow. We, citizens of lands deserted by the sun of civilisation, how should we wield our pens? Must we force literature to change its face and scuttle like a lizard through the cracks of rocks, struggling to survive like some mountain weed? Do we resign ourselves to the fact that our works are born into the world like deformed children, with a harelip here, a misshapen nose there, with hands and feet paralysed? Maybe, and yet … this acceptance of a misshapen, twisted face, a dwarfed body, is the natural and permanent predicament of writers who live under a totalitarian regime. Should they snuff out, with their own hands, the flame of freedom that burns at the bottom of their souls? Yes, that is the way it is … But freedom is the essence of literature and art; to snuff out this flame

Devastation, Ogoniland, Nigeria, 1995

The son of a forest ranger, Ken Saro-Wiwa, witnessed the destruction of Ogoni forests after Shell discovered oil in Nigeria in 1958. He became a dramatist and poet and, in 1992, his popular TV sitcom Basil & Company, about a poor man fighting a corrupt system, was cancelled by General Abacha's military dictatorship. Saro-Wiwa was instrumental in forming the Movement for the Survival of the Ogoni People which brought international attention to the environmental and human rights crisis in Ogoniland. It was only a matter of time before the military struck back. From 1993 to 1994, Nigerian troops attacked Ogoni villages, making thousands homeless. Above, a man sits in an oil spill. Photo: Detlef Pypke/Hollandse Hoogte

Environmental Degradation, Ogoniland, Nigeria, 1995

The devastation of Ogoni forests and waterways by Shell led to widespread gas flare sickness and corrosive oil spills. When the multinational oil company and the Nigerian government refused to halt the damage, the Movement for the Survival of the Ogoni People issued the first Ogoni Bill of Rights. As the movement's spokesperson, Ken Saro-Wiwa was arrested numerous times on spurious charges by the Nigerian military authorities. After his last arrest, he was accused of murdering four Ogoni chiefs who were his friends. Saro-Wiwa was held for ten months, tortured and then tried. In 1995 he was executed with eight others. Photo: Detlef Pypke/Hollandse Hoogte is to kill the very marrow of culture, the writer's sacred mission. If so, it is better to chase after a high-ranking position, a peaceful, humdrum existence. And yet this is often impossible … because literature can haunt you like a magic potion, like fate, like a debt of love contracted in a previous life, from which you can neither flee nor extricate yourself. A writer cannot trade in his dreams of creation for an ordinary life. And because of this, he is torn, from time immemorial, between two yokes. On one hand, the fear of power and the chains of earning a living, on the other, the passion for literature and art. In this situation, freedom is hidden like embers under a sea of mud. From time to time, here and there, it sends out sparks, but then subsides. In this same swamp, under a sullen sky, these fleeting sparks at once kindle the desire for freedom, and the fear of it. Like two famished wolves, both this terror and this secret thirst for freedom continually tear at the writer's heart. The superiority complex, the grandiosity that haunt the writer's secret, fantastic literary dreams, and the high idea he has of himself, clash violently and merge into an inferiority complex. And this complex – born of the writer's painful consciousness of his pitiful predicament in real life – is like a dangerous substance that gnaws, day after day, at his soul. In the writer's gaze you can see at once ambition and cowardice, rebellion and submission, the tears of humiliation mixing with gathering storm clouds.

Life slips by, and man grows wearier with each passing day, each passing month, each passing year in this incessant, hopeless, inner struggle. With such a mindset, literature prevaricates and can only produce masterpieces of allusion and dissimulation. While this is a particularly clever and touching method, it is also one that can backfire, as it is easy to abuse: the endless references to the past; the citations and metaphors; the art of using vague images and ambiguous words to indirectly allude to something; the craft of truncating and distorting the meaning of words. The writer employs all of these artifices, not to render his style richer, more seductive, but essentially to hide his secret thoughts, to dodge the knife of censorship. The writer must censor himself even as he writes. And instead of devoting his energy to narrative, to constructing characters and describing their development, or to weighing his words as he crafts a phrase, he spends it carefully preparing his replies for the authorities in anticipation of the day they will denounce his work. But these alibis and excuses only efface the more profound, essential thoughts that he wanted to share with his readers. And so, willingly or not, the writer transforms himself into a professional sophist, a perpetual liar. Lying is the fundamental character trait of men and women who live under totalitarian regimes; it is done as naturally as spring water flows into streams.

And yet there are people who, despite all the efforts in the world, will never be able to adapt to this environment. Unfortunately, I am one of them. I cannot and do not know how to lie. This was my greatest liability when I was born into this muddy country, this tiny tongue-strip of a land ravaged by many endless wars and storms. All around me live people who are both strange and familiar. I have always lived here with my compatriots, but I have never understood how both the hero and the slave can co-exist in them. For many years, I never understood my colleagues. When I finally did, I distanced myself. I have no talent for rhetoric or bad faith. I would be ashamed if one day I had to denounce my own writing, even though I realise quite clearly that self-abnegation is a clever and effective mode of Asian behaviour, a way of saving face for the authorities while assuring the writer and his writing. All the kings and lords and patriarchs in Asia are fond of melodrama; they love to see, at their feet, trembling and sobbing servants and serfs bowing their heads. Since ancient times, Asians have governed according to whim and inspiration rather than law. In the generation before me, in mine and even in the next generation, everywhere we can see this melodramatic, tear-jerking spirit. This makes me feel what Jean-Paul Sartre identified with precision in his novel, *Nausea*. Long ago, I decided to measure my life by the yardstick of happiness and not by the number of years. I decided to live as a free being, to create my own sun of freedom in this land of mud. And the instant I made this decision, I felt completely changed, happy. Completely happy in my absolute, painful solitude.

Am I crazy? Did I force myself, out of vanity, to create illusory feelings to console and delude myself? Many would say so; they cannot believe in my freedom. After all, what woman could pretend to be free when the police regularly summon her entourage and her friends and assign them to watch and spy on her, forcing them, whether they like it or not, to become informers? What woman can claim to be free with a security policeman at her heels the minute she steps into the same café the third time in a row? What woman could be free when her mail and all forms of communication and correspondence are routinely checked and arbitrarily confiscated? That is the way it is …

And yet I still think I am free. I say what I want to say and I write what I want to write, even if my writings will never receive authorisation to be published. In 1991, during the months I was imprisoned by the Vietnamese authorities, I still felt free. I thought what I wanted to think. I continued to be inspired by everything that was buried in my heart, which moved me. The interrogations and the three men facing me belonged to another world. That world had nothing to do with my inner world, with my real life.

The cell was filled with mosquitoes. All you had to do was stretch out your hand to catch them. I caught a lot of them. I also caught black bugs that swarmed in the torn, old cotton quilt they had given to me. It was stained with the dried blood of the previous prisoner, who had been stricken with dysentery. I chased bugs in the cracks of my wooden bed. I made battlefields with their corpses: the passage of Elbe in Boldartchuk's film *Liberation* and the battle of Waterloo in the film *Napoleon*. I compared the Russian filmmaker's direction with the Frenchman's, because I have always been a film-lover even though in this poor, muddy, famished country the cinema is a dream too distant, too extravagant. But I dreamt. And I continued to dream. With bugs' corpses for tanks and cannons, and mosquitoes for armies, I remembered the films that had once captivated me.

And I remembered my father. A man whom I loved with anger and resentment. A father who was both tender and unreasonably strict. He loved me, but he was incapable of freeing himself from his ossified principles, his feudal morality. I loved him, but I could not be other than a disobedient, rebellious child. During those moments, I missed him. Aside from my dreams of art, it was his memory that invaded my soul. I argued and quarrelled with him, defended myself, showered him with reproaches. Together, we sobbed out of anger and resentment. Sometimes this would happen in the middle of an interrogation, as I listened to questions and replied mechanically, like a tape-recorder someone switches on.

Thanks to that experience, I understood how Cervantes was able to write *Don Quixote* in prison. It is certain that he was free in his own space. He was free even in the middle of his prison cell. And this imaginary freedom is nevertheless so strong that in its thrall the outside world fades, weakens, and self-destructs. The outside world is powerless to the point that it has no further hold on the thoughts or the feelings of the writer. This freedom was created by the writer himself. A chimerical freedom. The kind of freedom born of a challenge to the hostility of the outside world. And this freedom exists like a fantastic sun that only one person can see, that illuminates and warms him alone.

This freedom is the writer's supreme power, his sacred act of stealing fire. No one can give it to him except himself. This freedom is the vital space of writing.

Is the quest for such freedom insanely naïve, pure madness? Perhaps … but we have to choose: live free to write what deserves to be written, or die. Talent? The heavens endow us with that.

Daw Aung San Suu Kyi, Rangoon,Myanma (Burma), 1995

In 1995, Nobel Prize laureate Daw Aung San Suu Kyi addressed hundreds of anxious Burmese supporters from the main gate of her family compound in Rangoon, the capital of Burma. Suu Kyi left her home on 27 December for the first time in about three weeks to pay respects at her mother's tomb on the eighth anniversary of her death. She admitted, 'I never predict what will happen in the future. That's the sort of thing astrologers do. [However] I hope that we will get to our goal quickly because the longer we have to stay under a dictatorship, the country suffers.' (Interview with Malu Halasa)

Photo: Manuel Ceneta/ANP

Going to the Movies, Afghanistan, 2001

A crowd of a 1,000 culture-starved Afghans rushed into the *Bagh* Tar cinema, the most famous theatre in Kabul that had been closed for the last five years. They wanted 'to catch the first show in town since the Taliban fled'. *Uroj* [Ascension] is a movie about Afghan mojahedin fighters defeating drunken Russian soldiers in the mountains of the famed Panjshir Valley. 'Seats for yesterday's screening were 3,000 Afghanis [Euro 0.79]. Women, however, were [still] banned ... "It was the first time I have ever seen a film and I loved it," said seventeen-year-old Omaid. "But now I would like to see a film about brotherhood and peace in Afghanistan."'
(Rory McCarthy, 'Showing Today, the Fight for Freedom', *The Guardian*, 20 November 2001) Photo: Alexander Nemenov/ANP/EPA

But freedom can only be built with self-confidence and human dignity. On this earth there are myriad paths to it. And I am not idiotic or senile to the point of believing that the road I have chosen is the only road. But I know that in this world everything has its price, that each human being is both the author of his destiny and the victim to the reactions this destiny elicits from others. When the Berlin Wall fell, we thought that the world would explode in shouts of joy from millions of human beings. The Stalinist state was crumbling. The dictatorship of the proletariat was shattered. People gazed, stunned, at the once distant blue horizon of their dreams: the azure blue of Freedom. And at that moment, tens of thousands of artists in the former Soviet Union and the Eastern bloc wept with happiness. The future of literature and art unfurled before their very eyes. Free at last, but those tears of joy had barely dried when a flood of tears of pain sprang forth. There was a long, embarrassed, sheepish silence. Then, a few writers dared express their anxious uncertainty and, finally, en masse, they acknowledged their impotence: they could not write anymore. I remember the bitter words of a Bulgarian poet: 'Once, for many long years, we dreamed of writing freely. Now that freedom is here, we have nothing more to say.'

This poet had visited Vietnam many times. She was an intelligent, beautiful, gracious woman. Her confession made my heart wrench. But I knew there was nothing I could do for her – for her and those who had shared her fate. Because freedom is not a treasure that can be stashed in a palace and then excavated, that will retain its value three thousand years later. Freedom is like human life. A fellow-traveller. We have to learn to live with it and to deserve it.

Once, there was a Chinese emperor who would only eat the flesh of a certain wild bird. The high-ranking mandarins sent out an order to capture these birds and to breed them in the Forbidden City in gardens covered with nets. They put the tiny baby birds, just barely hatched, in bamboo trunks, only allowing their beaks and claws to stick out. They fed them on precious grains and exotic fruit. As the birds grew, their bodies took on the shape of the bamboo trunks - plump, but stunted. When the cook split open the bamboo trunks, freeing them to kill them, these obese little birds took a few steps and then fell flat. That is what is called the principle of adaptation. Tens of thousands of writers and artists were bred like this under the socialist regime. Nothing but suffering, nothing but regrets. How many talents were withered and deformed like this?

Nevertheless, whatever the circumstances, there have always been free birds, a species indigenous to the vertiginous heights, finding happiness there. Amidst the storms. Amidst the solitude. Proud, even in that hardship and solitude. I can name one of them: Bulgakov. He didn't choose exile, like Solzhenitsyn. Like Pasternak, he stayed in Russia and accepted long years of oppression. He was isolated, spied on. He had to work in a brick factory, toiling at other tiresome jobs to survive. But he lived and he wrote as a free man. His works, *Heart of a Dog* and *The Master and Margarita* were written under the sun of freedom. And it was Bulgakov and his strong, noble, Russian soul who created this freedom.

Human history, according to the Christian calendar, is over two thousand years old. But even before the Christian era, the east went through the Warring States period. The west has been through the Crusades. Humanity has known both sadness and joy, suffering and happiness. And humanity has had time to reflect. She has passed down legends and fables, accumulated these alluvial plains in her subconscious. This is our heritage, along with all talents and handicaps that our ancestors have sown in our souls. For a writer, this spiritual heritage is more precious than all the material legacies of this base world. In my youth, by some coincidence, I read one of Aesop's fables. The image of the slave immediately captivated me. Thanks to this writer, I realised that freedom was the most powerful of all human aspirations, the most ruthless challenge. And that freedom was the measure of our humanity.

Aesop's last words, before throwing himself in the pit, were as follows:

> For love, I am still too green.
> For freedom, I am already ripe.
> Come, abyss, the road I have chosen.
> I will die, for in dying I shall become a free man.

Slavery has long since disappeared, but the aspiration to freedom is still a new yearning. For writers who have long lived in the lands of mud, the memory of Aesop's slave remains instructive, if they want to write with dignity. Aesop's freedom is the imaginary freedom of the writer, and it is the writer's imaginary freedom that is the precondition for the real freedom of all those who live around him. So I ask you, fellow writers, though you may suffer oppression, misery, opprobrium, imprisonment, even death, never give it up.

Translated from the Vietnamese by Nina McPherson

Marcel Khalifé, Lebanon
Arabic Coffeepot, 1995

In 1999, the day after Abdul-Rahman Chehab took over the new post as Beirut's investigating judge, he issued an indictment against the Lebanese singer Marcel Khalifé for 'offending Islam'. The singer had set to music 'Oh, My Father, I Am Yusif', a Mahmoud Darwish poem that interprets a Quranic verse. The case was dismissed due to lack of evidence. In 1997, a similar case was brought against Khalifé for singing Quranic verses alongside popular songs before the then Prime Minster Rafiq Harari halted the case. (Robert Fisk, 'Frontline: Beirut – Heavy Hand of Islamic Judiciary Condemns a Song from the Heart', *Independent*, 7 October 1999, p.19) CD cover: art designed by Emile Menhem, courtesy of Nagam Records

Poem by Mahmoud Darwish
Performed by Marcel Khalifé

'Oh, My Father, I Am Yusif'[1]

Father! I am Yusif
Oh father!
My brothers neither love me
nor want me in their midst.
Oh father, they assault me,
they stone me and
with insults they shower me.
My brothers wish me dead
so they give their false eulogies.
They shut your door before me,
and from your field
I was expelled.
They poisoned my grapevines,
Oh father!
When the passing breeze
jested with my hair,
They all became envious,
outraged at you and me.
What have I done to them, father,
and what loss have I caused?
Butterflies rest on my shoulder,
wheat bows towards me
and birds hover above my hands.
What then did I do wrong, father,
and why me?
You're the one who named me Yusif!
They pushed me down the well
and then they blamed the wolf.
Oh father! The wolf is more merciful
than my brothers.
Did I wrong anyone
when I told about my dream?
Of eleven planets, I dreamt,
and of the sun and the moon
all kneeling before me.

1. 'Oh, My Father, I Am Yusif' is the translation of 'Ana Yusif', a poem by Mahmoud Darwish, performed by Marcel Khalifé from the CD *Arabic Coffeepot* (Nagam Records NR1008; 1995)
Lyrics courtesy of Marcel Khalifé

Exile[1]

> I borrow seasons of an alien land
> To stay the season of a mind

Having proposed the question – *When* is a nation? – in my collection of essays, *The Open Sore of a Continent,*[2] I suppose I should have realised that it was only a matter of time before I would confront myself with one of its potential corollaries – *When* is exile? Speculations over that transposition did not however commence without some external stimulus. The theme of exile appears to hold great fascination for literary critics, mere artistic consumers, anthologists and festival directors of all artistic genres, and a week or two had hardly passed after my vanishing trick from my homeland before I began to be bombarded with enquiries about how exile was affecting my writing – oh, I forgot to add the interviewers, autograph hunters and the most casual encounters – *Are you still able to write? What does exile mean to your writing? ad infinitum.* Invitations from literary journals were not slow to follow, then desperate summons to conferences, seminars etc. all in the quest of the elusive quarry – both process and product – that bear the invisible stigmata of literature in exile.

Indignant, I refused to co-operate – no, I had not gone into exile, I was merely away from home on a political sabbatical – that, plus a dozen other variants of the Great Evasion, in which I lavishly indulged. Among those variants, one could argue that the one that remained in its own zone of subjective impregnability was that of identity. I was not in exile because I did not *feel* that I was in exile – I feel, therefore I am; I do not, therefore I ain't! I had not remotely begun to sense the beginning of an exile identity. Literary history and sociology are incomplete without colourful, intrigue-filled accounts of (national) colonies of exiles – a familiar enough categorisation for those literary and other artistic émigrés who swamped the congenial cafés of Paris both during the Tsarist era and following the Bolshevik Revolution. Richard Wright, James Baldwin remain among the earliest famous writers of the black American émigré colony and, towards the end of the Fifties, I also encountered the distinct Guatemalan micro-community, also in Paris. Yet even if, objectively, some equally obstinate critic would refer to me as having swelled the increasing stream of exiled Nigerian writers, professionals and intellectuals, he would be hard put to it – I insisted – to prove that my identity was thereby transformed and could now be described – not as African, Nigerian or Yoruba, but as – uniquely Exilian!

Of course I knew I had gone into exile! You don't plunge into the forest of a thousand daemons on a sputtering two-wheeler just for a brief change of environment in a neighbouring country – you go through the airport or use the autoroute. I had however closed my mind – I did not even have to think about it – I simply set up barriers against the acceptance of the condition of exile. Going into exile was one thing, I argued, arriving there was another – now who was to tell me that I had indeed arrived in exile? That unique status of going into, but not having arrived at, was a luxury I could bestow on myself with the authority of lines from Lenrie Peters:

Earth has nowhere to go
You are at the starting point
Jumping across worlds
In condensed time
After the awkward fall
We are always at the starting point

Those lines are from his poem, 'Parachute Men', and if ever there was an image that is appropriate and definitive on the liminal but dynamic condition of the exiled writer, the parachutist or free-fall glider is surely a front-runner. Those interviewers however, magazine editors and literary conférenciers are nothing if not persistent, and perhaps it was in an effort to sustain my stubbornness that I began to ask myself the question: *When* is exile? Other tantalising variants follow – *Where* is exile? etc. Is there a state of exile? For surely even an exile must exist in some space – physical and mental. Even more optimistically, there is that strong temptation to describe exile as simply a state of mind. Over any state of mind we may arm ourselves with the challenging power of the will and thus negate all debilitating tendencies that threaten the ego from the inescapable *fact* of exile. Still, the questions persist, prodded into being by a sensation of loss, of absence, however temporary, and by whatever strategies are adopted by individuals to counter the interruption in, or distortion of their routine sense of being.

But sometimes exile is indeed a place, and thus a newfoundland, to borrow the name of that desolate space, a wasteland that, for tropical blood like mine, must have been a naming ceremony of supreme self-consolation. And so, in both physical and other senses, one confronts the question: is there a moment when, on arriving there, one knows intuitively, and accepts that one has now truly arrived in exile? (For now, we may postpone the complex but real experience of exile as a state of mind that separates present consciousness from the originating zone of self-cognisance, in short, exile as the home of alienation.) Arriving in exile as a spatial change may happen to one in any number of ways, defining each individual's specific quality of exile. If the nature of departure from homeland has been marked by total rejection, by the necessity for a near-total obliteration of memory, then an encounter with an environment that is a complete antithesis of the place of setting out – from topography to emotive and sensory properties – may find the wanderer breathing a sigh of relief – oh yes, finally, I have arrived in exile. No more sounds, no more sights, textures or smells, no exhalation from any section of humanity that evokes the memory of home. To put it in more familiar terms, the wanderer shakes the dust of erstwhile habitation off his feet.

The opposite of course, may come to pass. Exile may hanker for a sympathetic environment; one that trails an umbilical cord to abandoned roots, as if a handful of earth has been sneaked into the baggage and delivered ahead of the wanderer at his destination. Mentally, the newcomer does the papal rites – kneels down and kisses the ground. There indeed, a close duplicate of habitation is recognised and adopted – while the self is schooled in a few minor adaptations. Or else schooled to exist in a kind of paradox, a state of tension where the mind simultaneously embraces an anchor in alien territory yet ensures that it stays at one remove from that alien milieu. This requires erecting a creative barrier, sometimes half-hearted but sufficient to distance complete absorption. In such an instance, the writer reflects present reality, but deflects its seductiveness through literary strategies of a markedly different temper from those that define or dominate the space that has given him shelter.

Ben Okri springs to mind as being an embodiment of that temper, always bearing in mind however

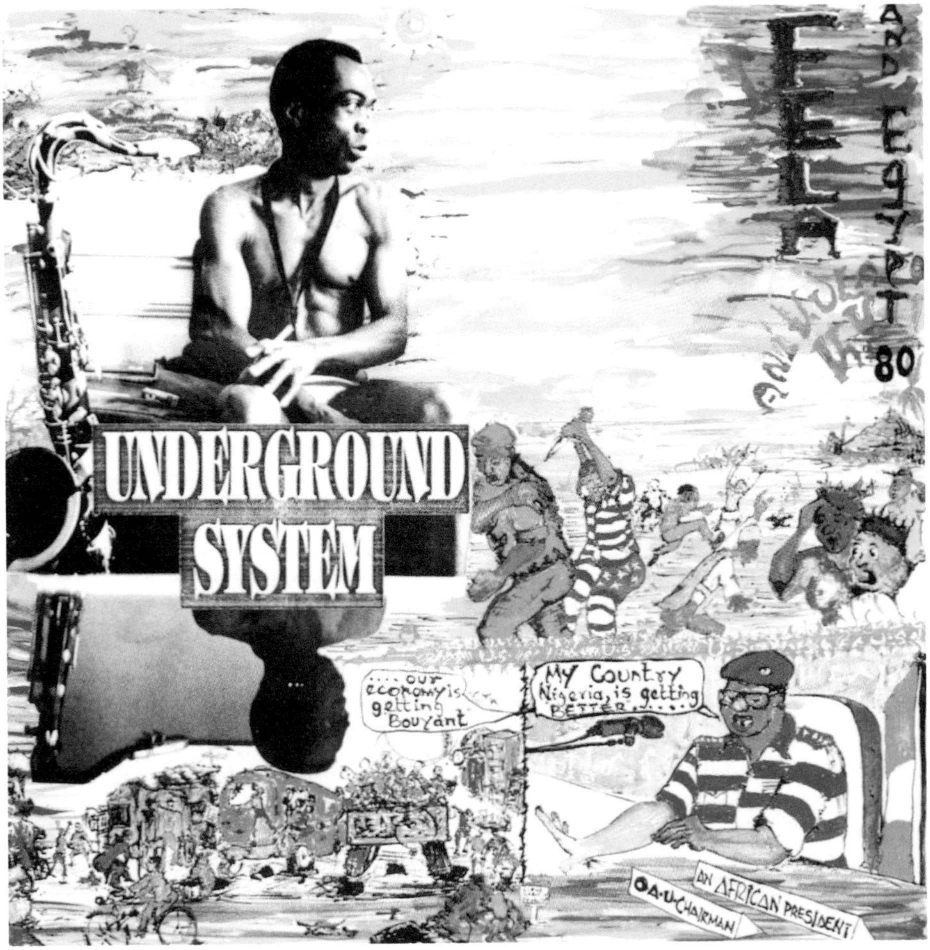

Fela Kuti, Nigeria
***Underground System*, 1992**

'We need to use everything we have to fight ignorance, oppression and exploitation. Music is one of the necessary means to carry out the human struggle for a better world ... I am using my music as a weapon,' said Fela Kuti in a 1989 interview. His weapon – amounting to 23 albums over the course of his lifetime – provoked persecution from the Nigerian military authorities. In 1977, soldiers attacked his compound, destroying recording equipment and throwing his mother out of a window. Despite a military ban, thousands of Nigerians attended his funeral in 1997.
(Rotimi Santorri, 'From Praise to Protest', *Index on Censorship* 6/98, p. 67) CD cover courtesy of FKO Music

'Underground System'[1]

We be about fourteen of us
We de make one club together
Everything na turn by turn
Reach – chairman na turn by turn

When e reach my turn by turn
When my turn by turn for chairman reach
Dem chop all of my turn by turn
Di money of my turn by turn
Di Chairman of my turn by turn
All of my turn by turn
Dem chop all of my turn by turn
Di money of my turn by turn
Di Chairman of my turn by turn
All of my turn by turn don turn no mess.

Main song:
I don sing song for great African men
Na Osagiefo Kwame Nkrumah be di greatest one
I don sing song for great African men
I don sing song against African thieves
Na Obasonjo be di biggest thief
I sing about and Abiola
I don sing song against African thieves

Ask many African young people today
Dem no know nothing about Kwame Nkrumah

Chorus: To know Nkrumah
Yeye leaders no fit dey
Chorus: To know Nkrumah
Yeye president no fit dey
Chorus: To know Nkrumah
African personality go show
Chorus: To know Nkrumah
African pride go de shine
Chorus: To know Nkrumah
Prosperity go de flow
Chorus: To know Nkrumah
Good good things go de happen

When one good man was rise for Africa today
Bad leaders dem go wan finish am O
When one good man was rise for Africa today
Useless people dem go wan finish am O
Dem go plan against am, lie against am
Lie against am, talk against am
Talk against am, plan against am
Lie against am
You no see Nkrumah no finish am O
You no see Seko Toure dem finish am O
You no see Lumumba dem finish am O
You no see Idi Amin dem finish am O
You no see Mandela dem wan kill am O

Anywhere all over di world
Young people dem go de look up to leaders
Wetin leaders di do di young people de do
One good thing African people de do
Few of dem go gather together
Dem go start one club
Dem go de contribute money together
Dem go de share di money when dem de contribute
But everything na turn by turn
One good thing about this matter be say
It is in di African tradition
For people to trust themselves ...

1. *Underground System* by Fela Anikulapo Kuti and Egypt 80, recorded as an LP (Kalakuta KALP013; Nigeria 1992), was also released as a CD (Sterns STCD 1043; UK, 1992).
Music and lyrics by Fela Kuti, published by FKO Music, © FKO Music

that his novel, *The Famished Road*, so deeply embedded in mythic reconstructions from homeland, did have its beginnings in earlier works, short stories, which were published while he was still in Nigeria. Living by choice in England, he peoples his habitation with beings of a world that is reminiscent of the abandoned terrain, even though placed at a heightened remove from that distant reality. Actually, this makes Ben Okri a prime candidate for that whimsical – well, half-serious – definition that I once proposed for the true temperament of the writer or the artist tribe in general: as a creature in a permanent state of exile, since his or her real vocation is the eradication of the barriers of reality (for reality, read intimacy, literal recognition). I was then giving voice to my growing suspicion that few creative terrains appear to be more congenial to the writer than such frontiers, the threshold of reality, and the immediate provocation of my re-examination of such a province was the predicament of Salman Rushdie: At that time, I wrote:

> Indeed, I am more than ever persuaded that this is what defines the breed – living the paradox that embraces, even interiorises the barrier, yet insisting that the barrier should not be there. And thus, charging at, manoeuvring past, slithering through, hurling imprecations and shaking the fists at ... simply insisting that the frontier be shattered, that the barricades be lifted, that human communication be not controlled, constricted or manipulated. For this activity takes place on all fronts – it is both elemental and social. Political. And this last results not infrequently in the writer himself finding the barricades sharply lifted at a critical moment of contest; the momentum carries him forward and, by the time he has regained balance, he finds himself across the frontier, the barricade neatly, definitively or temporarily lowered behind him. He is compelled to learn a new language of the space beyond the frontiers, the mores, customs, taboos ... in short, he encounters the new language of the frontiers of exile, its joys and anguish, its challenges. This tension has proved, over the ages, a life and death recurrence. The conjunction of both the physical and the elemental frontiers has surely never been more dangerously expressed, at least in this century, than in the yet ongoing drama of Salman Rushdie and the satanic regime of fanaticism. For Rushdie, the physical frontier has contracted, while the elemental remains – within the imperatives of creativity – innately expansive.

Since writing that, Salman Rushdie has been joined by Taslim Nazreen who, like Rushdie in his time, failed to recognise the definitive lowering of the barrier at the frontier of exile. What really took her home, I have wondered again and again? I understand that her mother was ill and dying, but I suspect that beneath such filial pull was also that periodic need of all creative people to recross the threshold of loss, to recharge the batteries of identity and thus engage in the ritual of the lifting of the creative frontier, an attempt yet again to wage war within the liminal zone, the writers' normal place of habitation that sometimes turns unbearably physical. Those creative frontiers, I cautioned, remain 'territories of hazardous navigation for the voyager, the writer, who remains a suspect émigré in a refugee camp, and whose status of semi-exile undergoes quite arbitrary forms of articulation.'

The recognition of frontiers can be overwhelming, and the condition of exile is the daily knowledge, indeed the palpable experiencing of such frontiers. Some writers are more susceptible to their debilitating effects and succumb – Arthur Nortje, the South African poet for example, or Rabearivello, the Madagascan poet, whose career reminds one forcefully that there is also a condition of internal exile. A mixed-up, identity-confused poet of potential genius, Rabearivello occupied a creative habitation whose true indigenes were thousands of miles away in France. He grew gradually into that extreme product of the colonial psychic divide, one leg across the threshold of his spiritual home, France. He applied again and again to be fully admitted and his frustration grew, as the prospect became more and more remote. Rabearivello, a product of the movement that came to be known as Negritude, occupied a very special creative space, unique to himself, and untouched by many of the social concerns that relieved other poets from the danger of alienation and a total retreat into a solipsistic creative existence. His true soulmates were Verlaine, Rimbaud and Baudelaire, with whom he shared, in the words of Ulli Beier, 'a disgust of reality'. I tend to express this differently: Rabearivello's world, the world within which alone he found his being as indigene and citizen, was simply the frontier zone of reality, that liminal territory to which we earlier referred, where the writer's passport requires no validation and accepts no restrictions. His craving however placed him among those writers who appear doomed to remain on the threshold of identity.

Rabearivello's anguish, assuaged only partially by retreats into a surreal imagination, however lay in that paradoxical sense of exile; the weight of a distant cultural longing. It overwhelmed him eventually, leading him to commit a very painful suicide. So did Arthur Nortje through an overdose of drugs, in a different clime, but no less a liminal inhabitant of a deceptively congenial environment. Nortje's poetry is permeated with the visceral protest of a sensibility that tries hard, but cannot reconcile itself with a condition of forced exile. He agonised over an existential impotence that commenced with the very political situation that had resulted in his exile – apartheid – which itself constituted another form of exile, an internal one, not self-induced, like Rabearivello's, but imposed by the insanity of the state. Like other victims of apartheid, the forces that controlled his existence effectively annulled his social being, crammed his self-awareness – like others – into a ghetto of internal exile, and eventually flung him into a wider field of alienation. Coming to terms with the contradictions of this liberating vista – England – that spelt freedom and self-realisation but one which, nevertheless, inserted a real territory of loss, of the dissipation of a once cohered self – in short, exile – did not come easy to Nortje's poetic sensibilities.

Dambudzo Marechera, the Zimbabwean – *Scrapiron Blues* etc. – by contrast, made no effort to come to terms with exile, except as a violent predator, whose real life excesses were only matched by his intellectual (but rather sophomoric) voracity. Exile was a provider, but not one that should be treated as a willing partner; it had to be a relationship of forcible extraction, as dues to a resentful guest from a resented host, whose resources must be laid bare for eclectic, even undisciplined appropriation. He was a vastly different spirit from Rabearivello, yet they shared one thing in common – a frank acknowledgement of an exterior cultural home whose threshold they never fully crossed. For Rabearivello however, it was a loving recognition; not so for Marechera, who did savour, at first hand, those foraging fields. But the denizens were mere intellectual acquaintances and his frustration at a tacit exclusion made him more demanding, less selective, and proportionately hate-filled and despondent.

If ever there was a writer who wore the banner of exile on his brow, it was Marechera. His eclectic, voracious appetite for the spoils of exile – that is, the insistence on an exile persona that feeds on the community of the alienated is a characteristic also of Syl Cheney-Coker of distant Sierra Leone, who actively sought kindred spirits from within the continent but also in literary careers from all over the world. This was strictly a younger, passing phase for Cheney-Coker, but it retains its validity both for its time, and for many others. What is significant about that phase is that this younger Cheney-Coker confesses a need to become an exile in order to find his creative persona:

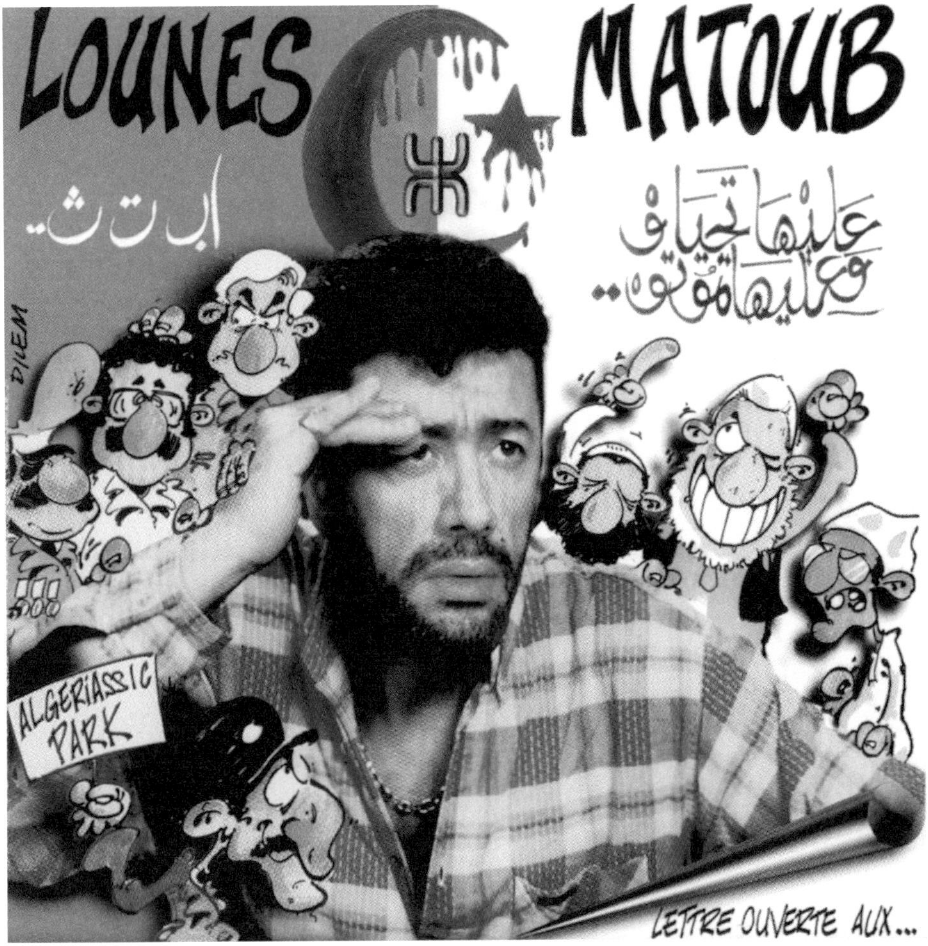

Lounès Matoub, Berber, Algeria
***Lettre Ouverte Aux ...*, 1998**

In 1978, Lounès Matoub's debut album *Ay Izem* [The Lion] 'was an instant hit and was quickly followed by a second, *Ayemma a'zizen* [Dear Mother]. When anti-government demonstrations swept through Tizi-Ouzou [in Algeria] in April 1980, his songs were the anthems of the protesters. Along with singers that included people like Lounis Aït Menguellet ... whose music had been in the forefront of Berber cultural resistance to forced Arabisation since the early 1970s, all his songs were banned. It did not prevent his impassioned defence of the Berber language nor his attacks on fundamentalists.' Matoub was murdered in 1998. (See page 45) (Judith Vidal-Hall, 'A Gig Too Far', *Index on Censorship* 6/98, p. 117) CD cover courtesy of Friends of Lounès Matoub

'The Revolutionary'[1]

Companion of the Revolution
Even if your body decomposes
Your name is Eternity
Go in peace, we will never fail you
Whatever happens
We will always be one of yours
The coffin awaits us all
Today or tomorrow
We are joining you
We will not allow adversity to
Break our will
Your death is our pledge

1. 'The Revolutionary' by Lounès Matoub appears on *La complainte de ma mère* (Melodie; France, 1996)
Lyrics courtesy of Friends of Lounès Matoub

Mother, I want to return to exile to be your poet

The mother is both his biological parent and the land with whom the poet has a tortured relationship, a tension of unrequited love and unfulfilled expectations, in short, the very embodiment of the poet's alienation which however he seeks to overcome with a willed passion of commitment:

my mother prevents my flight into myself
speaking to me through her silence through the beat of her heart
the sword fighting my days the lamp lighting my nights
when my heart sinks deep in the oasis
of its pain! she rejuvenates me calling back the me
that has died tracing the man-child to the poet
but finally, the lament:
without understanding the dictates of my soul

And yet, within that same poem, 'The Road to Exile Thinking of Vallejo', is the avowal of both umbilical ties of the mother/motherland that nurtured that same poetic persona, and the ironic, separatist consequences, nothing exceptional, and certainly not unique to this poet:

It is recorded then: I'll die in exile!
thinking of my Sierra Leone
this country which has made me a poet
this country which has honoured me
with the two knives of my death passed crisscross
through my heart
so that I can say to a bleeding mother:
Mother I am returning into exile to be your poet

What he wants to be, what he declares in accents of anguish in 'On Being a Poet in Sierra Leone' remains elusive – to be the breakfast of the peasants, the hands that help the fishermen bring in their catch, a hand on the plough that tills the fields, even, somewhat disturbingly – the national symbol of life. I say 'disturbingly', but perhaps 'awkwardly' states the case better, since there is something rather presumptuous about any writer striving to become a national symbol. However, the theme remains the same: a territory that separates desire and actuality, even when the tools of desire have been forged within the hearth of actuality. But actuality itself is dual – it is both present reality and the envisioned reality. In most instances, alas, that envisioned duplicate, the constantly receding actuality gradually evolves into a mere vision of possibilities, of potential articulation. And so the poet finds he must also separate himself from that source of inspiration, which also translates as the zone of obligation – in order to embrace it more fully, and to serve it more faithfully. Nowhere, I believe, is the pathos of this paradox conveyed more effectively than in his 'Letter to a Tormented Playwright':

remember Amadu how terrible I said it was
that you were in exile and working
in the Telephone Office in touch with all
the languages of the world but with no world
to call your own: how sad you looked that winter
drinking your life and reading poetry with me
in the damp chilly English coffee shops

It is a most apposite metaphor, truly evocative – 'in touch with all the languages of the world but with no world to call your own' – a true liminal centre of receptivity that is however located on the threshold of desired reality, seeking but never truly grasping a world it can call its own.

1. 'Exile' is from 'Thresholds of Loss and Identity', an unpublished lecture.
2. Soyinka, Wole; *The Open Sore of a Continent*: A Personal Narrative of the Nigerian Crisis, (Oxford: Oxford University Press, 1996)

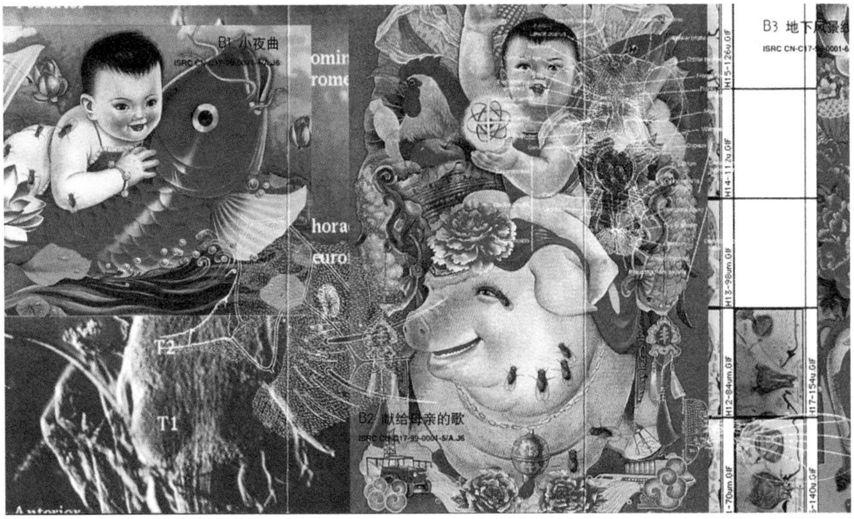

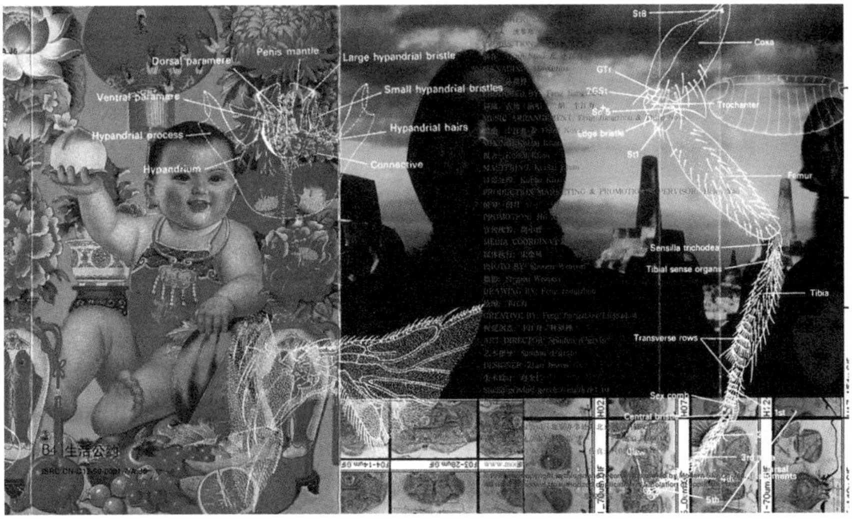

The Fly, PRC
***& Seven Die Fallen Love*, 1999**

From the Chinese press: ***Beijing Weekend*** called the Fly 'the first dirty band in China's music history'. ***Chinese Broadway*** describes their style as 'punk, mixed with Freudian craziness'. ***At Your Service*** maintains that 'Listening to their music is like getting stabbed'. From ***Drama and Movie News***, 'The Fly's music has a strong sense of dissension ... they sing of the need to express love frequently, just like a toad croaking everyday. "Man's dedication to his job is like a fly busily working around a pile of shit." ' The Fly's singer Feng Jiangzhou told ***Standard Magazine, Hong Kong Life***, 'The spirit of rock cannot be compromised.' (www.globalserve.net/~jiangy/thefly/excerpt.html)
Cassette cover designed by Song Yonghong.

'Nirvana'[1]

Since there is no light bulb in this village toilet
Since there is no full moon tonight
Since I can't fall asleep
Since I want to play with myself
I shape my fingers into a circle, to burn a match, gently
It lights up this smooth piece of wood
The tender whiteness of a girl's thigh
I put down my pants and sit on it
Outside the hut breezes are blowing gently
Everything seems so quiet here

I throw the burning match
Into the deep black hole under my ass
Outside the hut breezes are still blowing gently
The match burns with the soiled toilet paper, slowly
Everything seems so quiet
I close my eyes, and smoke is everywhere
Outside the hut breezes are still blowing gently
Fanning the fire stronger and stronger
Under my ass shine rays of light, rays of light
I will bring with me the thick smoke that fills the hut
Under my ass shine rays of dawn
I will bring with me the shit fragrance that fills the hut
My nirvana, my nirvana

1. 'Nirvana' by the Fly from the CD *The Fly!* (1996)
Lyrics and vocals: written and sung by Feng Jiangzhou, translated by Yiufan Chow.

Mohamed Fellag

Djurdjurassique Bled: Censorship[1]

Censorship has played havoc with Algerian television, our one national channel. Our dear national channel. As the adverts used to say: 'A binding force!'

There are three forms of censorship in Algerian television: political censorship, moral censorship and self-censorship. We won't talk about this last one. That's a private matter. Political censorship is quite simple. Whenever anything serious is happening on the political front, on TV we get animal documentaries. And as there are lots of serious problems on the political front – Jacques-Yves Cousteau has become a nationwide star. Fish, all day long! It's not a television set we're looking at – it's an aquarium!

Take what happened on 5 October 1988: 600 dead. There was an atmosphere of war throughout the country. People were hurrying home and switching on the TV to hear the news, so they could make out what was going on. Through the window you could hear nothing but the rattle of bullets, the cries of the wounded; you could see smoke from the fires. And on TV: 'This fish which lives at the bottom of the sea and feeds on plankton ...'

Algerians are now experts on plankton. But as they aren't stupid, they've become cunning. They've ended up decoding the animals. I remember, for example, at the end of the 1970s, they showed a documentary about a herd of elephants. The elephants were grazing in the bush. One of the elephants broke away from the herd, made its way to the elephant graveyard, collapsed and died. The next day, in the streets of Algiers, people were hugging the walls, looking to left and right:

> 'Psst, come here.
> What's up?
> Just come.
> What's happening?
> Boumedienne is dead.
> You really mean it?
> Yeah, I saw it on the news.'

Only Algerian TV uses real animals. The rest of the world has latex dolls.

But the type of censorship that has created the greatest havoc is moral censorship. The main casualty of moral censorship is – kisses in films. These days they cut all kisses. Up to a number of years ago they only cut the kisses if the couples were not married. If the actor and actress were not man and wife: '*Wallah,* don't touch her! You could have married her if you wanted to before you started filming.'

If, at the beginning of a film, an actor promises an actress that he will marry her at the end of the film: 'You can start kissing her right from the beginning, but as long as you're not actually married – just a light kiss, you understand? None of that heavy stuff.'

If the actors are married, there's no problem. They can kiss. We respect the customs and habits of other societies. But actors have to prove they're married. You have to be able to see them getting married in church or in the town hall. Failing that, well, let's see – for instance, Robert de Niro moves towards his wife to kiss her; in passing he shows his marriage certificate to the Algerian censor.

The result of all this is that every time we are sitting watching TV and an actor and an actress move towards each other to kiss, as soon as they are within ten centimetres of each other – Snip! The kiss is cut. Ping! The actors move backwards. This makes it impossible to follow the film. We've no longer any idea what's happening. When we see the actress recoiling, we say: 'What's going on? The actor must have eaten some rotten *merguez* [spicy North African sausage]!'

And if you see an actor kissing an actress at the beginning of a film – that means he's going to marry her at the end of it. So you know how it's going to finish. We're landed with a dud film. '*Nâaldine* [Fuck] this film!'

As you know, a film involves suspense, but for us the suspense is not: 'Who's going to kill her? Is he going to kill her? – No, let him kill her! What the hell do I care? That's their problem, nothing to do with me. He can kill all of them if he wants.' Our version of suspense is: 'Is he going to marry her at the end of the film?'

Take *Dallas*, 800 episodes, shown all over the world. In our part of the world, they cut all the kisses, the scenes of man and wife together, women at the swimming pool, scantily clothed, etc. The *Dallas* actors do nothing but work. Eight hundred episodes slaving away! All that's left are the working hours. These people aren't actors. They've been put there by an employment agency. It's not JR, it's Manpower.

Sometimes, in *Dallas*, you see JR – the hero of the series – at work in the office. He has arranged to meet his wife, Sue Ellen, at six o'clock in the evening. At a quarter-to-six he gets up with a pleased look on his face, puts on his jacket and goes to meet Sue Ellen … BANG! He is back again in the office! Only now his coat's a different colour.

Sometimes a young actor is in his car, a convertible. Three hundred kilometres an hour. He has arranged to meet his girlfriend, who is waiting for him, scantily dressed. You don't see her. They've cut her, but you know that's what's happened: you know from how fast the car has travelled. He arrives at her home, leaps from his car and is so excited that he runs up eighteen flights of stairs. When he gets to the girlfriend's flat, he rings the bell. And now what happens, in our version? There's the girlfriend's door. The censor looks at the rest of the story, finds another door and glues it in its place. Which means that the actor is standing there, all excited. 'WOW!!!' The door opens and – he's in the office!

In Algeria, *Dallas* is a documentary on the American way of office life!

So how do they actually do it?

Television has a censorship office. The films are shown. There's a guy with scissors – they're usually retired tailors from the Kasbah – who's on the lookout. The day he was taken on, he was told: 'You are the guardian of the moral temple. Make sure you don't let a kiss be shown which will destabilise the country. Be particularly careful with French films. The people in their films do nothing but eat and kiss. And sometimes they don't even eat! When you see a French actor and actress eating at table – start getting ready as soon as they reach the dessert. And if ever, during the dessert, the actor puts a cherry in his mouth and transfers it straight to his girlfriend's mouth: SNIP! And make sure you get back that cherry!

'If you happen to see an actor and an actress in a film walking on a pavement in Paris, New York or anywhere else, they're not doing anything wrong, let them walk; it's part of the scenario. If, after a time, you see them leaving the main street and turning into an alleyway, follow them. Suddenly they go behind a building – and you've lost sight of them. You suspect something's going on:

Willy Chirino, Cuba / U.S.
Asere, 1995

Power-played all over Havana, Willy Chirino's song 'La Jinetera' [The Rider] tells the story of Eve, a seventeen-year-old Cuban prostitute who plies her wares among American tourists, after her student activist boyfriend fled on a boat to the U.S. Chirino, originally born in Cuba, played Miami night clubs as a teenager and pioneered the Miami Sound, a fusion of Cuban, Brazilian and American musical styles. Since 1994, the Willy Chirino Foundation funds projects which supply the basic needs of food, water and medical care to underprivileged children and their families in the Americas. For its efforts, the foundation received a UNICEF award.
CD cover courtesy of Sony Discos

'The Rider'[1]

When the sun sets over the pier
Eve is preparing for action
Lying in wait for the tourists in Havana
For a few dollars she'll sell you her cherry.

Her mini-skirt reveals all
While she does the circuit
Where a few bucks buy you whatever you want
Make way for Eve, the rider.

Chorus:
She's only seventeen, but has had more adventures than Tarzan
Underneath her laughter, Eve, the rider, is crying for her Adam.

She's got a small room in Luyano
Where tonight she'll take what she's won
This is how she feeds her little seven-month-old girl
Appearances are never what they seem.

Her boyfriend was a student and an activist
For the party that breaks those who don't support it
When he woke up to the lie, he accepted the truth
And with four boards and an oar, to old Uncle Sam he fled.

And when the sun rises again over the pier
It's the same old routine, the same old thing
Living in a country where the future
Leapt over the wall and swam away.

I don't want my song to bring you down
But take this as a promise
That I will soon be singing in my land
Because I know Havana is waiting for me.

1. 'The Rider' is a translation of 'La Jinetera' by Willy Chirino from the CD *Asere* (Sony Tropical Label CDZ-81713 2-469801; U.S., 1995)
Music and lyrics: written by Willy Chirino, published by BN Tunes (BMI)

"Why have they gone behind a building?" There are thirty million Algerians who suspect something's going on. Some people even look behind the TV set. And if you suspect something's going on, well – cut the whole building. Get rid of the building and the actors along with it. "Get out!"'

And what about the families at home?

Usually the family members only see a film together at the weekends. The father gives permission. He's the one who issues a family film-viewing visa, after studying the television listings during the morning on the first day of the weekend. In other words on the Thursday. Our weekend is Thursday-Friday! Even our weekends are different from other people's. The whole world has Saturday-Sunday, and we have Thursday-Friday. Just like that! For no reason at all! It's nerve-racking! The French have Saturday-Sunday – and we have Thursday-Friday! There are three countries in the world with their weekend on Thursday-Friday: Algeria, Saudi Arabia and Libya. And if ever we have any trouble with these countries – well, that's the end of it. We'll have to have our weekend on Monday-Tuesday!

So, on Thursday mornings, the father buys the newspaper and studies the programme. At half-past-eight that evening there's *Vengeance in the Desert* with John Wayne and Rita Hayworth. It could be an Algerian film. We know all about the desert, and as for vengeance – we invented it. In the evening, all the family is gathered round the TV set. Sixty people in the living room. Cousins, neighbours – sometimes there are people who come to the house, have a meal, see the film and leave – and we don't even know them!

And they manage well the *meïdas* [small, low table] – the little oriental cakes – jasmine, all kinds of drinks, tea, coffee, Coca-Cola, *gazouze* [soft drinks]. The evening starts at eight o'clock. From eight to eight-thirty, there's the disinformation bulletin. All the animals come on! At 8.30, there's the weather forecast, but that only takes a couple of seconds: tomorrow 48°C.

Then the film starts. TATATATA! *Vengeance in the Desert*. John Wayne, Rita Hayworth – TATATATA! The credits disappear and you see the desert, the dunes, turned leaden by the sun. Suddenly a very small rider appears from behind the furthest dune, way off on the horizon.

'That's bound to be John Wayne. He's playing the main part, so you see him first!' The rider gradually comes up closer and you recognise him. Yes, it's John Wayne. His horse rears up, neighs. John Wayne gets off. He goes towards a mirage for a drink of water. The camera turns. Panorama. From the other side, another dune, another rider is approaching, very small, dressed in black.

'WOW! That's great! Someone's going to die right at the beginning! Terrific! That's the sort of film!!! Come on, come here grandma, come on, sit down! Don't be frightened, there's no need to hide behind the curtain, come on, I tell you! It's a film with people dying. It's not a love film. There's nothing to be afraid of.

'It's an Algerian film, there are only people dying in it. It's a comedy. No cause for alarm, we're all going to enjoy it. Sit down. There you are, you see that one, the second rider? John Wayne's going to kill him in a minute. John Wayne's very strong. He's stronger than Boumedienne!'

The second rider gets nearer. The closer he gets, the more the national silence descends. 'What's that? Ohhh! A WOMAN! What does she think she's doing in the desert? Haven't you got a family, children? Well, I wouldn't know, but surely there are a whole lot of things you should be doing at home – the washing, feeding your offspring, instead of wandering around in the sand. Not only that, John Wayne is behind the rock. If he sees you, there's nothing he wouldn't stop at! Bah, call that a film! There's no fun in it any more! Go on, grandma, I think it's time to go and put the tea on again, go on. Go and put it on, I tell you! Go on, girls, go with her; she needs help. That's it, let it boil until the cows come home. And drink it out in the kitchen!'

The second rider has arrived. It's Rita Hayworth. She gets off her horse. John Wayne has heard the sound of neighing and turns round. He sees her. 'Wow, but I know that one – we're in the same film!' John Wayne smiles. Rita smiles. Throughout Algeria people are no longer smiling.

The actor advances, the actress advances. The closer they get to each other, the more all the muscles in Algeria are tensing. Hair is standing on end. The actor advances, the actress advances. The censor in his studio is raring to go, ready to draw his scissors. 'Oh, dear me, they want to put me to work right away. But, by Allah, you're not going to touch her! You don't know Mohmoha – off you go, I'll give you a head start. In a couple of seconds you're going to find yourself in a saloon and you won't have the slightest idea what's going on!'

The actor advances, the actress advances …

Half the viewers avert their gaze from the TV – and look at the light bulbs on the ceiling.

'That's a 60 watt, isn't it?'

The actor advances, the actress advances …

You hear a squeaking sound as toes put on the brakes inside shoes. That's the main cause of shoe-wear in Algeria. It's the only country in the world where shoes wear out on the inside.

The actor advances, the actress advances …

One guy takes a glass of tea, raises it to his lips: 'Ah, it's good, this Coca-Cola!'

The actor advances, the actress advances …

There's another guy with a cigar in his hand. He has put it out on his father's arm and his father hasn't even noticed.

The actor advances, the actress advances …

Just as they are facing each other, ready to kiss, at the very same second, throughout the country, you hear the sound of fifteen million ears being boxed.

'WHAM! Off you go, go and do your homework! You're not doing any schoolwork these days! I've noticed – you're not working!

'But, Papa, I'm top of the class!'

'Well, I want you to be more than top. What's better than top, before number one? Zero! Right, you'll be a zero! And you, go and get me a glass of water!'

'But Papa, they've cut off the water!'

'Well, just stay there until it comes on again!'

The actor and the actress kiss – and the censor draws his scissors. SNIP! SNIP! He circumcises the film and the film becomes *halal* [permitted in Islam].

Since the arrival of the satellite dish, our national channel has done its best. Confronted with other cultures, other channels, competition, it has been forced to operate on their level.

You won't believe me! An absolutely incredible thing happened a few years ago. Well, incredible these days, but true. Algerian television showed a documentary about a clinic, a maternity hospital with babies – stark naked! Not a bad start, hey? It's wonderful, marvellous, amazing.

LONG LIVE ALGERIA! HURRAH!!! LONG LIVE ALGERIA!!!

Translated from the French by Hazel Wachters

1. '*Djurdjurassique Bled*: Censorship' was performed as an encore on 15 May 1999. The script was originally published in French, *Djurdjurassique Bled* by Mohamed Fellag; Editions Lattès, Paris, 1999.

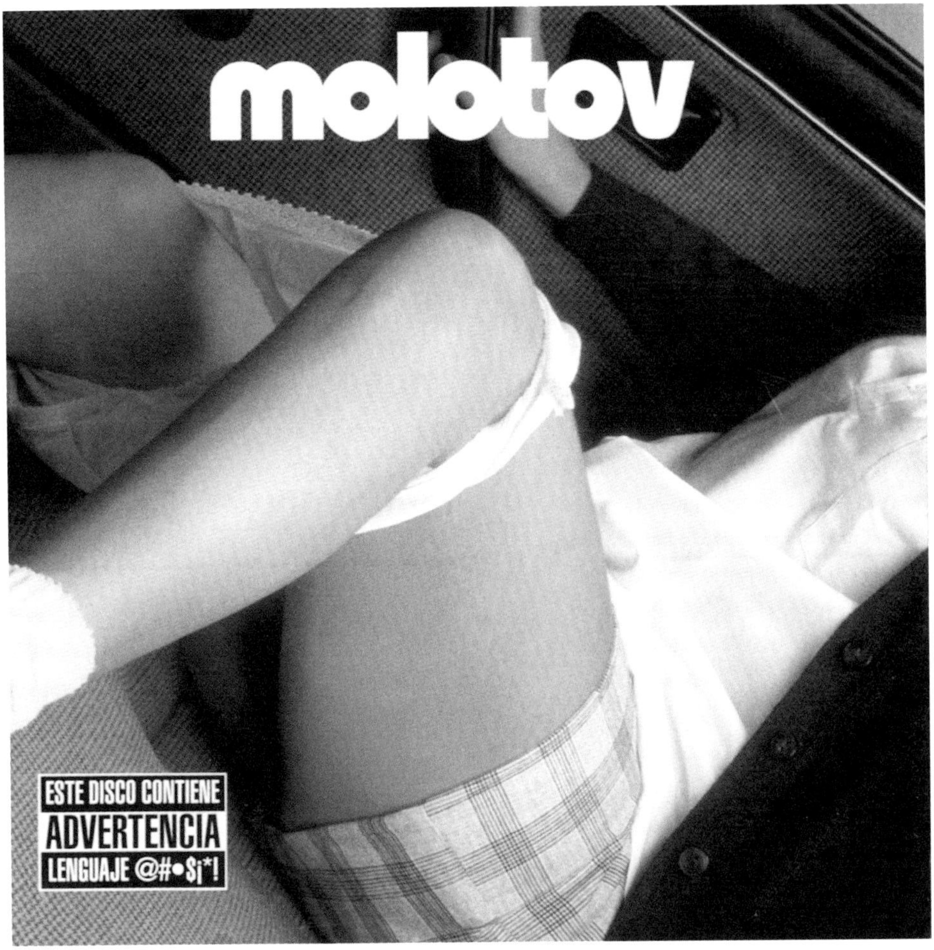

Molotov, Mexico
Dónde jugarán las niñas, 2000

The Mexican rock/hip hop band Molotov causes insult wherever they go. In northern Mexico, a bishop headed a PTA [Parents Teachers Association] campaign to prevent the band from performing live. At the daily Mexico City newspaper, *Variedades*, the band has been accused of being 'offensive' and 'polluting' Mexico. While in Spain, gay and lesbian groups attempted to have the group jailed for their controversial song 'Puto', derogatory slang for homosexuals. In 1998, Molotov's debut album *Dónde jugarán las niñas* [Where the Little Girls Play] sold 700,000 copies and was nominated for a Grammy. Their second CD *Molomix* was produced by the Beastie Boys. (See page 82) CD cover © 2000 Surco Records/Universal Music Group

Molotov

'Gimme the Power'[1]

The police run a protection racket
Although they live thanks to your money
If they treat you like a criminal
It's not your fault, just thank the *Regente*.[2]
You must rip it out by the roots
You must change our Government
The bureaucratic people
And those who want more and more.
That is why I complain and complain
Because here in my new home I am not a fool any more
That worries about the Government
And with the ones that are getting rich.
People who live in poverty
Nobody does anything for them, and nobody cares
The top people hate you
And more people would like to chop off their heads
If you give power to the powerful
They will try to get you faster.
Because we used to be a world power
We are poor, we have no leaders

Chorus:
Give me, give me, give me,
Give me all the power
To get on the mother
Gimme all the power
So I can come around and fuck you
Because we weren't born hungry
We don't have to ask ourselves, what are we going to do?
If they label us as lazy sods, we are not ...
Viva Mexico – Bastards!
Let's feel the Mexican power,
Let's feel that we are all brothers

Just because we are many and eat well
Doesn't mean we have to follow the idiots
These people move us around wherever it suits them
It is our blood that's keeping them alive,
And hot bread is keeping them alive
Our people's bread.

Molotov

'Puto'[3]

Fuck the man that doesn't jump and skip
Fuck the man that doesn't shout and swear
Fuck the guy who conformed
Fuck the man that believed the news
Fuck the man that takes our bread
The man that doesn't do what he wants
A fucker he is born and a fucker he will die.

Murderer: kill that fag
What does that fucker want?
He wants to cry, he wants to cry.

1. 'Gimme the Power' is a translation of 'Dame todo el power' by Molotov from the CD *Dónde jugarán las niñas* [Where the Little Girls Play] (Universal Music 75031; Mexico, 1997)
2. Mayor of Mexico City
3. 'Puto' by Molotov is also from the CD *Dónde jugarán las niñas*

Malu Halasa

Songs for a Civil War: Algerian Raï, Rap and Berber Folksong

> 'You listened to gossip and you were in a hurry.'
> Cheb Hasni from 'Ma Tabkis, Hadha Maktubi'
> [Do Not Cry, This Is My Destiny]

Raï singers, who were not afraid of being murdered, returned to Algeria for Cheb Hasni's funeral in 1994. Immediately afterwards, Chaba Zahouania, who sang with Hasni on his first hit 'We Made Love in a Broken Shed', went straight to the airport and flew out of the country. Another popular woman singer, Chaba Fedela – wearing a *hijab* Islamic headdress in an effort to blend in with the 10,000 mourners – also left the country and returned to Paris, with her husband Cheb Sahraoui, where they now live in exile.

Hasni, 26, was known for his sentimental Raï love songs. He was gunned down in the Gambetta district of Oran – or Wahran in Arabic – the city of his birth. He had spent the previous night, like countless Raï singers before him, performing in one of the city's clubs. The frenetic, dancing crowd shouted '*Ah, ya Raï!*' to encourage Hasni to sing until dawn. The next day he was on his way to a soccer match when he was killed. If the Islamicists were trying to send a message to the 75 per cent of the Algerian population under 30, they failed. Hasni's death caused a run on Raï cassettes, increasing their value fivefold.[1]

Hasni was murdered four days after the kidnapping of the 42-year-old Berber singer Lounès Matoub, who was later freed and finally murdered in 1998. Popular *Raï Rebels* producer, 47-year-old Rachid Baba-Ahmed, and the 28-year-old singer Cheb Aziz also fell in the war of attrition that has been taking place against Algerian intellectuals, artists, journalists and political activists since the government cancelled elections against the popular Front Islamic du Salut (FIS) in 1992. An estimated 70,000 people have been killed in Algeria's brutal civil war. As a result, Raï's most popular singer, Khaled, whose lyrics were banned in his own country the year of Hasni's murder, refuses to go home. 'I'm not a politician, only a messenger. But in some countries, to sing about life is by its nature a political act.'[2]

The 'Prince of Raï' Cheb Mami makes a point of returning annually to Algeria to renew his family and artistic ties. 'First of all, it's my country,' he stresses. 'I need Algeria, to rebuild my reserves there. Obviously, I have to take precautions. But once I'm in the bath, I forget them straight away. On each trip to Oran, I am rejuvenated. It's too easy to say you are afraid.'[3]

Khaled, Mami, Zahouania and Fedela, together with Sahraoui, all have flourishing careers inside and outside the communities of people from the Maghreb in Paris and Marseilles. Raï's engaging mix of flamenco, rock, reggae, hip hop and funk, accented with traditional North African instruments such as the *derbouka* (a goblet or hand-drum) and the *gasba* (a rosewood flute) has intrigued foreign audiences since 'Didi' by Khaled reached the French Top Ten in 1992. Ironically, the western country responsible for Algeria's violent colonial past – and some insist France is not neutral in the current turmoil – is where Algerians fleeing the war find refuge. Clearly Raï arrived in France as a minority or immigrant music, but popular culture rarely operates in a vacuum. Consequently, a variety of Maghrebi influences have been infiltrating French pop with the rise of bands such as Gnawa Diffusion, Lojo, and Orchestre de Barbès, which play a distinctive blend of popular and traditional music from around the world.

The origins of Raï

> 'It was a single bed and my love and I slept in it
> He scratched my back and I gave him my all'
> Cheikha Remitti from 'Al-Habib al-Chatar' [Clever Lover]

Raï would have remained a little-known, regional sound played in Oranaise bars and cabarets, but it made the same journey that characterises other 'vulgar street music'.[4] Like American blues and rap, it travelled from obscure grassroots origins to the heart of dominant mainstream culture, propelled by its difference and vivacity.

In the 1920s, the Bedouin forms of *chi'r el-melhoun* – Arabic folk lyrics – were sung by itinerant Algerian *chioukh* – the plural of *cheikh*, an honorific title meaning 'venerable sir'. These formal songs about the night sky and the desert held little relevance to Algerians, who, forced off their lands by French colonialists, had become a poverty-stricken, migrant workforce. They laboured in the vineyards around Oran, which had once grown cereals for domestic consumption. Their free time and little money were spent in the city's seaside bars and clubs, where Raï was born in the Twenties.

It was the *cheikhat* – the plural of *cheikha*, originally a title of respect for women well-versed in art and poetry – who sang, danced and drummed for both men and women at traditional festivals, circumcisions and weddings. However, once these 'venerable ladies' went looking for work in the cities, like many destitute Algerians before them, they found their main audiences in the male-only hashish dens, in cabarets – which bordered on brothels – or during the *gasra* [a stag party for wedding feasts]. The *cheikhat* improvised songs about women's intimate lives in a colourful Wahrani patois which lent itself to risqué punning and innuendo. Shunned by respectable society, the *cheikhat* were known to their fans by adopted nicknames and were rarely photographed without their veils. The exception was Cheikha Remitti, whose crude lyrics ridiculed the French and the Muslims. Her first national hit in the 1950s 'Charag, Gatta' [Tear, Lacerate], about virginity, outraged conservative Algerians.

Remitti grew up homeless, sleeping in hammans [public bath-houses] and in the shrines of local marabouts or local saints. She had been given her nickname by French soldiers in a café after she kept ordering another drink, saying '*Remettez*' in French – 'give me another'. Her first improvised verses were topical, inspired by the terrible epidemics, such as the plague that was mentioned by Camus – a *pied-noir*, also born in Oran – in the novel *The Plague* published in 1947. However, most of her songs were about the hardship of women's lives, as more and more Algerian men had to move around their own country or even go abroad to find work, or about women's love affairs, sometimes with independence fighters. Her uncommonly gritty lyrics cut to the quick of normally clandestine sexual politics, as in one song about the repugnant attitude of old men towards their young brides: 'Does the saliva of revolting old men have anything to do with clean saliva of young women?'[5] Early 78 rpm recordings for Pathé in 1936 earned her the nickname of the Piaf of Raï. Raï comes from the Arabic root *ra'i* [the verb to see] which also has myriad meanings – opinion,

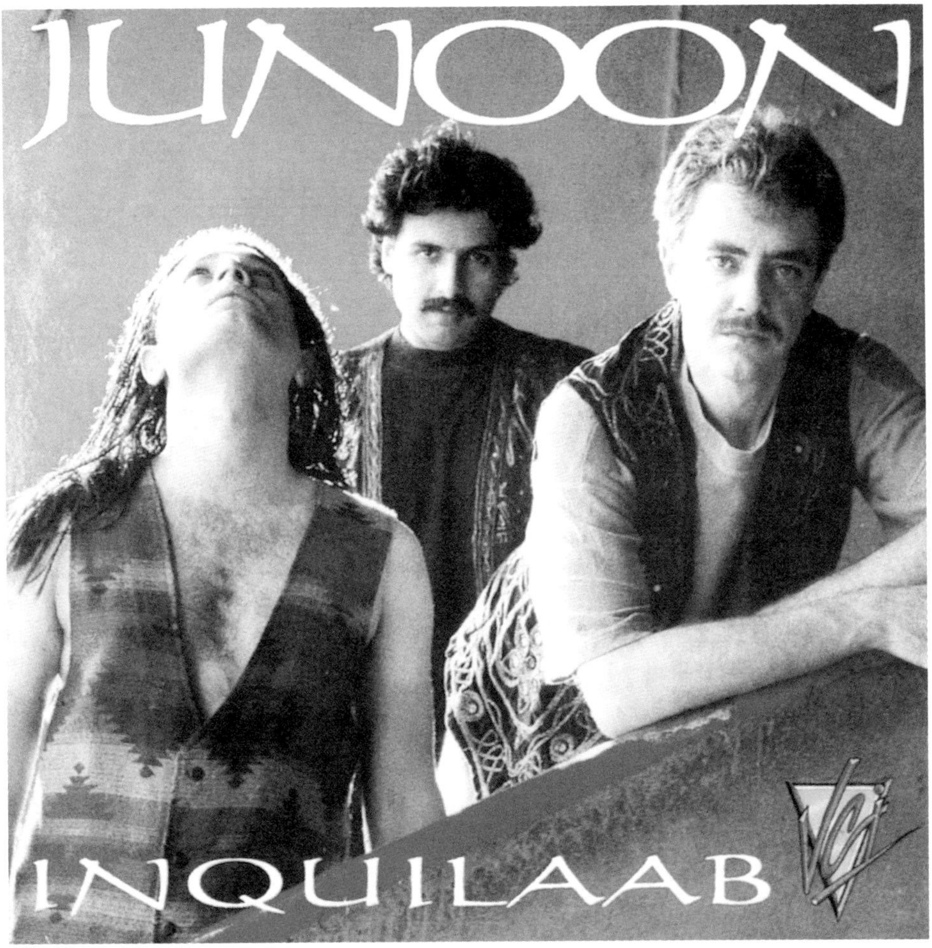

Junoon, Pakistan
Inquilaab, 1996

Although the rock trio Junoon has been banned from Pakistan state TV and radio, they find fans in unusual places. After their hit 'Ehtesaab' [Accountability], the band worked for weeks to get permission to play Karachi's Nishtar Park, an area known for its militant Urdu nationalist leanings that is ringed by Islamic religious schools. Despite permission, there was no electricity on stage, until Junoon guitarist Salam Ahmad approached a local mullah who recognised him as the author of the spiritual song 'Saeen' [Saint]. Once Junoon agreed not to play during the call to prayer, a cable was set up from the school to the guitar amps. (See page 162)
CD cover courtesy of Junoon

'Bulleya!' [Bulleh Shah][1]

Bulleya, who am I?
I am no believer in a mosque
And I have no pagan ways
I am not pure. I am not vile
I'm no Moses and I'm no Pharaoh
Bulleya, who am I?

First and last, I see the self
I recognise no second to it
No one is more knowing than me
But, Bulleh, who is it that I am?
Bulleya, who am I?

Water nor dust are neither what makes me
I am not flame. I am not wind
I am not pure. I am not vile
I'm no Moses and I'm no Pharaoh
Bulleya, who am I?
Bulleya, who am I?

– Bulleh Shah

'Aleph'[2]

Cryptic Sciences? Enough already!

The first letter is all you need
Aleph is all you need
Knowledge hardly comes in dozens
And who's to say how long you'll last?
Cryptic Sciences? Enough already!
Aleph is all you need

You read heaps and write heaps
And bury your head in books
Light is everywhere but where you are
And you haven't a clue how to reach it

Marking time in extra prayers
Climbing a minaret and screeching
Mounting a pulpit and preaching –
All this has nothing to do with knowledge
Cryptic Sciences? Enough already!
Aleph is all you need.

Aleph is all you need.

– Bulleh Shah

1. Bulleh Shah (1680-1757) was a Sufi poet whose poetry transcends religions, castes, creeds and borders. His poetry, which embraces secular and human values, remains popular with ordinary people who throng his shrine in the city of Kasur in Pakistan. After Partition in 1947, official promotion of Urdu as the language of Muslim nationalism entailed semi-suppression of Shah's humanistic and secularising poetry written in the Punjabi language. The lyrics of 'Bulleya!', first written by Shah, were adapted by Junoon from the Persian poem by Maulana Jalauddin Rumi, the poet mystic who founded the Sufi Mevlevi order of the whirling dervishes.
2. 'Aleph', also by Shah, takes its name from the first letter of the Arabic and Hebrew alphabet. According to legend, at an early age Shah was a terrible student. During his first alphabet lessons, he would not recite beyond the first letter Aleph. When teachers scolded him, he answered, 'But Aleph is all you need!' – the reasoning being that Aleph is the first letter in the name of Allah.
'Bulleya!' [Bulleh Shah] and 'Aleph' by Junoon appear on *Parvaaz* (EMI/VIRGIN; Lahore, 1999), the group's fifth album which is dedicated to the poet. Song Lyrics: translated by Andy McCord, © Nameless Music LLC

advice and judgment, among others. Raï also embodies the concept of freedom of expression. However, after Algerian independence in 1962, the new authorities became more intent on controlling the outspoken music. The rapid Arabisation programme begun by the post-independence government of Colonel Boumedienne, nostalgic for Nasser's pan-Arabism, banned the *cheikhat* from singing in public. They were replaced by young men with high, feminine voices.[6] Many *cheikhat* either returned to their original training ground, the *meddahat* female orchestras, singing ritual and religious songs to women only, or they performed at weddings, using slang and vulgarities that would not be tolerated in the newly-sanctified public sphere. Raï went underground and its improvisation, teasing and allegorical bawdiness were only accepted within the closed quarters of Algerian family life.

Pop-Raï

'The young girl wants to get married
The divorced woman wants to break loose
The married woman wants a divorce
The married woman wants to break loose
The married woman wants to go wild ...'
Khaled from 'Hada Raykoum' [It's Your Opinion]

The country's social strictness was at odds with the times. On the radio, Algerians were listening to the Rolling Stones, the Beatles and James Brown. The new directness made an impression on Cheb Khaled: 'Nobody sang about sex, so we all went wild when we heard James Brown on the radio singing "Sex Machine". But we could hardly understand the lyrics, so we were all asking: "What is this sex machine?" Once we found out, there was no stopping us.'[7]

Khaled and his friends were also listening to a new music coming from just over the border from Morocco. Nass el Ghiwana merged politicised lyrics with percussive beats. Algerian musicians were keen to take advantage of the public's appetite for new instrumentation. A relatively inexpensive sound technology, the synthesiser, provided a range of quirky, never-before-heard sounds. This, coupled with a drum machine and, later, electric guitar and violin, sax or trumpet, provided a new musical backing. Modern Raï or 'Pop-Raï', to distinguish it from earlier forms, was to gain a reputation among western music critics from 1979 as Algerian rock'n'roll, but its song patterns are highly traditional. The spoken dedications recall the beginning of *cheikhat* songs. Also, as Tony Langlois analyses in *Popular Music*, the call and response between the synthesiser and the drum machine have their antecedents in traditional wedding music that uses the *ghraita* (double reed shawarm pipes) and the *tabl* (a large double-headed drum). These same patterns are also duplicated in the relationship between the trumpets and the snare and bass drums in western Algeria and eastern Morocco. He observes: 'This example of syncretism is clearly the result of colonial culture contact; instruments have changed, but the role and social context have remained largely unaltered.'[8]

Messaoud Bellemou began playing the trumpet in Ain Temouchent's municipal brass band and his early recording 'Ya Rayi' [My Raï] from 1975 predates the Pop-Raï explosion on the world music scene. This begins, according to critics, with Bellemou's 1979 hit with a singer and actress Fedela Zalmat 'Ana M'Hlali Ennoum' [I Don't Care About Sleep Anymore], a song she had written with her girlfriends. Fedela started singing when she was eight and caused a scandal as a drinking, mini-skirted teenager in the 1976 television film *Djalti*. She adopted the stage name 'Chaba' Fedela – meaning young – to distinguish her from previous generations of *cheikhat*. She and her husband 'Cheb' – also young – Sahraoui, a classically-trained musician from the Oran Conservatoire, had a follow-up hit six years later with 'N'sel Fik' [You Are Mine]. They are considered Algeria's Sonny and Cher.

However, the Cheb who became Raï's undisputed king, crowned in Oran's first Raï music festival in 1985, was the rakish Khaled Brahim, the son of a retired policeman. Like other Raï singers, Cheb Khaled performed at weddings and cabarets. When he was fourteen, he recorded his first 45 single, 'Trig Lici' [The Road to School], about a long walk up the hill to school, a song that brought him national notoriety. Growing up, Cheb Khaled played guitar, bass, accordion and the harmonica and listened to an impressive range of music from Um Kalthum to Edith Piaf, Elvis and Johnny Halliday. The 'Cheb' was dropped after he moved to France.

Khaled and Cheb Mami had similar experiences as teenage performers and both benefited from the rise of cheap cassette recorders. Unlike television, cassette recorders encouraged grassroots musical forms to flourish, through the technology's interactive nature. The proliferation of tapes also meant that singers no longer relied on hostile state radio to play their social criticism. With the new technology came the rise of the *éditeur*, a manager and producer who made financial and artistic decisions, as well as arranging for singers to record in the twelve-track or the few available 24-track recording studios. An *éditeur* also handled the manufacturing of the cassettes and their distribution to small shops. Khaled complained that he never made any money from his music in Algeria, but nobody else did either. Profits from the Raï explosion in the west never filtered back to the small labels in Algeria. Again, the parallels between early blues, rap and Raï performers are striking, particularly when it comes to matters of payment.

Obviously, before the Algerian civil war started, Raï singers went to France as economic refugees looking for opportunity, much like the Kabyle Berbers from the mountainous district outside Algiers who became Parisian cab drivers. In 1986, Cheb Mami arrived in the French capital ostensibly to buy equipment, with the attitude '... of a tourist who was not in the slightest interested in the Eiffel Tower or the Louvre. My tourism was the Pigalle sound-system shops.'[9] Paris was the door to New York and the rest of the world, but life in the west was not without its cultural misunderstandings and often blatant racism. During the 1991 Gulf War, Cheb Mami was banned by French radio stations and his concerts received bomb threats, due to the fact that Algeria supported Iraq, as did Le Pen and the French fascists.

While Raï was intriguing foreign audiences abroad, it was still causing repercussions back home. Some of it had been sanitised and sentimentalised for family audiences, but 'dangerous' songs about sex, looking for sex, drinking and getting drunk were considered *'ayb* [shameful] in respectable company. Human rights activist Marc Schade-Poulsen learnt the finer distinctions when he went to live in Oran. Some dutiful sons did not listen to Raï in front of their fathers, although they played 'dubious' cassettes in the company of their adoring mothers. Some sisters did not play it in front of their brothers or parents, while there were brothers who were too embarrassed to listen to it in each other's company.[10]

Khaled framed his songs within the context of local place names in and around Oran, and his audiences loved hearing about a broken affair on the Boulevard Front du Mer, where many Raï singers were photographed for their cassette covers. But locality rarely translates well in the global marketplace. Once *Khaled*, his first album for the French Polygram subsidiary Barclay, was released in 1991, showcasing a new international sound provided by ambient avant-garde composer

***Algerap*, Compilation of Algerian Rappers, 1999**

'Hamma and Untik [are] stars of Algerian rap ... Completely banned from Algerian state radio and television, they draw vast crowds wherever they appear – Paris, Algiers, Marseilles. Along with [groups like] K2C, De Men, K Libre and Cause Toujours, they ... recorded their first hip hop compilation for Virgin ... In France they sing mainly in Arabic. Their calls to revolt and contempt for government speak across the divides of race and language to all who are excluded by unemployment, homelessness, racism, the life of the ghetto in the barren, urban wastelands of metropolitan France ...' (See page 45) (Chawki Amari, 'In the Land of Raï', *Index on Censorship*, 3/1999, p. 168) CD cover courtesy of Virgin Music France

Darkman & K-Rime

'The Outcome'[1]

In Algeria,
running rumour,
annoying critique,
compromising words,
a real outrage to the impious,
constantly diving among the noise.

Intik

'Words in the Air (Tragedy)'

Now I'm going to the heart of the subject,
To speak about those who have been mistreated,
I'm talking about the children who have been burnt to ashes,
We are like birds in a cage, that can no longer fly,
Thirsty for freedom.

Algerian rapper Sofiane[2] remembers why he started to rap:
'On 5 October 1988, I was twelve ... I cut my classes to join other Algerian [students] at the demonstration, without really knowing why I was doing it. Anyhow, I just wanted to blow off steam. I was young and I'll never forget that day. It was the first time I saw the uniforms of the blue helmets[3] and, in front of my eyes, weapons. For the first time I heard the sound [of gunfire]. It was also on that day I tasted teargas ... Like everybody else in the Souk el Fellah I picked up a pair of Stan Smiths[4] and the coins scattered on the floor. But when I saw kids beaten up by the blue helmets and overheard that some were even killed in Bab el Oud, I immediately went back home where my terrified mother was waiting for me. I understood nothing of what I had lived through or seen that day. It is only with maturity that I have come to understand the whys of those events and the reason I rap, "Fed up with promises, we call SOS. Fed up with those shut ups, many mothers have suffered, like your mother and mine."'

Translated from the French by Mai Ghoussoub

1. The raps, 'The Outcome' and 'Words in the Air (Tragedy)', are translations of 'Constat' and 'Des Paroles en l'Air' from the CD *Algerap* (Virgin France, 1999)
   Lyrics: 'Constat' by Darkman + K-Rime, 'Des Paroles en l'Air' by Intik.
2. Sofiane, *Libre Algérie* No. 02 du Lundi 28 Septembre au Dimanche 11 Octobre 1998. He is the founder and leader of the rap group, Hamma Boys. He raps on 'The Shade of Nothingness' with De Men on the CD *Algerap*
3. 'Blue helmets' is slang for the Algerian riot police whose helmets are blue
4. Stan Smiths are popular Adidas sneakers

Michael Brooks and pop producer Don Was, disgruntled Oranaise complained to music critic Langlois from *Popular Music* that Khaled's songs were 'not about anything'.

That album featured the single 'Didi' and sold two-and-a-half million cassettes in Egypt.[11] After one of his concerts nearly caused a riot in Cairo, the song was taken off the airwaves by the Egyptian government. It was so popular in India that the singer recorded a Hindi version. The bigger the music became the more it bothered Algerian extremists. Khaled was pragmatic: 'I know I am at the top of a list of well-known people the fundamentalists want to kill. I don't have bodyguards, just tight security during concerts. Even so, I get scared.'[12]

In 1998, he was accused of wanting to play in Israel at a time when Arab artists and musicians maintained a cultural boycott. This is not the first time Khaled found himself in the hall of mirrors that is Middle East politics. After *Le Monde* asked him about sales of his first record in Israel, he explained somewhat expansively that he had been born under a French flag, his godmother was French and his bass player Jewish and that the Arabs and Jews are cousins. After the subsequent public outcry in Algeria, Khaled later retracted his statement.

East meets west: the new musical hybrids

> *'Je voudrais être un fauteuil/dans un salon de coiffure pour dames*
> *pour que les fesses des belles âmes/s'écrasent contre mon orgueil'*
> [I would like to be an armchair in a hair salon for ladies/
> so that the bottoms of these beautiful souls/get crushed against my pride ...]
> Gnawa Diffusion from 'Ombre Elle' [Her Shadow]

For North Africans, Marseilles is the gateway to the west. The tangle of tiny streets from the Vieux Port to Gare Saint-Charles, where thousands arrive from the Maghreb each weekend for shopping and visiting, have been derided as 'the Cashbah' (sic).[13] Because Algeria was a possession of France, it has stronger historic and political ties than other French colonies in North Africa. But it is the Algerian immigrants who have brought Raï into direct contact with French culture. Consequently *le style beur* has become more than a fleeting exoticism and rising Raï stars storming Paris have become household names. Two such singers joined Khaled for a celebration of *algérainité* [Algerianness] at POPB in Paris in 1998. The event was recorded and released as the live, double CD set *1,2,3, Soleils*. The second *Soleil* was 21-year-old, fresh-faced singer Faudel and the third was Rachid Taha who had been scathing about France when he had been the lead singer of the *beur-franco* punk band Carte de Séjour, named after the country's green card. Their song 'Douce France' was described by world music critic Andy Morgan in *Songlines* as a subversion of Charles Trenet's classic French eulogy.[14] Taha also had a hit in 1993 with 'Voilà Voilà' at a time when the Front National was making headway in the municipal elections.

Taha's solo work with the techno producer Steve Hillage has taken Algerian popular music to startling levels. In his explanation of the title song in the CD's liner notes, he explains his unique approach: 'I started out with the idea that "Olé, olé" comes from Allah. Actually it is from "yallah", which means onward. In some Arab orchestras, the music stops and you know someone's going to say some great poem with the music, and everyone else is saying "Yallah, yallah". It's a big deal, you know, it's Allah. In flamenco music, in certain parts of Andalusia, they say "olleh", and it's even closer to Allah. The story is also about betrayal.' Taha's second CD, *Diwân*, illustrates the history of Algerian popular music through song. Taha mentions both the trumpeter Bellemou and

 Sheik El Hadj Mohamed el Anka, the founder of *chaabi* – Algerian popular song – who broke from the Arab Andalusian music of the past with his emphasis on gritty realism. *Diwân* also includes songs dedicated to the working-class singer and composer Dahmane el Harrachi who wrote on themes close to Algerians living abroad: exile and loss. Taha is one of the first Algerian musicians to marry the experiences of exiles in a foreign land with the new, ultra hi-tech musical culture that confronts them. But they are not the only people being influenced by strangers in their midst.

'French kids know Raï the same way white, British youth culture knew reggae in the Seventies,' according to Justin Adams, a guitarist formerly with Jah Wobble and Sinéad O'Connor. An expert on Arabic and African music, Adams plays a mixture of Malian blues and North African rhythms on his debut CD, *Desert Road*. He also produces world music bands, including Lojo from France.

'For the past ten years, a few French groups have taken North African and African influences and formed mixed bands with musicians from these countries, who were either born in or living in France. The fact that bands like Gnawa Diffusion from Grenoble and Lojo from Anvers – two towns far from Marseilles – incorporate Maghrebi influences in their music show just how inextricably French youth culture is linked to North Africa.'

The frontman in the five-piece Gnawa Diffusion is Amazigh Kateb, the son of the Algerian independence novelist Kateb Yacine. Amazigh moved to France at the age of sixteen. His band Gnawa Diffusion mixes *gnawa* – a 3,000-year-old trance-musical tradition of black, Saharan slaves – with rock, pop, reggae, even French chanson. Amazigh, who was given a Berber name meaning 'free man' – unusual for a Muslim Algerian – accents his country's diversity by playing *chaabi*.

'It's not a problem that we are Arab and Islamic in our culture,' he points out during an interview at the 1999 WOMAD [World of Music Arts and Dance] festival in Reading, 'but Algerians are a lot of other things too – Gnawa, Berber ... In my country we have a model. To be Algerian, you have to make an effort. Don't eat on the street during Ramadan, and if your sister wears a short skirt you'd better be macho or you're not "Algerian". These are not questions about identity. This is the social model of the Front de Libération National (FNL), which wants all Algerians to be the same. Now the crisis for the Algerian people is to act like individuals.'

Away from his native city of Algiers for a decade, Amazigh knows that he would not be allowed to make his music in his homeland and appreciates the freer cultural climate in France. Bands who play more than 42 shows a year earn a subsidy from the French government.

Even in France, it's important for Amazigh to sing in popular street Arabic. 'In North Africa, we don't feel good about ourselves. We wait for westerners to say our music is "groovy". We shouldn't be ashamed of our language and our popular sayings. You have to have a local consciousness in the language, as well as in the politics. We have to be free.'

Without a distribution deal for North Africa, the band's two CDs are not sold there. However, Amazigh is aware that illegal cassette copies are turning a profit for the pirates. This has been a long established and reliable cultural trade route. Algerian exiles in the west have always relied on France to provide them with a platform from which to address their homeland, and historically Algerians back home have been keen to listen.

Journalist and novelist Lakhdar Belaid-Serhani remembers that his own parents, who were living in Paris, bought the cassettes of Slimane Azem, the banned and exiled Berber singer. Belaid-Serhani's parents made additional copies onto cassettes that had no name written on them or had the names of other singers written on them. These were then smuggled into Algeria, where it was a crime to possess any tapes by Azem, although he was played loudly in remote Berber mountain villages. For the 30 per cent of the Berber population living in Algeria, their fourteen dialects were virtually

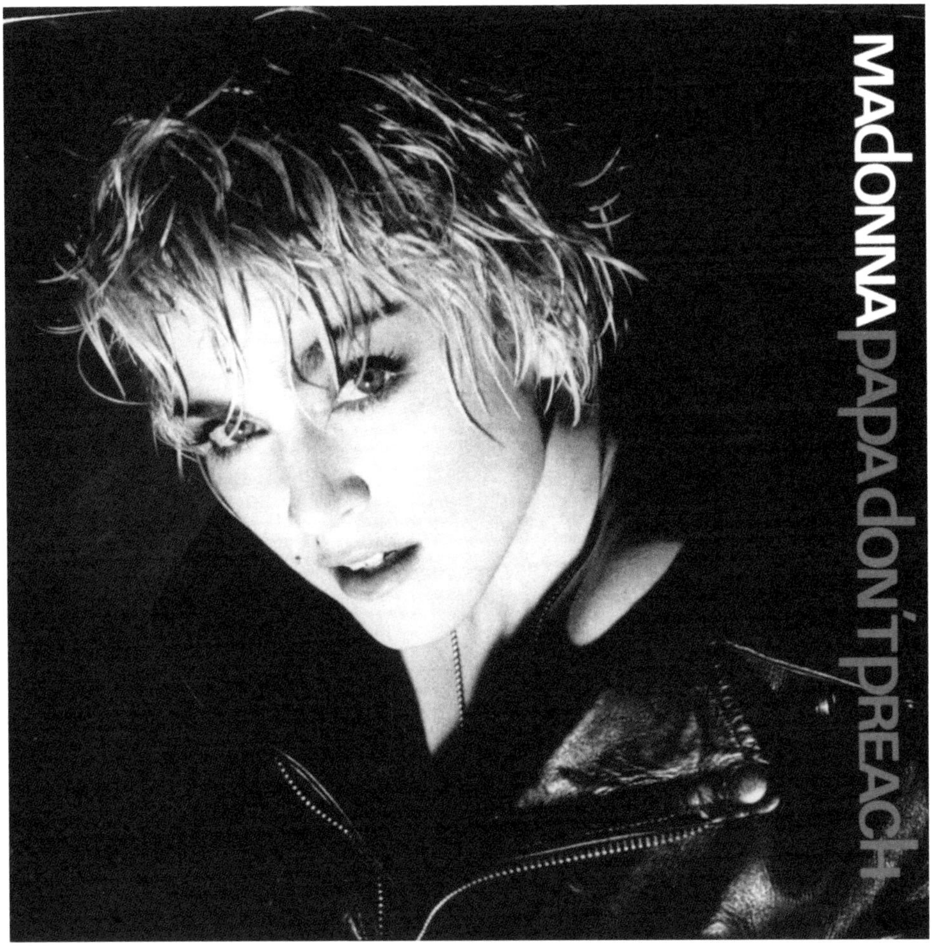

Madonna, U.S.
'Papa Don't Preach', 1986

'Too many kids are getting pregnant ... I don't like the message, but I do like the beat,' said a teenage girl about Madonna's 1986 hit 'Papa Don't Preach'. The single, about keeping an illegitimate baby, was criticised for promoting teenage pregnancy. Planned Parenthood of New York asked radio stations not to broadcast it. The organisation requested that a quarter of the song's earnings from Madonna's record company Warner Bros. went to responsible teen sex programmes. (Georgia Dullea, 'Madonna's New Beat Is a Hit, But Song's Message Rankles', *The New York Times*, 18 September 1986, p. B1) Single cover courtesy of Warner Bros. Records Inc.

'Papa Don't Preach'[1]

Papa I know you're going to be upset
'Cause I was always your little girl
But you should know by now
I'm not a baby

You always taught me right from wrong
I need your help, Daddy, please be strong
I may be young at heart
But I know what I'm saying

The one you warned me all about
The one you said I could do without
We're in an awful mess
And I don't mean maybe – please

Chorus:
Papa don't preach, I'm in trouble deep
Papa don't preach, I've been losing sleep
But I made up my mind, I'm keeping my baby
I'm gonna keep my baby, mmm ...

He says that he's going to marry me
We can raise a little family
Maybe we'll be all right
It's a sacrifice

But my friends keep telling me to give it up
Saying I'm too young, I ought to live it up
What I need right now is some good advice, please

Daddy, Daddy if you could only see
Just how good he's been treating me
You'd give us your blessing right now
'Cause we are in love
We are in love, so please

1. 'Papa Don't Preach' was the first single from Madonna's *True Blue* album, 1986.
Words and music by Madonna Ciccone and Brian Elliot © 1986 Elliot-Jacobsen Music Publishing Co., USA, Warner/Chappell Music Ltd., London W6 8BS, reproduced by permission of International Music Publications Ltd.

made redundant when Modern Standard Arabic became Algeria's official language after the revolution. In 1998, two weeks after the Berber singer Lounès Matoub was murdered by a faction claiming to belong to GIA (Groupe Islamique Armée), the government extended the Arabic official language law and made it a punishable offence for politicians to address Berber crowds in a dialect they could understand.[15]

When the dominant language no longer reflects everyday experiences, then a music which relies on the spoken word can be threatening. Although Algerian rap, banned from state radio and television, has become the latest 'pariah' music, it continues in the country's lively tradition of musical poetry. Hamma and Intik are rappers in a burgeoning new scene and have played to vast crowds in Algiers, Paris and Marseilles.[16] Their rhymes about inadequate schooling, high unemployment, no opportunity, Islamic extremism and ineffective government speak volumes to disaffected youth, whether they live in an Islamic society or in a Parisian *banlieue* [suburb].

Concerts, whether rap or Raï, are a chance for Algerians to meet as a community and renew cultural ties. In 1998, Belaid-Serhani saw a Parisian concert by Cheb Mami, the singer who has said he wants to combine the '*tchtche*' of the suburban rappers with Oranaise Raï. When he sang his song 'Bledi' [My Country], a hush went through the mixed audience of Algerians and French. Many people, the journalist observed, were on the verge of tears.

'For a number of French,' Belaid-Serhani concludes, 'a good Arab is someone who looks like them. This creates an inferiority complex in the French Muslim population but a singer like Cheb Mami builds self-confidence and reconciles Algerians with their past.'

As the crowd spilled out of the concert hall that evening, some Algerians might have pondered the curious state of affairs: the ability of some of their countrymen to find artistic freedom in situations often xenophobic and racist. However, thought and expression censored in one part of the world can flourish unexpectedly in another, where only a few people – maybe two or three – gather together and remember their country and culture. For Algerians, young and old alike, music has become an integral part of their national identity. Whether celebrated at home or in lonely, foreign cities abroad, it remains their last bastion of free expression during a pitiful civil war.

1. Boustany, Noura; 'For Raï, There's No Oasis in Algeria', *The Washington Post*, 2 July 1995, p. G02. Boustany also describes Cheb Hasni's murder and funeral at length.
2. Myers, Paul; 'Mixing It in a Mad World', *The Guardian*, 16 May 1997, p. G2T/23
3. Belaid-Serhani, Lakhdar; 'Cheb Mami', *L'Evènement du Jeudi*, 3-9 December 1998, p. 100
4. Sweeney, Philip; 'Algerian Raï – The French Connection', Hanly and May, eds.; *Rhythms of the Worlds*, BBC, London, 1989, pp. 48-57
5. From interviews with Cheikha Remitti conducted by Amel Tafsout, an Algerian anthropologist and dancer living in London.
6. Virolle, Marie; *La Chanson Raï*, Karthala, Paris, 1995
7. Myers; ibid.
8. Langlois, Tony; 'The Local and Global in North African Popular Music', *Popular Music*, vol. 15, 3, 1996, pp. 259-272. Langlois, who used to live in Oran, also gives a detailed description of the duties of *editeurs* in Raï, as well as local audience attitudes.
9. Belaid-Serhani; ibid.
10. Schade-Poulsen, Marc; *Men and Popular Music in Algeria: The Social Significance of Raï*, University of Texas, Austin, 1999
11. 'Raï', North Africa website: www-bcf.usc.edu/~~ccline/mag/nafrica.html
12. Strauss, Neil; 'Singing of a Beloved Homeland, Fearful of Going Home Again', *The New York Times*, 30 April 1995, Sec. 2, p. 33.
13. Sweeney, ibid., p. 265
14. Morgan, Andy; 'Algerian Raï. Pop Goes to Algeria', *Songlines*, summer 1999, pp. 24-32.
15. Azad, Arif; 'Clash of Language', *Index* Online, 24 July 1998: www.indexoncensorship.org/news/algeria240798.html
16. Amari, Chawki; 'In the Land of Raï, in: *Index on Censorship*, 3, 1999, p. 168. Amari's article – at www.multimedia.com/algo/texte/rap – was translated by Judith Vidal-Hall

Discography

CDS

- Cheb Hasni: *Raï Love* (CMM/Buda Musique 82854-2; France,1994); *Rani Mourak* (Gafaiti Productions GP 02; France, 1994)
- Cheb Zahouania: *Le meilleur de Chaba Zahouania – La reine du raï* (Blue Silver 50347-2; Paris)
- Chaba Fadela & Cheb Sahraoui: *Hana Hana* (Mango/Island Records CIDM 1005;UK) *And You Are Mine* (Mango/Island Records ZCM9827; UK) are both considered seminal albums, but they are out-of-print; *Walli* (Gafaita Productions GP 08; France) is available.
- Cheb Mami: *Saïda* (Totem/Blue Silver 50368-2; France, 1994); *Meli Meli* (Virgin 7243 8 47123 2 7; France, 1999) includes 'Bledi' [My Country]
- Cheb Khaled: *Sahra* (Barclay 533 405-2; France, 1996) featuring the hit 'Aïcha'; on *Kutché* (Sterns STCD 1024; UK, 1987) Khaled - still with the 'Cheb' in the front of his name – worked with Algerian jazz musician Safy Boutella for the official Riadh el Feth Cultural Association in Algiers; *Hada Raykoum* (Triple Earth/Sterns, TERRACD 102; UK, 1986) early pop Raï from the mid-Eighties; *Khaled* (Barclay 511 815-2; France, 1991) including the worldwide smash hit 'Didi', produced by Don Was; *N'ssi N'ssi* (Barclay 519 898-2; France, 1993) - last two CDs only available from Barclays, in France.
- Cheikha Remitti: *Cheikah Remitti: Aux Sources du Raï* (Instute du Monde Arabe 509 09-2; France); the legendary Cheikha with Fripp and some members of the Red Hot Chilli Peppers on *Sidi Mansour* (Absolute Records Absolcd 2; France, 1994); *Cheikha Remitti: Les racines du raï* (CMM/Buda Musique 82874-2; France)
- Bellemou Messaoud: *Le Pere du Raï* (World Circuit WCD 011; UK, 1989)

Raï's French and British Connection

- Faudel: *Baïda* (Mercury 558 311-2; France, 1996)
- Rachid Taha: *Olé Olé* (Barclay 529 481-2; France, 1995); *Diwân* (Barclay 539 953-2; France, 1998); Made in Medina (Ark 21 ABKcd1006, France, 2001)
- Justin Adams: *Desert Road* (Wayward Records 701; London, 2000)
- Gnawa Diffusion: *Algeria* (7 Colors Music/Musisoft CDS 7369-SD 40; France, 1999); *Bab el Oued Kingston* (7 Colors Music/Musisoft CDS 7370-SD 40; France, 1999)
- Orchestre National de Barbès: *Orchestre National de Barbès* (Tajmaat 7243 8 44009 27; France, 1997) is a live concert recording; *Onb Poulina* (Samarkand 8475532; France, 1999)

Berber Music

- *Lounès Matoub: Lettre Ouverte Aux …* (Blue Silver 846327-2; France, 1998); *La Fichta Kabyle* (Beur FM/ Blue Silver 8440462; France, 1997)

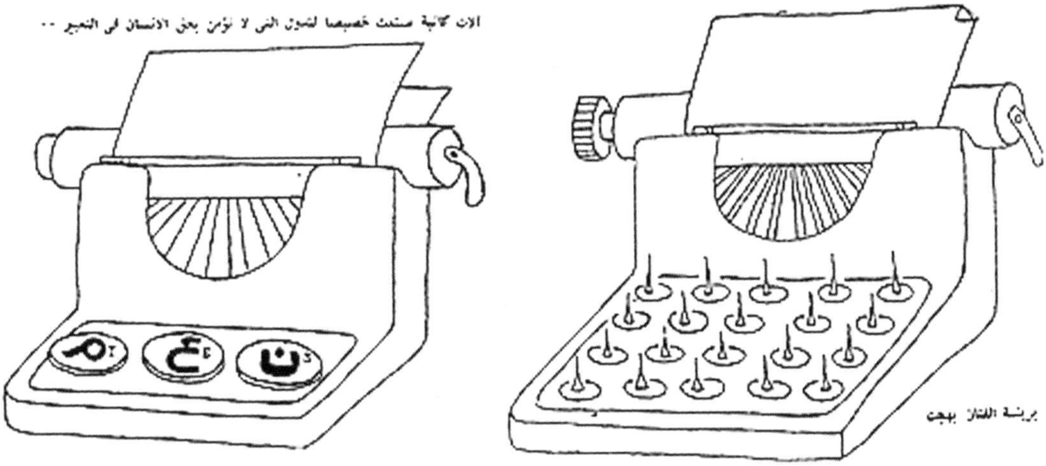

Bahgat, Egypt, 1985

Prominent Egyptian caricaturist Bahgat is part of a generation of radical artists and writers formed by Nasser's July Revolution. In his cartoons, Bahgat attacks political and socially sensitive issues such as polygamy and black stereotypes in the Arab world. Banned from drawing for a decade under President Anwar Sadat, Bahgat created the memorable cartoon dictator, Bahgatos, once he was allowed to publish again. The above customised typewriters, from a 1985 Arab Human Rights Organisation report, were created for 'governments opposed to freedom of expression'. The three-key machine types out one word – yes. *Index on Censorship,* www.indexoncensorship.org, Cartoon/egypt/egypt/html) Cartoon courtesy of Bahgat

Ali Farzat, Syria

Ali Farzat's cartoons posit an alternative to the seamless web of the official narrative. He too must operate within the parameters of the permissible. But he too probes the limits and tests the sensibilities of Syria's censors ... Farzat's cartoons demonstrate his trenchant political acuity; his reputation as Syria's foremost cartoonist suggests that his understanding is shared by many Syrians. When Ali Farzat was dismissed from [the newspaper] *Al-Thawra* [Revolution], circulation reportedly dropped by 35 per cent until he was reinstated one month later ...

>>

Ahmed Al-Mukarram

Sudanese Culture in Exile

> ... How could midday possibly go by without there being in some place a man who sits contemplating a fish in the river of his alienation, and the evils which still abound ...
>
> Sudanese poet Atef Khairy from *The Book of Doubt*

Nine years ago, the ferry Saq Al Na'am carried me far away from my country of Sudan. As the boat ploughed through the waters of the Nile, now contained within the banks of Lake Nubia, the world's biggest artificial lake, I could not believe I had escaped the large prison Sudan had become. A military coup against a pluralist democratic government had brought the Islamic fundamentalists to power in 1989. Under a totalitarian religious regime, all spaces of freedom, of expression, of speech, even the freedom to differ, had been abrogated. Instead, religious arrogance prevailed as democracy, human rights and the legitimate rights of minorities were compromised.

Leaving my country had been an ordeal. The new government didn't want journalists going abroad. As a result, all travel required special permission from the Ministry of Culture and Information, followed by authorisation by the under-secretary of the ministry. I was finally allowed to leave on the pretext that I was going 'to look for a publisher for my works on literary criticism'. Despite obtaining the necessary documentation, I was not totally convinced that I was going, until I found myself on that bitterly cold night in December, 1991, on board Saq Al Na'am. Although I knew that the nightmare was over, anguish still tore at my heart. Grim political conditions had forced me to abandon my home. Beside me on the ferryboat were scores of young Sudanese who were also determined to emigrate. All of us seemed to carry the same conflicting feelings, relieved by our departure, but apprehensive about a dark, unknown future.

The boat steered its way stealthily to the widest part of Lake Nubia to the northern rim of my country, where Wadi Halfa once stood on the Sudanese-Egyptian border. In the early Sixties, the High Dam was built and Wadi Halfa was submerged under the lake, a massive body of water in the heart of what seems a never-ending desert. Intercepted by hillocks and dunes, it eventually merges into the great African desert that solemnly leans on the outer fringe of the valley of the Nile, which for centuries winded its course, tirelessly cutting through large stretches of hot, tropical wasteland.

The ferryboat was bound for Aswan, and then Cairo. Since the Nineties, the Egyptian capital has become a safe haven for an estimated two million Sudanese, including a multitude of Sudanese writers and thinkers, who managed to flee the inferno of their homeland. A Sudanese opposition paper issued abroad[1] published a report which maintained that 116 Sudanese intellectuals and artists had either died a normal death or were victims of repression by the government in Khartoum, over the last ten years. Dubbed as the death list, the roster contained names of singers like the famous Khogly Osman who was stabbed to death by a young fanatic in the Artists' Union headquarters in the city of Omdurman one sad night in the mid-Nineties. Commenting on the violence against intellectuals and artists, Haider Ibrahim Ali, the director of the Sudanese Studies Centre in Cairo, said, 'Such a nighmarish atmosphere has been created by the regime, which is directly responsible for the cases of death among Sudanese intellectuals – in their various forms.'

According to a Sudanese researcher from the opposition, once those who took charge of the cultural activities fully digested the cultural ideology of their extremist religious party, they braced themselves to uproot evil and launched one campaign after another against cultural institutions in a purge to eliminate 'idolatry and pleasure seeking'. As a result, the national library and the broadcasting station in Khartoum came under fire from the 'enlightenment campaigns' which resulted in the loss of most of its archive of registered music, and its audio and visual resources on the pretext of 'their incompatibility with the Islamic state ...'[2] The new religious dictatorship pre-emptively removed all the emerging forces of the civil society and the intelligentsia from the institutions of the state. Brute force, torture and repression were some of the weapons used by the regime to fuel religious fanaticism among the younger generation.

Few realised the effects of a religious dictatorship on national unity. Those who witnessed it first-hand for themselves soon realised it was better to leave the country. Many preferred life in exile, particularly in Egypt, which has historic ties to Sudan, although it is true that no matter how harsh the conditions in one's country, the country of emigration can never, by any means, be a substitute. Other hardships awaited the Sudanese refugees in their new home. As explained in the introduction to a 1996 report prepared jointly by the Near East Institution and the Centre for Development Services in Egypt entitled 'Assessment of Needs: Women's Health, and the Economic Needs of the Sudanese in the Arab Republic of Egypt': 'Over the last decade, an increasing number of Sudanese came to settle in Egypt in search of stability. In fact the majority of the Sudanese in Egypt suffer from unemployment, and depend for their livelihood on transfers from their relatives and friends in all parts of the world.'

To address some of these problems, newly formed Sudanese cultural centres and civil society organisations – including maternity and childcare, and assistance for students fleeing the devastating civil war – all helped Sudanese refugees suffering hardship. Over the last ten years, the Sudanese in exile centres and cultural groups enabled the refugees to express the tragedy of their homeland while at the same time binding them to their national culture and reinforcing the roots from which they came. For Sudanese intellectuals and artists, it was an opportunity to continue their creative work and produce a culture opposed to dictatorship, one that is tolerant and democratic, a culture of peace for a country that has been eroded by civil war. As a result, Sudanese culture in exile has emerged as a vigorous and effective movement on the banks of the Nile.

Sudan's multicultural society

At the centre of Sudan's current conflict is the problem of identity, which stems from the sheer size of the country. This Arab-African nation with an ancient pluralistic civilisation and a contemporary ethnic and cultural diversity with profound differences extends over a large territory from the equator in the south, to latitude 22 in the north. It stretches from the edge of the Ethiopian highlands to the east, to the Darfour highlands and Jebel Mara near Lake Chad to the west in the very heart of the continent. In terms of its varied geographical climate, its widely varied cultural, ethnic, linguistic and religious diversity, Sudan is a true replica of Africa.

With an area estimated at one billion square kilometres, which places it as one of the largest African nations, Sudan's problems are further compounded by the diversity of races and ethnic groups who survive side by side. The population of Sudan is estimated to comprise 570 tribes, races and ethnic groups that speak nearly 595 languages. Arabic is the common language ...[3]

Ali Farzat, Syria

The popularity of these cartoons and [the fact] that one picture can convey to the literate and the illiterate audiences a widely understood critique of official political life suggests the power of Farzat's work: the moment the meaning of a Farzat cartoon dawns inside one's own head, the censor has been circumvented, and one's own sense of unbelief affirmed ... To the extent that Farzat's cartoons communicate unbelief in the regime's rhetoric, they represent a victory in the contest against enforced falsehood ... Farzat's cartoons offer concrete, detailed criticism of the distance between rulers and ruled, of political oppression, corruption, inequality, exploitation, and conformity. (Lisa Wedeen, *Ambiguities of Domination: Politics, Rhetoric, and Symbols in Contemporary Syria,* Chicago: University of Chicago Press, 1999, pp. 107-108)

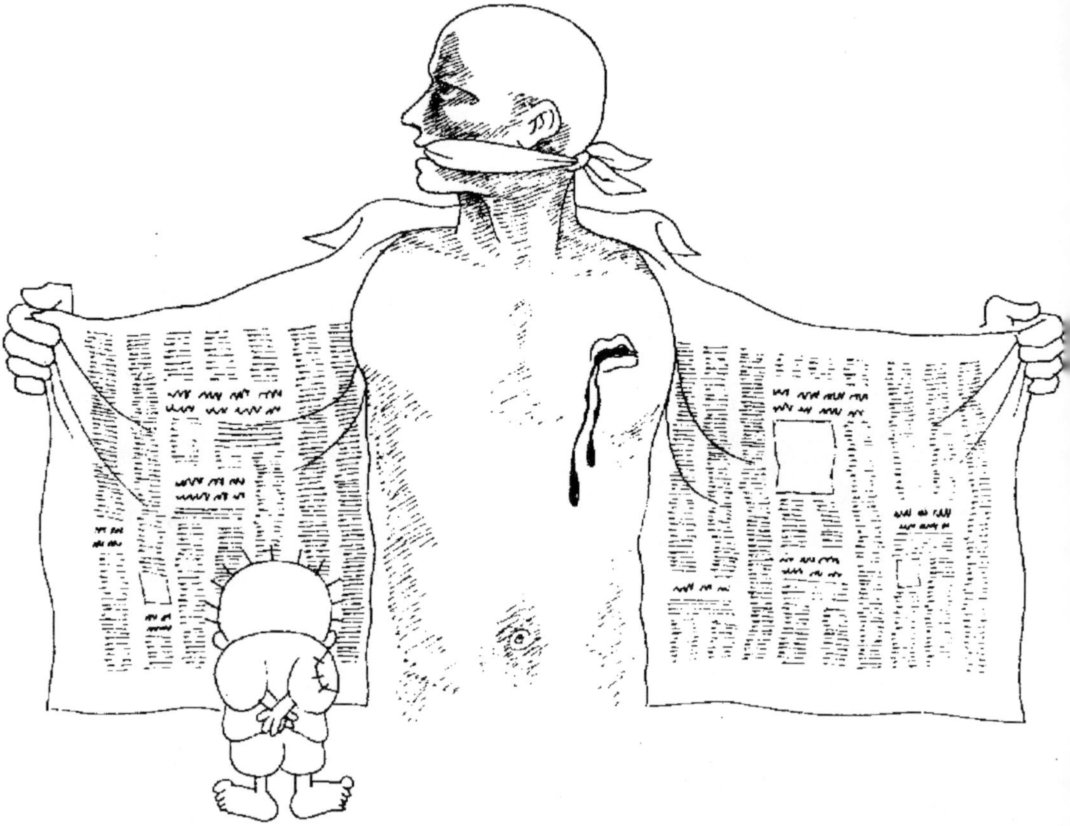

Naji Al-Ali, Palestine, 1980

Naji Al-Ali was born in 1936 in Galilee, Palestine. Following the establishment of Israel in 1948, he was forced to flee, along with hundreds of thousands of Palestinians. His family settled in the Ein Al-Helwe refugee camp in southern Lebanon. He spent the rest of his life in exile, shuttling between Beirut and Kuwait. In 1985, he was expelled from Kuwait and moved to London, where he was shot at close range on his way to work on 22 July 1987. After five weeks in coma, he died aged 51. The assassin remains at large ...

>>

Sudan's unique characteristics and its specificity as 'Arab-African at the same time'[4] has generated results contrary to expectations. Thus Sudan was considered politically marginal in that it was neither Arab nor African, and neither Muslim nor Christian.[5] In the midst of this equation charged with racial and social contradictions, and against a backdrop of conflicting identities that raged in the country, it seemed understandable that rounds of violence and counter-violence should plague the country. To understand the situation, a thorough reading is needed of the consequences of the colonialist period and the 'methods used by colonialism to dominate the country. Such methods ... have created the social and economic disparities in Africa. They are responsible for the duality and contradictory approaches to racial conflict, and for the vast number of incompatible patterns of change in social and economic relations and in terms of racial development ...'[6]

In the case of Sudanese national rule over the last four decades, we can clearly observe this pattern of development. The ruling élite, mostly from the north, envisaged Sudan as Arab Muslim. Meanwhile the élite in the south viewed Sudan as African with an Arab breeding. The disparity reflects the essential characteristic of Sudan as a country with a split cultural and civilisational identity between its Arab Muslim north and its African south with a predominantly Christian element. Despite the national conflict and structural rift, 'the development of the cultural and political conflict between the "authority" in the north and the "opposition" in the south (mostly armed), has generated more than a political faction. It has led to the rise of a movement for the unification of the factions in the south just as it enabled certain traditional political forces in the north to opt for a peaceful dialogue motivated by the belief that the crisis could be settled by peaceful means.'[7] By adopting an extremist religious position, the current government is rejecting the option of peace through dialogue and placing obstacles in its path. The government of Sudan is dictating Arabism and Islam as the final identity for Sudan.

Inclusion: cultural festivals

So the very first question for Sudanese in Cairo was how to expand Khartoum's official definition of identity and include – rather than exclude – all of the country's different ethnic and tribal groups. One of the most successful ways has been through cultural festivals. Two were organised by the Sudan Culture and Information Centre, originally formed in 1995 by a group of Sudanese intellectuals with the purpose of mobilising their potential in the 'country of emigration'. The festivals brought together a total of nineteen Sudanese exile communities and groups originally from the country's north and south: Abukaya, Al Shalak, Dinka, Yarul, Dinka Aqar, Nuba Al Jibal, Al Bagga, Dinkabur, Al Zandi, Dinka Awil, Al Ashuli, Nuba Al Shamal, Al Latuka, Al Belinda, Dinkarik, and women's groups, Women's Education, Al Wasat and Suq Al Gemal.

The first one, held in August 1995, at the American University in Cairo, drew 35,000 visitors during the six-day event, which highlighted Sudanese folkloric dance, rituals and religious practices, as well as seminars and other relevant cultural activities. The second, under the theme 'Creativity in Sudanese Culture' and the banner 'Wherever we go, Sudan shines', was held in September 1996. Among the festival objectives was to hold cultural dialogue between Sudanese ethnic groups and to break – as far as possible – language barriers between the participants through the use of a common body language in music and dance. According to the Sudan Culture and Information Centre, the festivals were adopted as an optimal means to consolidate the culture of peace as an antithesis to cultural repression or the dominance of one culture over other cultures in Sudan today.

 Domains of creativity: from seminars to the arts and newspapers

In 1998, a report from the International Organisation for the Rights of Writers estimated that 332 writers were subjected to exile and expulsion from 70 countries, the majority of whom were from the Third World. The report explained that among the total of 107 Arab writers, 22 are Iraqi poets and novelists and some twenty are Sudanese writers living in Switzerland. This is the first time specific figures have been given of the number of Sudanese writers in exile. However, the figures are only for Sudanese intellectuals living in the west. While there are no recognised statistics of Sudanese intellectuals and artists who lived in Cairo over the past decade before they were relocated (under the auspices of the UN resettlement programme), their involvement in Sudanese cultural events sponsored by organisations, such as the Sudanese Studies Centre, the Sudan Culture and Information Centre, the Centre for Nubian Studies and Al Karma Group for Plastic Arts, among others, has been undeniable.

The Sudanese Studies Centre, first established in the Moroccan city of Rabat then moved to Cairo in 1992, has been paramount in raising awareness of the community in exile of cultural, conceptual and political issues. In the second issue of the centre's publication *Kitabat Sudaniyya* [Sudanese Writings] of which there have been eight issues, an editorial discussed the role of intellectuals and artists in exile as a high priority in the Sudanese struggle:

> The need for cultural initiatives like *Sudanese Writings* is greater today than in any other time in the past. To the sceptics who question the futility of writing or establishing research centres in exile, it may be said that writing provides us with a temporary homeland which shields us against accepting and acquiescing to exile, and dispersion and consequently to spiritual disintegration and fragmentation, and the quest to escape through fantasy and oblivion ... Any kind of cultural initiative that is opposed to the state of decadence in Sudan today is a desirable and highly valued contribution ... for the emergence of a broad cultural front, or the creation of a cultural forum which rallies all intellectuals opposed to the discourse of ignorance, hostile to democracy, pluralism and freedom.

The message produced a swift reaction on the part of Sudanese intellectuals living in Cairo. Suddenly new centres with a range of interests sprang up, all with financial support from international donor organisations

Today, exiled Sudanese in Cairo lead busy cultural lives. Every week societies or groups for students, women and human rights hold numerous political and cultural seminars. Over the last decade, the Sudanese Studies Centre has held the majority of these functions, which draw participants from among Sudanese and non-Sudanese academics and experts specialising in Sudanese affairs. Some of the titles include 'Seminar on Democracy in Sudan – Historical Background, Current Situation and Perspectives for the Future' (1993), 'Cultural Pluralism and the National State' (1994) and 'Psychological, Social and Cultural Effects on Sudanese Children in Countries of Emigration' (1997).

The last of these specialised seminars included 'Project for the Sudan ... Beginning of a Century and End of a Millennium' launched by the ambitious Documentation Centre. The seminar was dedicated to the world-renowned Sudanese writer Al-Tayeb Salih, who wrote the pivotal Arab classic novel, *Season of Migration to the North*. Held in August, 1999, on the occasion of the writer's 70th birthday, the seminar at the Supreme Council for Culture in Egypt was the

Naji Al-Ali, Palestine, 1984

Al-Ali's work was characterised by an unwavering commitment to the rights of the Palestinian people and the portrayal of their plight and bitter struggle against Israeli occupation and oppression. Furthermore, he devoted himself to the poor and the underprivileged, campaigning against the absence of democracy, widespread corruption and gross inequality in the Arab world. For him, the Palestinian refugee was not confined to a specific geographical area but transcended into the whole of the Arab masses. Al-Ali's cartoons always included the bare-footed little boy, Hanzala, who turned his back to the reader in rejection of the world around him. (See page 106) (Khalid Al-Ali for the Friends of Naji Al-Ali) Cartoons reproduced with the permission of the Naji Al-Ali family

Youssef Seddik, Tunisia
***Si le Coran m'était conté: Abraham*, 1989**

Youssef Seddik has published several volumes of what he considers a comic strip version of the Quran. In a clear attempt to reach the widest possible audience, Seddik has brought out his sacred strips simultaneously in French and Arabic editions. The scenarios have all been prepared by Youssef Seddik, but the illustration is the work of a number of French artists ... *Newsweek* printed the charges that Seddik's strips visually stereotype Arabs (negatively is implied). With the series' multiple artists, this would be difficult. (Allen Douglas and Fedwa Malti-Douglas, *Arab Comic Strips: Politics of an Emerging Mass Culture*, Bloomingdale: Indiana University Press, 1994, p. 103-104, 107) Caption and cartoon © 1994 Allen Douglas and Fedwa Malti-Douglas largest Sudanese cultural rally in the last twenty years. It was attended by Sudanese exiles in Cairo, as well as writers and students from Sudan and from around the world. Nearly 60 research papers and studies were presented, focusing on: 'Culture and the Building of the National Democratic State', and the problems, specificity and strategy of 'Sudanese Culture: Present Situation and Future Prospects' – all to be published by the centre. The seminar closed with the adoption of a 'Sudanese Cultural Declaration', which denounced the culture of war and adopted the culture of peace for the twenty-first century.

Another vibrant area of cultural activity has been art. A prominent artist who participated in the Cairo Biennale, Hassaan Ali Ahmad has exhibited throughout the Arab world, in Africa and in Europe. By celebrating his Nubian descent in his painting, he believes that art 'does not only challenge our memory and contemplation, but urges us to address the present struggle and forge the future'. For him, exile has been an introduction to the rest of the world. In 1996, he won the grand Japanese Noma prize for children's drawings. Ali Ahmad is also known for his posters, T-shirt designs and magazine and book covers.

From a younger generation of artists, Mahmoud Seif Al Islam has exhibited three times since 1996 in the Berlin-Cairo gallery in the Society for German-Egyptian Friendship. Seif Al Islam headed the now closed Al Karma for Plastic Arts, which held several collective exhibitions the last of which was the art workshop in collaboration with the Centre for African Studies in the American University in Cairo entitled, 'Feathers as a Raw Material in Works of Art'.

If Sudanese artists are a living testimony that the creative communication with their national culture has not been severed despite the civil war, filmmakers are documenting life in exile. Another artist is the Sudanese film director Hussain Sharif whose *Snatching the Amber* is a landmark in contemporary Sudanese documentary films. Currently, Sharif is working on a joint project with Atiyat Al Abnoudi, the pioneering Egyptian documentary filmmaker, on the film project, *From the Diary of Exile*. The 54-minute film, produced by the Sudanese Human Rights Organisation in Cairo, deals with the problem of emigration and asylum of intellectuals in Egypt. Sharif is working on a new documentary, entitled *Letters from Abroad*.[8]

However, the most vigorous contribution of Sudanese intellectuals in Cairo to culture has been in the field of publishing. Their publications in exile far outnumbered their publications prior to exile. In 1994, the Sudanese Centre for Information and Strategical Studies began with the main objective of conducting a statistical study of the conditions of Sudanese refugees and has published six issues of its magazine *Al Nafidhah* [The Window]. The Sudanese Studies Centre alone published nearly 45 titles about topics relevant to the Sudanese problem, as does the International Printing and Publishing Company. Another publishing venture, Dar Al Katib Al Sudani, founded by a number of writers and intellectuals, operates as a shareholding public company to ensure that books would find their way to the readers not necessarily through the official channels for book marketing and publication.

Daily newspapers have also contributed to the community-in-exile. On 17 April 1993, the first issue of the independent daily *Al-Khartoum* appeared on the streets of Cairo. Started by the proponents of democracy, who fled the military dictatorship's siege of freedom of the press, the newspaper resumed publication outside Sudan. *Al-Khartoum* has become an important and reliable source of information about events in Sudan. In effect, its readers from around the world also contribute, since *Al-Khartoum* makes a point of publishing their letters and any news of the repressive regime. In this way it has also become a symbol and an ideal for Sudanese democracy. Another daily newspaper, *Al Itched Al Dawliah* is the mouthpiece of the Democratic Union Party.

Other publications belonging to opposition parties include: *Sudanese Issues* by the Sudanese Communist Party, *Al Hiwar* published by the Democratic Party and *Al Haq* published by the Movement of Modern Democratic Forces. Other publications in English include *Sudan Dispatch* published by the Sudanese Development Initiative Abroad.

From newspapers and the arts to seminars and festivals, Sudanese culture in exile remains a much-needed bastion of free expression for the myriad groups, tribes and individuals who, discriminated against by an Islamic government in Khartoum, are proud to be Sudanese. Not only do Sudanese cultural organisations in exile educate and provide information about the community in exile, they also act as barometers of their country's shifting political situation: the newspaper *Al-Khartoum* has moved back to Khartoum, while the Sudanese Studies Centre has opened a branch office in the city.

1. Al Bilal, Mu'waiya and Ahmed Mukarram, Abdel, 'Tahqiq Thaqafi' [A Cultural Account], *Mulhaq Hadarat Al Sudan* [The Civilisation of Sudan supplement] (February 2000) pp. 6-7
2. Bola, Abdalla, *Shagarat Nasab Al Ghul Fi Mushkilat Al Hawiyya Al Thaqafiya wa Huquq Al Insan fil Sudan* [The Genealogy of the Ghul and the Problem of Cultural Identity and Human Rights in Sudan], Masarat Jadida, p. 7
3. Harir, Sharif, et al., *Sudan: Short Cut to Decay*, translated from the English by Mubarak Ali Uthman and Magdy Al Naim under the title, *Al Sudan: Al Inhiyar aw Al Nahda* [Sudan: Collapse or Renaissance] Cairo, Centre for Sudanese Studies, p. 13
4. Ibid, p. 11
5. Ibid, p. 11
6. Ismailova, Rosa, *Racial Problems in Tropical Africa*, translated from the Russian by Sami Al Razzaz under the title, *Al Mushkilat Al 'Irqiya fi Ifriqiya hal Yomkin Halliha?, Dar Al Thaqafa Al Jadida*, p. 109
7. Mousa, Hassan, '*Shobhat Hawl Al Hawiyya: Mulahazat Hawl Ishkaliat Al Fan wal Hawiyya Fil Sudan*' [*Suspicions About Identity: Remarks about the Question of Art and Identity in Sudan*] *Kitabat Sudaniya*, No. 4, p. 7
8. *Letters from Abroad* is funded by the Prince Claus Fund

Abdulrrahim Yasir and Raid Nouri Arrawi, Iraq, 1989

An Iraqi cartoonist told *Al-Hayat* art critic Ismael Zayer that when a cartoon is drawn, usually 'four people in the magazine approve it'. Cartoonists in Iraq rarely comment on social and political affairs. With the press owned by Saddam Hussein and his son Uday, the majority of cartoons reflect internal government struggles. In Arab cartoonists' and journalists' organisations, Abdulrrahim Yasir (top) represents his country around the world. 'Raid Nouri' Arrawi (bottom) was awarded the Republic of Iraq Saddam Hussein Award before leaving the country 21 years ago. Both cartoonists were included in *Al-Majallah Magazine* Festival of Arab Cartoons at London's Kufa Gallery in 1989. Cartoons courtesy of *Al-Majalla Magazine*, London

Sid Ali Melouah, Algeria, 1999-2001

Considered one of Algeria's leading cartoonist and comic artists, Sid Ali Malouah incurred the wrath of Muslim fundamentalists. Due to several attempts on his life since 1995, he went underground. Melouah now lives and works in exile. In the top left cartoon from 2001, the man exclaims, 'On the occasion of the commemoration of March 8, I declare that all women are free,' and then he adds, 'Except for my wives, of course.' Right, executioner makes a mistake in 1999. Bottom centre, a father suggests in 2000, 'My son you must go to school to become a prime minister.' The son replies, 'I'd rather *not* go to school and become president.' (*Index on Censorship,* www.indexoncensorship.org/Cartoon/algeria/algeria.html) Translated from French by Veronique Whittall, cartoons courtesy of Sid Ali Melouah

Albie Sachs

A Conceited Look at Creating Free Space for the Artist: Texts, Subtexts and Contexts[1]

The activist speaks

There is no conceit like that of a survivor of an assassination attempt. It was only a year after I had lost an arm and the sight of an eye through a hit-squad car bomb that I found myself opening an exhibition of art from southern Africa at the Kulturhuset in Stockholm. Speaking with the magnified serenity of a near-death survivor, I felt I could say what I liked. My first statement was: 'We don't want your solidarity!' The hallful of Swedish art curators was shocked. 'We don't want your solidarity!' I repeated. A hundred faces tightened at my ungracious remark. 'The solidarity was to bring the works and the artists here; we appreciate that.' The faces relaxed into friendly Swedish smiles. 'Now we want real criticism. If you like the work, tell us. If you don't, tell us. And if you're puzzled, ask us to explain. We don't want solidarity criticism!' The audience was relieved, but my conceit was not yet exhausted. 'And I think that we should stop saying that art is an instrument of struggle.' Once more the tightness. I was the fifth speaker. Each one of the previous members of the panel had intoned the words that art was an instrument of struggle. 'I suggest we ban these words for five years.'

I little realised that my provocative and light-hearted proposal was later to spark the most intense debate on culture that South Africa had ever known. A paper which I wrote on the subject for a seminar organised by the Cultural Department of the ANC in Lusaka was subsequently republished by various South African newspapers and put in anthologies in different parts of the world. Re-reading it now reminds me of the double pressures under which artists worked in those hard and relentless days of struggle, and which today's artists connected with popular struggles must face. The obvious pressures were those of the repressive apartheid state that banned free expression, prohibited publications and imposed censorship over all forms of artistic expression. Writers were locked up; many went into exile. In response, the anti-apartheid movement brought artists together in a solid front against repression (and I am happy to say that the Netherlands played a specially valuable role in this process). The friendships built up in the course of shared danger and conjoined idealism continue to this day, but we paid a price, a heavy, heavy price.

'Our artists' – I now quote from the ten-year-old paper – 'are not pushed to improve the quality of their work, it is enough that it be politically correct. The more fists and spears and guns, the better. The range of themes is narrowed down so much that all that is funny or curious or genuinely tragic is extruded. Ambiguity and contradiction are completely shut out, and the only conflict permitted is that between the old and the new, as if there were only bad in the past and only good in the future. Whether in poetry or painting or on the stage, we line up our good people on the one side and the bad ones on the other, occasionally permitting someone to pass from one column to the other, but never acknowledging that there is bad in the good, and even more difficult, that there can be elements of good in the bad; you can tell who the good ones are, because in addition to being handsome of appearance, they can all recite sections of the Freedom Charter or passages of Strategy and Tactics at the drop of a beret.

'And what about love? We have published so many anthologies and journals and occasional poems and stories, and the numbers that deal with love do not make the fingers of a hand. Can it be that once we join the ANC we do not make love any more, and that when the comrades go to bed they discuss the role of the white working class? ANC members are full of fun and romanticism and dreams, we enjoy and wonder at the beauties of nature and the marvels of human creation, yet if you look at most of our art and literature you would think we are living in the greyest and most sombre of all worlds, completely shut in by apartheid. It is as though our rulers stalk every page and haunt every picture; everything is obsessed by the oppressors and the trauma they have imposed, little is about us and the new consciousness we are developing.

'Listen in contrast to the music of Hugh Masekela, of Abdullah Ibrahim, of Jonas Gwanga, of Miriam Makeba, and you are in a universe of wit and grace and vitality and intimacy, there is invention and modulation of mood, ecstasy and sadness; this is a cop-free world in which the emergent personality of our people manifests itself. Their music conveys genuine confidence because it springs from inside the personality and experience of each of them, from popular tradition and the sounds of contemporary life; we respond to it because it tells us something lovely and vivacious about ourselves, not because the lyrics are about how to win a strike or blow up a petrol dump. It bypasses, overwhelms, ignores apartheid, and establishes its own space.

'Dumile, perhaps the greatest of our visual artists, was once asked why he did not draw scenes like the cruel one that was taking place in front of him: a crocodile of men being marched under arrest for not having their passes in order. At that moment a hearse drove slowly past and the men stood still and raised their hats. "That," he said, "is what I want to draw."'

Some months later, Mandela is freed, I am back in South Africa participating in a heated public debate on my tongue-in-cheek banning of the words 'art is a weapon of struggle'. After the debate, someone 'from the struggle' comes up and throws her arms around me: 'I'm a dancer,' she says, 'and I love tap dancing, but I didn't dare do it for years because I thought it was bourgeois and an aspect of cultural imperialism. Then I read your paper and went out straight away and did it for half-an-hour. My dream now is to attend an important ANC conference and jump out of a cake and do a tap dance for all the delegates.' I knew then without doubt that my paper had been right.

The judge speaks

Did I say there was no conceit like that of a survivor of an assassination attempt? Well, I was wrong. There is the institutional, if not personal, conceit of a judge of the highest court in the land, one who can set aside laws, even those passed by the country's first democratically elected parliament and signed into law by none other than Nelson Mandela. One of our tasks has been to insist that the state does nothing to inhibit all the multiracial, multicultural, multi-faith people of our diverse and conflicted country from feeling that they have an equal place in the sun (or, because we have too much sun, an equal place in the shade). When the court was asked to decide whether or not it was constitutional to prohibit the sale of liquor on Sundays, Good Friday and Christmas, that is, to select out Christian holidays for the prohibition, this is what I wrote – you

Chawki Amari, Algeria, 2000

Widespread protests followed the arrest and detention of Chawki Amari, the Algerian political cartoonist. He was taken to Serkadji prison after the daily newspaper *La Tribune* published Amari's cartoon showing two figures talking beneath houses festooned with Algerian flags: 'Is this for 5 July?' – the country's Independence Day. 'No, they're hanging out their dirty linen.' The examining judge called the cartoon 'an insult to the national emblem' and threatened prosecution under Article 160 of the Penal Code, which stipulates five to ten years for 'anyone who deliberately and publicly tears up, defaces or defiles the national symbol'. Amari was given a three-year suspended sentence. He presently lives in exile. Cartoon courtesy of Chawki Amari

Jerry Robinson, U.S., 1982

In the Seventies, American editorial cartoonist Jerry Robinson learned that Francesco Lorenzo Pons, the cartoonist known as Paco, had been arrested and sentenced to six years in jail by the Uruguayan military junta. 'He had been certified a prisoner of conscience,' Robinson explains, 'He didn't kill or throw bombs. He drew and wrote against the regime. He was treated worse than people who robbed or murdered.' Robinson and Amnesty International campaigned for Pons. He was released a few months before his term ended. Robinson's cartoon about human rights abuses was first published by the Chicago Tribune/New York News Syndicate and appeared in newspapers across the U.S. (See page 106) (Interview with Malu Halasa) Cartoon from *Human Rights* will note that the language is stiffer, and it should be read with the appropriate gravitas, but I like to feel that the quest for freedom was the same:

> One of the functions of the constitution is to protect the fundamental rights of non-majoritarian groups, who might well be tiny in number and hold beliefs considered bizarre by the ordinary faithful. In constitutional terms, the quality of a belief cannot be dependent on the number of its adherents nor on how widespread or reduced the acceptance of its ideas might be, nor, in principle, should it matter how slight the intrusion by the state is.
>
> What may be so trifling in the eyes of members of the majority or dominant section of the population as to be invisible, may assume quite large proportions and be eminently real, hurtful and oppressive to those upon whom it impacts. This will especially be the case when what is apparently harmless is experienced by members of the affected group as symptomatic of a wide and pervasive pattern of marginalisation and disadvantage.
>
> Even if there is no compulsory requirement to observe or not to observe a particular religious practice, the effect is to divide the nation into insiders who belong, and outsiders who are tolerated. This is impermissible in the multi-faith, heterodox society contemplated by our constitution.

This was a tiny, benign and purely symbolic example of the state imposing a single world-view onto the whole nation. At the other end of the intolerance continuum, however, is state-backed fanaticism, which surely must be one of the greatest threats to artistic creation in the world today. Communal passions are manipulated with a view to acquiring or maintaining state power. Religious emotion is heightened and abused to achieve the lowest and least spiritual of ends. Artists are oppressed not only by walls of censorship and the threat of violence, but also by crashing waves of intolerance and incomprehension. Without dialogue and rights of conscience, we are lost; artists flee for their lives and art goes underground. An open society does not mean that anything is permissible, that grossly exploitative behaviour goes unrestrained. It does, however, require that all the multiple voices of humanity have a chance to be heard.

The creator speaks

The final conceit belongs neither to an assassination survivor, nor to a judge, but to all of us would-be artists. When I was young I used to get confused between the words 'creature' and 'creator'. Now I find it a happy confusion, and I dedicate the last portion of my essay to the creatures/creators of the world. In my capacity as one of them, I offer you four simple statements.

First, all creators need to be placed and displaced at the same time. Space is never empty, even though it may be invisible. It is always between something and something else. By its nature it is bounded and relational. Artists are never completely alone, nor should they wish to practise their craft in an existential limbo. We live in our world, in our countries, in our cities or farms, in our homes, in our bodies, in ourselves, in our histories, our memories and our languages. Space for the artist repudiates none of these things, but acknowledges them all. In Africa the problem seems to be to capture the experiences of being out of sync, fractured and disoriented but to discover underlying harmonies so that we can recall experience in a synchronised, integrated and oriented way. In Europe – I suggest with continuing conceit – it would appear to be the other way round. Thus, whereas we Africans strive for ways of capturing and soothing an over-tormented reality, you Europeans seem to need to torment and trouble an over-bland one. (Occasionally, I should add, our Euro-Afro-Afro-Euro writers, our Breyten Breytenbachs and our J.M. Coetzees, tell of torment in a tormented way – and how brilliant they can be!)

Secondly, even while we want to be alone, we want to be together. For my struggle generation, togetherness was everything. We found it much easier to love our neighbours than to love ourselves. Yet now we are slowly and painfully learning to love ourselves. There is a fine African word in our constitution – *ubuntu* – that signifies the connection between individuality and community. We are all human beings, because each of us is a human being; each one of us is a human being, because we are all human beings. Africa has much to give the world.

Thirdly, nothing is more globalised yet lacking in global meaning than the word globalisation itself. It is spoken of everywhere, usually pessimistically, as something inevitable that frees economic potential, but at a terrible cultural and human price. Yet modern transport enabled me to fly here, the microphone permits you to hear what I am saying, we manage to see films, read books and enjoy cultural exchanges on an unprecedented scale from all over the world. The internationalisation of economic relations is not in itself an evil. What is evil is our near-universal subordination to money, to greed and to the values (or lack of values) of a few. I draw a distinction between globalisation and universalism. Globalisation presupposes that a technique, a philosophy or an image starts in one part of the world and is spread unchangingly to cover the whole globe. Universalism is just the opposite. It emanates from all over the world and is brought in and distilled as the common experience of humankind, representing something shared and in constant re-creation, to be generalised and appreciated by all. Unfortunately, what we are getting is increased globalisation of ever more attenuated experience. Even worse, instead of communicating experience, we all end up simply experiencing communication.

Fourthly, 'We each give what we have to give.' These simple words of the Mozambican artist Malangatana (one of the 1997 Prince Claus Award laureates) have helped me many times in my personal as well as my public life, and they are indeed what I give to you today. 'We each give what we have to give.' He made the statement when he was opening an exhibition of his paintings in Vienna. 'I thank you, good people of Austria,' he said, 'for supplying pipes and cement to my poor country. In exchange we give you what we have, and what we have is ... a song.' The fact is that Europe has steel, Africa has music. Much of our continent is poverty-stricken and tortured, but most of our people sing, and sing beautifully. There is a musicality that goes with being, a spirituality that is part of ordinary existence, and a delicacy of speech, posture and laughter that informs all communication. People learn in their communities to dance, sing, adorn themselves and produce beautiful objects. My dream is that this rich source of creativity will find projection in high works of art that can be universally enjoyed. I recall the excitement at the Royal Shakespeare Company in London some years ago when the so-called *Zulu Macbeth* brought the World Theatre Season to an end. The performers were cooks, gardeners, office workers and factory operatives, unskilled in modern theatre. Yet they tapped into a deep, participatory cultural tradition. It was their culture, it was my culture, it was world culture. The most sophisticated audience in the world rose to stamp and cheer.

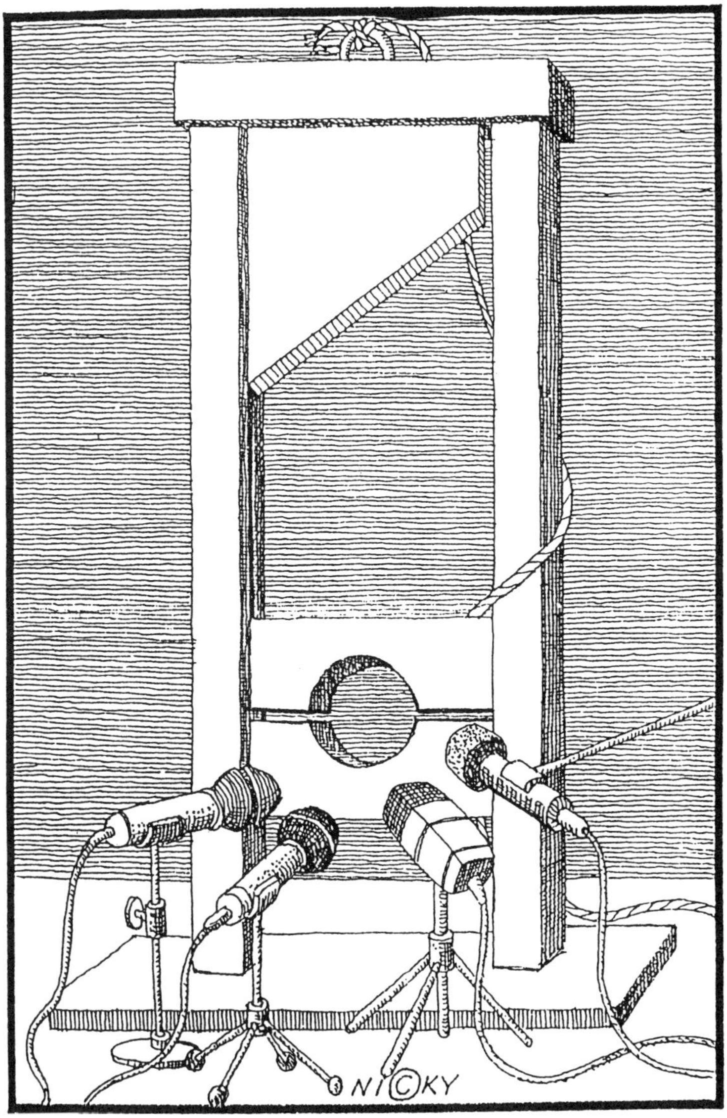

Ni©ky, Bulgaria, 1989

Nicolas Pecareff, who signs his cartoons as Ni©ky, is one of Bulgaria's foremost cartoonists. Known for his askew worldview, his humour transcends languages and political systems. This cartoon of a guillotine giving a press conference was included in a cartoon exhibition and catalogue for the 1993 UN Human Rights Summit in Vienna. Ni©ky published his first cartoons in a local newspaper at the age of fifteen and has been included in seventeen group shows from Denmark and France to Cuba and the former Yugoslavia. Since 1980, he has been honoured with one-man shows in the Czech Republic and Bulgaria. (Cartoonists & Writers Syndicate)

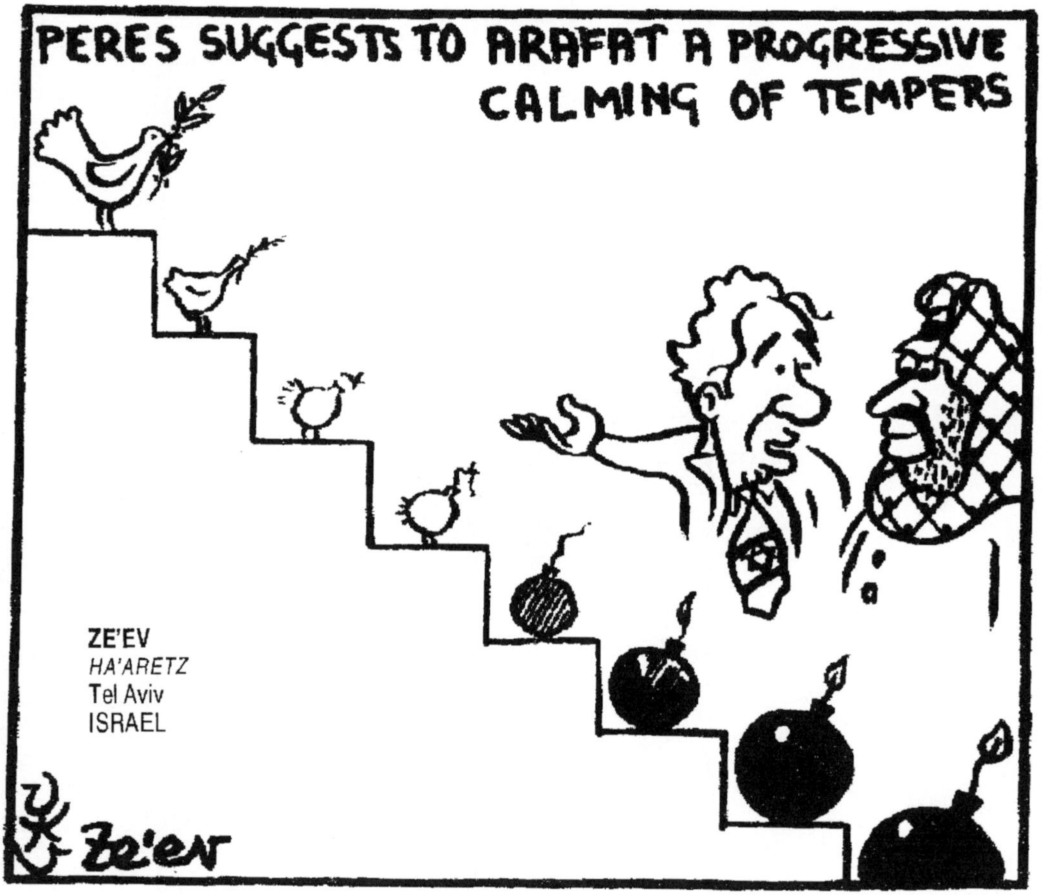

Ze'ev, Israel, 2001

Yaacov Farkas, who is simply known as Ze'ev, moved from Hungry to Israel in 1947. For several decades, his cartoons have appeared regularly in two national daily newspapers published in Tel Aviv, *Ma'ariv* – where his work is currently in print – and *Ha'aretz*. Ze'ev's cartoons are characterised by an inventive political symbolism that is on the sharp end of the Arab-Israeli conflict. Above, Peres shows Arafat the dangerous steps of the peace process. The seventy-eight-year-old cartoonist has received numerous awards, including the 1993 Israel Prize, the country's highest civilian honour. (See page 106)

The judge has the last word

I end as I began, quoting from myself, a one-time freedom fighter, now a writer and a member of the new establishment. I have been normalised – I have become so legitimate that I even insist that the state conduct itself in legitimate fashion! My conceit fails. I face the world with the same apprehension and the same eagerness for applause as anybody else.

The remarks that follow are from a judgement dealing with de-criminalising sodomy. They were addressed to members of the gay and lesbian community who had approached the court for relief, but they could have referred to artists or to any group anywhere in the world that chose to live the truth of their lives in their own way. The passages I will quote deal with space for love, intimacy and creation in an open society, and centre on the right not only to think differently, but to be different and to live differently. Where difference is acknowledged, art flourishes; where difference is suppressed, art becomes fake and conformist.

> From today, a section of the community can feel the equal concern and regard of the constitution and enjoy lives less threatened, less lonely and more dignified. A love that for a number of years had dared openly to speak its name in bookshops, theatres, film festivals and public parades, and that has succeeded in becoming a rich and acknowledged part of South African cultural life, need no longer fear prosecution for intimate expression. A law, which has facilitated homophobic assaults and induced self-oppression, ceases to be. The courts, the police and the prison system are enabled to devote the time and resources formerly spent on obnoxious and futile prosecutions, to catching and prosecuting criminals who prey on gays and straights alike. Homosexuals are no longer treated as failed heterosexuals, but as persons in their own right.
>
> Equality should not be confused with uniformity; in fact, uniformity can be the enemy of equality. Equality means equal concern and respect across difference. It does not presuppose the elimination or suppression of difference. Respect for human rights requires the affirmation of self, not the denial of self. Equality therefore does not imply a levelling or homogenisation of behaviour but an acknowledgement and acceptance of difference. At the very least, it affirms that difference should not be the basis for exclusion, marginalisation, stigma and punishment. At best, it celebrates the vitality that difference brings to any society.
>
> In the past, difference has been experienced as a curse, today it can be seen as a source of interactive vitality. The constitution acknowledges the variability of human beings (genetic and sociocultural), affirms the right to be different, and celebrates the diversity of the nation.

Artist and non-artist alike, we will most comfortably and creatively fill the spaces which life allots us if we do so as we are and not as someone else tells us we ought to be, and if we do so, we must do so with the pride and serenity that can only come from calm and peaceful self-affirmation.

1. Albie Sachs delivered the speech 'A Conceited Look at Creating Free Space for the Artist' at the 1999 Prince Claus Awards ceremony which took place at the Royal Palace Amsterdam on 8 December 1999.

Carmen Boullosa

Indecency Is Their Religion: Molotov and Mexican Rock[1]

Yes is no

We Mexicans have a particular trait: we hide behind a complacent 'yes' or an apparently amicable silence. It is extremely difficult to obtain a direct 'no' from a Mexican, a negative answer, a challenge. The word 'no' is considered to be an unutterable discourtesy. Like 'no', or its opposite 'yes', the true yes, many truths frequently remain unspoken. Friendliness and 'good manners' hide an aggressive moment that ferments in the silence.

'Say yes or no!' But to ask this is a demand that exceeds courtesy and any possible response. 'Are you asking me to say yes?' The unaccented 'yes' is the most common reply you are likely to hear in popular Mexican language. The harshness of 'no' is shunned to avoid both discourtesy and confrontation. Among equals a gesture is enough. But if the question is asked by somebody in a different social class (Mexico is so shamefully classified), the straightest answer would be, 'Let's see', 'a little', 'by and large', 'perhaps', or the unaccented 'yes'.

'No, it's nobody.'

There is a joke, which is commonplace in Mexico. It is the dialogue between a servant and the 'lady of the house'. The lady asks, 'Who is it?' 'It's nobody, madam, it's me.' To be nobody, so as not to offend the tyrant, and to never say 'no', in order to avoid dealing with the consequences of a challenge of whatever sort, is a proverbial elegance of Mexican social engagement. This is not just a matter of class. It is not only those who work in today's conditions of slavery, or those who have no access to a dignified lifestyle, that would rather pretend to be nobody or forever negate themselves in order to be polite, friendly and 'elegant'.

On 1 September 1999, the president of Mexico gave the annual State of the Union, which he is required to give. He did what has been traditional for decades since the first presidents: he said nothing. He replied like a domestic servant and consigned acts and realities to silence: 'It's nobody, gentlemen, it's me.' In his yearly address, the president began by talking about education, but he failed to mention the strike of Universidad Nacional Autonoma de México, which began in June, and each day appears less likely to reach a positive outcome.He lectured about the growth of our agriculture, but to the surprise of the audience and the nation, he did not mention the extreme poverty of the countryside. He spoke of tolerance and negotiation, but not a word about the time-bomb of Chiapas, nor the growing military presence in that state. He praised the growth and health of our economy, but failed to mention the massive foreign debt and the scandal that shook public opinion: after auditors found that a portion of the $40 million assigned by the Mexican state to rescue the banks ended up as an illegal donation for the president's political party, the PRI. On confirming that the public accounts would not be diverted in the 2000 presidential elections,

Suave Veneno, *Telenovela*, Brazil, 1999

Telenovelas, or soap operas, in Brazil are considered 'an authentic product of mass popular culture' which 'have illustrated and disseminated the urban and industrial changes that have taken place since the Fifties'. They have also 'been politically effective. From the Sixties to the Eighties, *telenovelas* provided one of the few forums for cultural expression at a time when Brazil underwent one of its harshest authoritative and anti-democratic periods ...' They have always charted social changes. In *Suave Veneno* [Tender Poison], the female character Nana 'was the pretext for another issue ... intimacy in the course of the life of older and independent women'. (See page 118) (Laura Graziela Gomes, 'The Case of Brazilian *Telenovelas*') Television still

Rakhshan Bani-Etemad, Iran
***The May Lady*, 1998**

***The May Lady*, the first personal film by Rakhshan Bani-Etemad, 'bears a definite female signature ... She now gives several reasons for the misery and restricted life of Iranian women: personal doubts, the norms of the males who wield all power, the legal system based on the Islamic norms of the *Shariat* (in which women have no right of guardianship, no right of divorce other than in exceptional circumstances)'. In 1998 Bani-Etemad won a Prince Claus Award.** (Elli Safari, 'Rakhshan Bani-Etemad: Between Love and Duty', *1998 Prince Claus Awards*, The Hague: Prince Claus Fund, p. 50) Director: Rakhshan Bani-Etemad, producers: Ali-Reza Raissian and Jahangir Kosari, still photographer: Asad Naghshbandi something which, according to his unsustainable version, has never happened, he went further into the religion of silence. The illegal donation, it was later proved, had been used for the electoral campaigns of both the president of the country and the governor of the state of Tabasco. That is the 'spoken' truth, in this particular case, hidden behind a cloak of silence. The religion of silence allowed them to state that: 'There will not be electoral manipulation of public finance in the year 2000, just as there never has been in this period of government.' If it was not the custom in daily Mexican life to avoid facing a direct 'no' or 'yes', or if it was not both good manners and elegant to deny what is obvious ('It's nobody, madam, it's me', 'a little bit', 'in a minute', 'it seems that way') in order to avoid irritating the other, or to resolve that which could upset or could cause irritation, then the discourse that is comfortable with lies as big as Jonah's whale would not be intelligible.

Stirred up

In this obedient silence, obviously, the parameters often get mixed up. The bandit and the 'good guy' connive under the same disguise, a cloak that covers up and does not indict. Intuition has a high value. It is necessary to raise the antenna like an ant to decipher what is being said, as the ears do not perceive the most important part of the message: the silence. Under the cloak of silence, all are equal, your enemies and your friends.

Against this silence a new kind of weapon has arisen in the form of certain popular bands. Rock bands combine commercialism and what is commonplace with a single aim: to break with the religion of silence. Breaking with the 'good manners' that confound people, interweaving elegance with spoliation, injustice with discretion, or impunity and intolerance with what is correct.

Rock with words

Two decades ago, having a rock band singing in Spanish meant being condemned to non-commercial circuits and being excluded from the mass media. A heroic band named the Tri, which called itself 'Three Souls in Mind' in the Sixties, but then became the populist and assertive Tri – an abbreviated way of saying 'three' in Spanish – enjoyed mythical fame and a wide following. The band's audience was far removed from the benefits of a state representing itself as the creator and means to Mexican modernity or a gateway to it. The Tri was not modern: it was aggressive rock played in front of masses of people dancing on bare earth, in roofless venues. The people followed it. It was a select audience of irreverent youth, where anyone could say anything without the law of silence or the law of education. The Tri, with a very elementary discourse but without censorship, would rave about things which used to be left unsaid due to decency and 'good manners'; there was swearing, crudity, obscenity, etc.

After the Tri there came composers and bands with a more intellectual discourse for a more select, better educated and literate public. Jaime López tried to be more populist when he recorded cumbias, trying a grassroots sense of humour. He is the highest exponent of this trend. But for him, Briseno, Botellito de Jerez and others, isolation was an inevitable punishment. They were not commercial. No recording label wanted them and television, then controlled by Televisa alone, showed no interest in them. Radio also turned its back on them.

Now, twenty years later, rockers like the band Molotov have entered the market with expressions and words much more unutterable than those used by the Tri or any other marginal group of previous decades. Many of their utterances are made in a frankly infantile spirit and are arrogantly bad mannered. Both convention and good behaviour are out. The new language of the bands permits anything to be said. To parody the ballad singer Paquita la del Barrio, indecency is their religion.

The first Molotov record cover shows a provocative scene: a close-up of a woman taking off her knickers. Like this image, the lyrics are worrying. What is it all about? Are they shameless, misogynist homophobes – one of their songs shouts 'Puto' [abusive slang for gay] – or are they deliberately politically incorrect? The only thing that is certainly true is the latter: they are politically incorrect. Furthermore, they exclude any political language, their final objective is to provoke and to be popular. They provoke their elders and seduce all young types of people, in sharp contrast with the public the old rock bands sought to please: university students, the educated, the intellectual or the necessarily rebellious or inevitably marginalised audiences. The Molotov boys take in their iconoclastic irreverence, stated in such a crude manner that it seems involuntary, and listen joyfully to words formerly heard only in the most obscure corner of a low cantina.

Like Molotov, there are other rock groups, irreverent and at times brainless, that do not hold back from speaking out. Some have begun to record marginal songs of the 1970s. Others, the majority, invent their own songs, believing they are saying it all. The truth is that they speak out for the sake of it. They have broken the mantle of silence with a muscular, not intellectual, force. There can be no middle way because their only enemy is silence. They attack silence as elegance and the mediator of good manners, the complicit silence that cloaks equally the bandit and the 'good guy', creating moral confusion. Currently what they utter is scrambled, mixing accusation and homophobia, rebellion and misogyny, combat and stupidity, but they have an aim: to make an assault on silence.

To be irate, oh how great!

We go back to the image that adorns the cover of the Molotov album. A young woman is taking down her knickers on the back seat of a car. Getting worried? It is certainly a discomforting image for the viewer and doubly so for women. It is not necessary to be a feminist to feel that some moral dimension is not being addressed. Do Molotov intend to shock feelings the image provokes? It is not necessary to be a member of a closed order of some semi-ecclesiastical association of *pater familias* to feel that something is being stamped on. There is a violent, ignorant and macho gaze; the gaze of the musicians who, as it became clear in an interview, confessed to not knowing the meaning of the word 'homophobic'. Molotov considers another three possibilities regarding the same album cover. The owner of the CD can cover up the girl who does not cover herself up, or provide protection from the obscene gaze by exchanging the CD for a multicoloured cover. The other covers are not figurative. They are completely inoffensive. They could not offend anybody and they are careful to 'say nothing'. Molotov's proposal is to propose that there can be another proposal. Shout, do not speak. Do not mediate. Do not express yourself. Break the cloak and circle of silence.

'Puto'

Let us return to the song that has caused so much of a stir in the Mexican media, 'Puto'. The most disrespectful pejorative used against a homosexual is rooted in popular jargon with the meaning of

Tomas Gutierrez Alea and Juan Carlos Tabio, Cuba
***Guantanamera*, 1994**

***Guantanamera*, a satirical film about a family having problems burying a relative in 1990s recession-hit Cuba, met with criticism from Fidel Castro. Just as the film didn't mention communism or Castro, the Cuban leader didn't identify the production by name. He stated that poking fun at tragedies was unpatriotic and counter-revolutionary. Cuba's National Film Institute, which provided financial backing for *Guantanamera*, erupted under the controversy. Its president, Alfredo Guevera, resigned though he hinted Castro had been influenced into making the criticism through 'inadequate channels'. The 1994 film was scripted by award-winning novelist Eliseo Alberto and the film's co-directors, Juan Carlos Tabio and the late Tomas Gutierrez Alea.**
Directors: Tomas Gutierrez Alea and Juan Carlos Tabio, producer: Gerardo Herrero. Photo courtesy of BFI

Tian Zhuang Zhuang, PRC
***Blue Kite*, 1993**

The Chinese government stepped in during the post-production of Tian Zhuang Zhuang's 1993 film *Blue Kite* and prevented its completion. The story of a young boy and his family's survival through two decades of China's political upheaval from the 1950s was a subtle look at what constituted revolution and counter-revolution in rapidly shifting social climates. Criticised for being made 'without permission' it was banned for its implicit criticism of China's former political rule. Lagging film sales and competition from neighbouring countries encouraged the government to relax its censorship regulations. Zhuang Zhuang was removed from the blacklist in 1995 but has faced problems producing projects since *Blue Kite*. Director: Tian Zhuang Zhuang, producers: Fortissimo Film Sales, Longwick Film Production, Beijing Film Studio. Still: reproduced by kind permission of Fortissimo Film Sales, Amsterdam coward, without manhood, without 'balls', worthless. If somebody is very 'puto', they have no value and are traitors to themselves. Popular speech conflates in one word those beings of a particular sexual orientation with those incapable of expressing any preference at all. What does the song allude to with its 'puto'? I believe it refers to neither the coward nor the homosexual, since in the songs of Molotov there are no direct signifiers. They shout, to break the silence, but the words do not have any more meaning than a shout. Their intention is to become a sign. This is a risky game, as there is an element of ignorance mixed in their project. 'Puto,' shout the adolescents at their parties, and '*Dame, dame, dame, dame todo el power; dame, dame, dame, dame todo el poder*' [Give me all the power], the words of another song. As is obvious in these lines, neither subtlety nor high literature is among their characteristics (in contrast to the skill of Jaime López). Repetitive, tiring, almost pre-verbal: Molotov gesticulates. They run no risks. The market has embraced them, thus avoiding showing too much the worrying album cover. The 'Puto' song is not heard on the radio or on television, but there is not a single adolescent that does not know it. The video of the song is shown only at parties and at concerts, and it is self-censored – images of plasticine figures play childishly before the eyes of the spectator without suggesting or inviting any suggestion. Meanwhile Molotov sells records wholesale and has penetrated the market notwithstanding the barriers of Mexican correctness and silence. Despite their purposelessness, or due to it, they are a catalyst for freedom. Freedom to call things by their name, for example. Even though they play with confusing terms.

The song with the chorus '*Dame, dame, dame, dame todo el power*' is played constantly on television and on the radio. It is not necessary to stress that the group plays around with English. It is a group from the north of Mexico close to the frontier. But it does not sing border songs. Many of their lyrics jump at the opportunity to transgress English and poke fun at it. If two decades ago a group had composed lyrics in Mexico, it would have had to dream of crossing the border to sing from there in English, in order to enter the Mexican market. Now Molotov makes fun of the English language, muddling it and stripping it down. The group has conquered the markets of both countries, and a few more, including Spain and some other Latin American countries. Not only does Molotov transgress English, it also transgresses traditional melodies.

From the bare earth to the screen

The bare earth on which the anti-establishment bands performed helped to convince the listeners that their music was innovative, regenerative, destructive of old formulae, a bomb against 'the system'. The minority that listened to them was convinced that they were different.

The crowds of young people in the past had to address their parents as *usted* – like French *vous* – as a sign of respect. They observed all forms of courtesy and inherited the tradition of silence. They also used to say 'cilantro' for a herb common in Mexican cuisine, which in fact is called culantro, but sounds like *culo* [arse], something improper and unspeakable. Young people today swear loudly in unison, saying words, which would have been unspeakable, while dancing at parties in the family home on floors of marble, or of bare earth. Three decades ago, no one could even dream of swearing in front of a woman. Now women themselves swear together. This daring behaviour is what interests me. Now they shout '*Dame todo el power*'. Will they demand it at the July presidential elections? Will they make accusation the rule? Will they talk about the facts with the appropriate words? Will they attempt to correct the system in this way?

I dare to say yes. Today these songs are demolishing the religion of silence, despite their inaccuracies.

However, tomorrow, when the silence is broken, the conventions that acted as a cover-up to an unjust and treacherous élite – one which had inherited the colonial order and its 'good manners' – will also be broken.

When the president finished his State of the Union address, it fell upon the speaker of the House of Deputies to reply. The occupant of that post belonged to one of the opposition parties, the PAN (the Mexican right wing). Breaking with convention, as did the deputy from the PRD (the left or centre-left) the year before, he responded to the president, asking him directly and naïvely for a clearer account. Failing in every way to comply with traditional Mexican 'elegance', he demanded the truth to be told, thus breaking the cloak of silence. The revolt, which erupted, was unimaginable. The deputies of the previously single party of government, the PRI, booed and moved to drag him from his place, alleging that it was unpardonable discourtesy and that his speech was 'partisan'. The most curious thing is that his speech was not partisan at all: he belongs to a right-wing party. He had spoken of social injustice and extreme poverty, which are two issues that are of little interest within the ideology of his party.

Between the fracture and aperture

If musical groups like Molotov say what could not be said before in public, it is because they clearly represent the break-up of the Mexican submission to silence. This fracture has travelled through their music into the mass media. In the president's last State of the Union address, we find evidence that even in those corners, where the silence was most enduring to the point of being almost sacred, the 'noise' that breaks it is heard, '*Dame, dame, dame, dame todo el power*'... and the totalitarian control of the PRI will, it seems, soon be buried as part of a miserable past, when the truth, that 'yes' or 'no', was always excluded from the presidential address year after year. The citizens remained in silence and the truth was expressed only by the facts. The word was never tarnished through the representation of our social necessities or the errors and unpunished injustice of those governing us. But now, even the House of Deputies has joined this 'indecency' that contravenes the 'decency' of silence. Unfortunately, when the word gained power over silence, something blew up in front of all Mexicans, similar to what we find in Molotov. Not accustomed to a direct and clear account, the deputies of the PRI exploded in rage, shouting incoherently, incapable of showing a minimum of civility. This civility would allow dialogue and meaning to protect the space required to build a more democratic society, a greater space for freedom, an opening for justice and respect for human rights. But those lacking in tolerance shouted against the man who, candidly, signalled how much silence there was in the annual presidential address.

'It is not worth listening again to the idea that "everything is fine", knowing that poverty has increased dangerously within the country,' said the deputy of the PAN. Molotov is in the mass media, and there is rage in the House of Deputies. This is the transition through which Mexico is now passing, the space that has been opened in a horizon of suicidal and oppressive silence. A more articulated, more 'decent' political discourse will reach this country, one which listens and speaks with all the letters of the alphabet. Once verbalised, the horror of the truth might then be addressed.

Translated from the Spanish by Jaime Flórez

Deepa Mehta, India
***Fire*, 1996**

Deepa Mehta's film, *Fire*, won fourteen international awards but opened to immense scandal in India in 1998. The story of two unhappily married sisters-in-law who fall in love with each other caused riots in major cities as protesters vandalised theatres. Prominent filmmakers backed Mehta who went to India's Supreme Court for protection of artistic freedom. The censor board reviewed, then re-released the film without any cuts, though demonstrations continued. Right-wing activists stated the lesbian love story would 'corrupt' Indian women. Meanwhile a Bombay politician claimed that lesbianism didn't 'exist' in Hindu society.
Director: Deepa Mehta, producers: Bobby Bedi and Deepa Mehta, still photographer: Dilip Mehta, Canada/India 1996

>>

Deepa Mehta, India
***Water*, 1999**

Filmmaker Deepa Mehta's production *Water* in Varanasi, India, ended before it could begin. Hindu fundamentalists, including Uttar Pradesh state government officials, destroyed the sets. They claimed the story of widows was a 'Christian conspiracy' which 'maligned' Hindu culture. The script was reviewed twice by the central Government and approved both times. Yet Mehta faced state government-provoked demonstrations, death threats and effigy-burning. After a week's delay, shooting finally commenced. Within hours a protestor jumped into the Ganges river in remonstration, a stunt performed three times before he got attention. In response the state government suspended the shoot for 'disrupting law and order', effectively halting production. Director, producer and writer: Deepa Mehta. Photo: Raveendran/AFP

1. Carmen Boullosa wrote 'Indecency Is Their Religion' when Ernesto Zedillo was the president of Mexico – before PRD's Vicente Fox won the 3 July 2000 presidential election and broke PRI's 71-year stranglehold of corrupt, single party monopoly over the country's politics.

Recommended Listening

compiled by Juan Aura

Mexican rock bands and singers in order of their appearance in 'Indecency Is Their Religion'

- The Tri: *Una leyenda viva llamada el Tri* [A Living Legend Called the Tri] (WEA 7020; Mexico, 1990) includes songs like 'Casa, comida y susteno' [Home, Food and Maintenance], 'El desempleado' [Unemployed], 'Como una lombriz' (taken from the phrase *feliz como una lombriz* [happy as a worm]) and 'Nuestra realidad' [Our reality]; *Indocumentado* [Undocumented refers to an illegal Mexican worker in the U.S] (Warner Music 7270; Mexico, 1992); *Cuando tú no estás* [When you're not here] (Warners 1; Mexico, 1997)
- Jaime López: *Nordaka* (Prodisc 27091; Mexico, 1999).
- Paquita La Del Barrio: *Acábame de matar* [Finish killing me] (Musart 81233; Mexico, 1994) with sentimental love songs like 'Mar y cielo' [Sea and Sky], '¿Qué estoy haciendo aquí?' [What am I doing here], among others
- Molotov: *Dónde jugarán las niñas* (Universal Music 75031; México, 1997) includes songs like 'Que no te haga bobo Jacobo' ['Don't let Jacobo make a fool of you'] about establishment figure and TV news presenter Jacobo Zabludowsky, 'Chinga tu madre' [Fuck your mother], 'Gimme tha Power', 'Puto', '¿Por qué no te haces para allá?... al más allá' [Why don't you move ... to the other world] 'Cerdo' [Pig] and 'Quitate que ma' sturbas (perra arrabalera)' [Move, you make me mo' sturbate – dirty bitch]; *Molomix* (Universal Music, 75192; México, 1998) including mixes of the band's controversial and popular songs like 'Puto'; *Apocalipshit* (Universal Music 153 770-2; Mexico, 1999) including songs like 'Rastaman-Dita' [a play on the words 'rastaman', 'Maldita' and 'cursed'], and 'Parásito' [Parasite].
- Cafétacuba: *Re* (Warner Music 9678426; México, 1994); *Avalancha de éxitos* [Avalanche of Hits] (Warner Music CX16718 2; Mexico, 1996) is a covers CD, including previously popular songs such as 'Chilanga Banda' by Jaime López, 'No Controles' by Ignacio Cano (made famous by the pop group Flans), 'Alármala de Tos' by the group Botellita de Jerez, 'Metamorfosis' from the underground group Axis, 'Cómo te extraño mi amor' by the Sixties rock solist Leo Dan, plus 'Ojalá que llueva café' by the Dominican Juan Luis Guerra.
- Control Machete: *Mucho barato* [Very cheap] (Polygram, 534 349-2; México, 1996); *Artillería pesada* (Polygram 538 944-2 (29); México, 1999)
- Poncho Kingz: *Plan de Contingencia* (BMG 743215256021; México, 1997).
- Santa Sabina: *Babel* (BMG 743213825724; Mexico, 1995).
- Maldita Vecindady Los Hijos Del Quinto Patio: *Rock del milenio* [Rock of the Millennium] (BMG 74321-64411-2, Mexico, 1992) including 'Pachuco' [referring to a Mexican living in the U.S.] and 'Mojado' [slang for a Mexican working in the U.S. without papers]
- La Lupita: *Caramelo macizo* [Hard candy] (BMG 74321; Mexico, 1998) including songs like 'Mexican Soap Opera' and 'Al caer el mall' [When the mall comes]

Websites on Mexican Rock:
www.molotov.com; www.universal.com and www.loquesea.com for MP3 downloads

Ernesto Ortiz Hernández

The Cuban Sociocultural Journal *Vitral*: The Freedom of Light

In a colonial house, a *vitral* [vitrail] or a stained-glass window evokes a feeling of fragile welcome. Upon entering, brush strokes of light create the delights of a harlequin: a Havana-blue leg, a sapphire colour below, shading above, half the face aglow, an emerald pupil; serene ... a sweet image for the siesta, a tranquil *danzón*.

In the westernmost province of the island of Cuba, when the word '*vitral*' was mentioned it did not at first conjure up this prismatic image. This is not because stained-glass windows have become increasingly rare, but because by June 1994, a journal of the same name had been founded. The journal's purpose was defined in its opening line as 'a space for transparency and the multicoloured light of our society' that seeks 'to contemplate the limits of our current co-existence in order to emerge, collectively, from this state of prostration through the pathway of creativity'; a journal that shocked readers, eliciting joy in some and, in others, the desire to throw it out the window.

Background

The Spanish poet and essayist Antonio Piedra wrote that the first time he was in Pinar del Río, one of those clandestine street vendors of rare and second-hand books recognised him as a foreigner and sidled up to him. With a voice that could equally have been offering a thriller or indeed an old and yellowed, erotic magazine, he recommended a certain journal, warning, 'Careful, it's from the church. It has some interesting stuff, but it won't last long.' For Piedra, this story acted as a leitmotif for his critical analysis of a journal then in its first year of publication. It was, he wrote, 'a time of great literary harvest, bearing visible positive fruits.'[1]

Five years later, the impact of the journal is considered a sociological phenomenon. With a growing readership, the journal has extended the frontiers of its message, despite the fact that its achievements have been made in technologically unsatisfactory conditions and distributed through informal rather than official channels. *Vitral* is the voice of the Centro de Formación Cívica y Religiosa [Centre for Civil and Religious Instruction] (CFCR) of the Pinar del Río diocese, an organisation directed by Dagoberto Valdés.[2] The journal is financed by the centre, which receives funds in the form of co-operative aid from CAFOD, a branch of the Roman Catholic Church in England offering support to the Third World, from ADVENIAT, a German Roman Catholic organisation, and from the Italian Episcopal Conference. The journal's print run has increased from an initial figure of 300 to some 3,500. The figures are still insufficient for its voracious readership, due in part to the vendor's first words, which surrounded *Vitral* like the halo of a medieval saint and never abandoned it.

Pinar del Río, formerly one of the most backward areas of the country, had more than 200 different publications in the first 60 years of the century. There was a powerful tradition of

Al-Jazeera – www.aljazeera.net

The Arabic 24-hour satellite network Al-Jazeera is changing the way news is disseminated not only in the Near and Middle East but also in the rest of the world. After the 11 September 2001 terrorist attacks in New York City, it was the only news organisation to obtain live film footage of the U.S. bombing of Kabul 26 days later on 7 October. Closer to home, Al-Jazeera is known for presenting opposing viewpoints, a journalistic standard that has caused difficulties for the network. In Bahrain and Saudi Arabia, its news reporters have been barred, and in Algeria, the authorities pulled the plug on the channel after a lengthy report on the country's civil war. Al-Jazeera was the recipient of the Principal 1999 Prince Claus Award. (See page 173) Website © Al-Jazeera, 2000

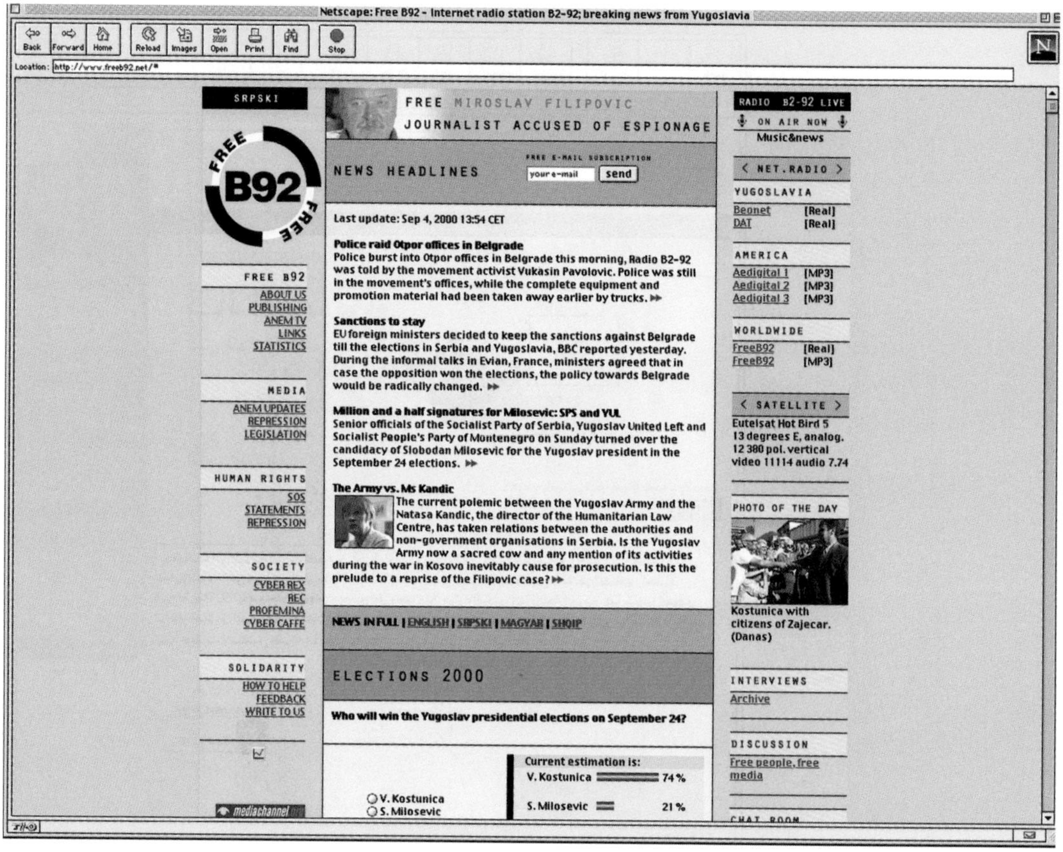

FreeB92 – www.freeb92.net/index.phtml

Independent broadcaster Radio B92 was established in 1989 as the most popular source for music and news information in Belgrade. Its promotion of peaceful activism and free speech gained ground with the internet broadcast of its radio programmes starting in 1995. The international public tuned in to get uncensored and unbiased coverage of events in the Balkans. In 1999, immediately before the NATO air strikes, the Serbian government banned its transmission. When the authorities took over the station, appointing its own management, the original team resigned en masse. With assistance from the Amsterdam-based coalition HelpB92, they re-established themselves as B292, followed by the website FreeB92 a month later.

freedom of the press which went through the same process as that experienced by commercial establishments, unions, political parties, etc., – the same active civil society that achieved the triumph of the Revolution and, upon radicalisation, began to disintegrate. In 1994, due to the shortage of paper and raw materials resulting from the ill-termed 'Special Period' crisis, there was only one single newspaper in the whole province. The official paper of the local Communist Party limited itself to publishing a weekly edition. Naturally, the national press continued to circulate and fashioned – together with radio and television – what Václav Havel called the 'daily panorama of the people': that web of opinions, news and slogans which remind each individual where he or she lives and what is expected of them. Owing to its excesses, monotony and hollowness, this web soon ceases to be recognised, but it still succeeds in promoting certain values, attitudes and forms of behaviour and attempts to condition peoples' responses to certain sets of signals.

Against this background, a vigorous and renowned group of writers and young artists from Vueltabajo began to bolster limited and scarce resources. They viewed with pleasure the explosive rise of a journal which proclaimed itself to be free of filters that might impoverish its creative substance, a journal in which anyone can read things that some would dare not say, that others do not want to hear, and which has on its cover a motto with that ever-dangerous and precarious word 'freedom'. '*La Libertad de la Luz*' [the Freedom of Light] is the subtitle of *Vitral*.

Under a totalitarian state, the simple fact of a publication on the margins of government structures creates a conflict regarding the use of media. On one hand, there is a body of rules leaving little room for manoeuvre or severely censoring independent initiatives in matters of publishing or broadcasting; on the other, there is the voice of those who think (and I quote Mons. José Siro, Bishop of Pinar del Río, in an interview published in the first issue of *Vitral*) that, 'During these years of revolutionary government, the church has never had the necessary freedom to fulfil its mission.' Let us not forget that the Cuban bishops, six months before, had publicly proclaimed their message, 'With love, there is always a way', which reflected to a large extent the difficult conditions in which Cubans live. The national press aggressively attacked the message without even publishing the text.[3]

Motivated by self-assessment, one which sought to understand the signs of the times around the theme of the incarnation – a concept that dates back to the 1986 Cuban National Ecclesiastical Congress in Havana – the church identified itself with the anguish and joys of the population.[4] It enhanced its ability to convince people and bring them together, by boldly denouncing the causes of the nation's moral decay and by sympathising with the hopes of all Cubans.

However, church and government relations were entering a delicate phase. The difficult economic situation provoked a tension, which was a catalyst for conflicts. It was clear that the country was going through the *homo guevarianus* crisis (referring to the new man expected to emerge from a well-planned and historically conditioned process). But what do the large-scale protest marches mean to the lives of our people? What do the lives lost on the sunken rafts mean? The incitement to crush the enemy and get even? 'What difference does it make that, according to the news, those who confront the citizens who cry freedom and the citizens who throw stones at shop and hotel windows are civilians too? What purpose does it serve anyway, to call the streets of our cities battlefields and to summon the people to arms for the cause?'[5]

This violence stemming from intolerance and from the incapacity to hold a dialogue – the ultimate and most profound root of which is injustice – has not prevented *Vitral* from telling the truth at the right time, as advocated by José Martí, the Cuban poet, writer and lawyer (1835-1895). The journal has a form of expression, which does not impose itself upon people. It makes the reader a participant, not only by adopting a literary style full of questions, allusion and figurative expressions but also through its central focus on human beings, their dignity and their capacity to transcend.

Positive aims

Vitral makes its denouncements but does not dwell on the negative. It asserts the positive values of Cubans, their potential and their strength, which allows them to transform an adverse reality in their favour. In this sense, and on balance, its articles can be considered stimulating and full of hope – ultimately an argument in its defence. And when we say *Vitral*, we are referring to the hundreds of collaborators who dare to be free and are fully aware of, and some are suffering from, the consequences of expressing and writing different ideas, according to their conscience. They are people from the widest spectrum of creeds and ideologies, the majority being non-Catholics and under the age of 35. They take responsibility for their opinions. Their criteria are often non-specialised. They are citizens who exercise their right not to live a lie.

To cultivate virtue, to reconstruct the nation, to reconcile a country divided by frontiers or ideologies: these are the aims of the journal, which calls together Cubans from Cuba and the diaspora, and men and women of good will. *Vitral* is devoid of any constraint other than the elementary principal of respect owed to any person and to the opinion of others. In this way it has been an incentive for pluralism, freedom of action and for the exercise of individual responsibility.

Vitral places a priority on ethics and the promotion of human and civic values, in the hope that these may lead to a true understanding of freedom and responsibility. It adopts a style, which, while interacting with the reader, simultaneously promotes the value of self-determination. The journal seeks to rebuild and strengthen a network of the groups, associations and nongovernmental organisations, which make up civil society and strive for a greater level of autonomy and participation. If the journal manages to survive, despite the many pressures confronting it, this will be due to the careful, respectful way in which it expresses itself and the fact that its influence transcends ecclesiastical and even national spheres.

A variety of artists contribute prolifically to the work of *Vitral* and participate in the alternative activities organised by the journal, such as concerts, exhibitions and readings. *Vitral* has promoted underground rock and salsa groups, and fashion and theatre groups. Its pages are designed by visual artists and their work also appears on the front cover – in full colour since July 1997 – and in reviews and analyses by major critics. Posters and catalogues have also been designed for numerous exhibitions.

As for the contributing authors, they do not write only for the journal. They also take part in literary competitions and make use of the *Vitral* publishing house. The CFCR also publishes the children's magazine *Meñique* [Little Finger], in which both children and adults participate. *Vitral* has supported various official literary events such as the Ibero-American Congress on the life and works of the poet and lawyer Dulce María Loynaz (1902-1997). It has collaborated on the rock fanzine *Cruzada* [Crusade] and is also one of the promoters of *Ilusión* [Illusion], another rock magazine, as well as the independent literary magazine *deLiras*. All of these publications are from Pinar del Río and are part of a recent movement, which to a large extent has been inspired by *Vitral*.

Of the 30 or so Roman Catholic publications that exist in varying forms today in Cuba, *Vitral* distinguishes itself for its sociopolitical engagement. Even though the Christian religion has an

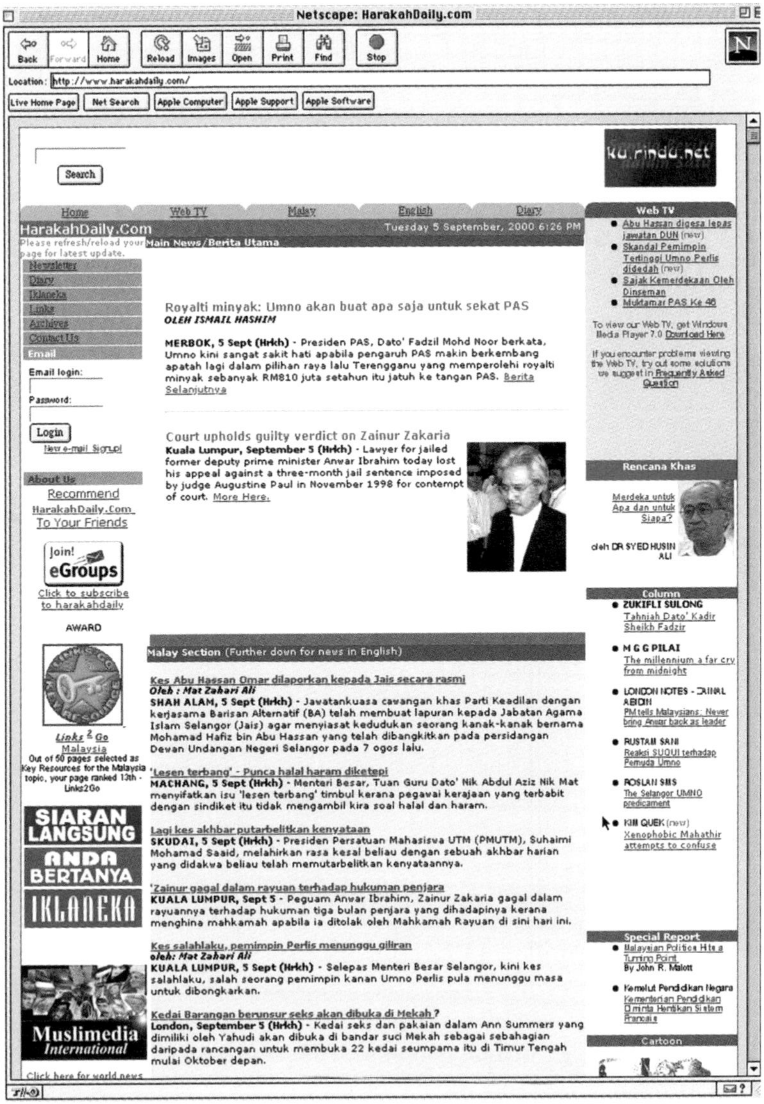

Harakah Daily – www.harakahdaily.com

With state-enforced regulations governing print and television media in Malaysia, a free press was in danger of becoming obsolete. However, with Prime Minister Mahathir Mohamad's determination to advance IT technology in his country, the internet has spawned a generation of uncensored political and social reports. The opposition party PAS (Malaysia Islamic Party) newspaper, *Harakah Daily*, went online and HarakahDaily.com recounted current affairs without threat. When former Deputy Prime Minister Anwar Ibrahim was charged with alleged sexual offences, the international press hit Malaysian news net sites to get the inside story. Harakahdaily.com launched Malaysia's first web television with news and talk shows in May 2000. (See page 146) Website © HarakahDaily.com, 2000

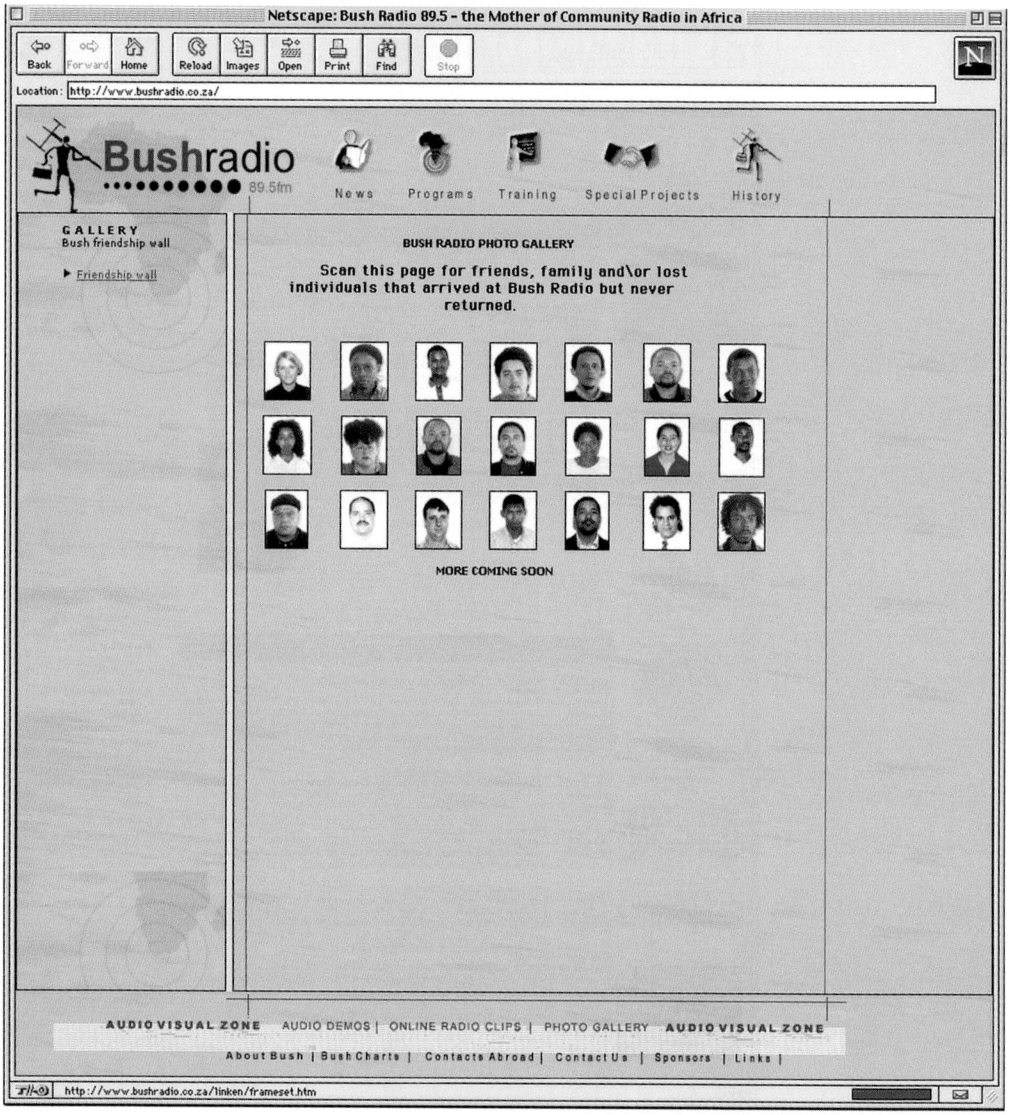

Bush Radio – www.rnw.nl/realradio/community/html/history_bush_radio.html

'We have no desire to be popular ... we strive to be necessary, an entity without which our lives cannot be maintained.' Bush Radio's broadcasting to Western Cape communities in South Africa has lived up to its motto. This first black-run station got its licence in 1995 after international pressure on the government. Health bulletins about AIDS and other medical issues, as well as missing children announcements, are transmitted in between news coverage and literacy workshops. Saturdays are exclusively for children, with a focus on human rights issues. Broadcasting training has remained the goal of Bush Radio, with over 500 graduates, including young offenders from local prisons. Website courtesy of Radio Netherlands, © 2000 unavoidable social dimension, on occasions it is only understood within its cultural context, detached from politics – that 'eminent form of charity', of which many popes have spoken. The journal insists that separating one thing from another is alienation and demonstrates the manner in which the lay regard service for the common good as their right. We observe the impassioned precision of Father Manuel H. de Céspedes, advisor to *Vitral*:

'The church has the very grave responsibility of helping in the political training of all of its members, so that each one takes upon himself, from his own personal set of circumstances, the duty of serving the community. This service may for some include meeting up freely in groups or political parties in order to evangelise the political status quo, in order to seek, obtain, retain and exercise political power.'[6]

Dialogue

Of course, with such objectives in mind, it has been an arduous path for the journal. There was one point which was hardly even recorded as a news item in the pages of the journal, but which I do not wish to ignore. This was the meeting between members of the editorial committee and persons of various ranks from the government and Communist Party authorities, perhaps prompted by the pope's visit to Cuba. The content of this dialogue, started by the Government, was leaked little more than a month later in the Mexican weekly *Proceso* of 7 July 1997. This leak was used by the journalist Homero Campa as the basis for formal protests to the Government, criticising *Vitral*. Even though it is not the only publication with a religious profile, it is the journal's social content that 'causes irritation: they criticise the excessive taxes which inhibit the incipient private sector, the laws that, in their judgement, violate individual liberty and even a person's privacy, the manipulation of the education system to serve their ideology, the narrow-mindedness of the cultural bureaucracy, etc.'

However, *Vitral* considers that the five hours of animated discussion were conducted in a frank and positive climate. It was hoped that these meetings would continue after the pope's visit to Cuba. But there is no indication that such an experience, which took place in an atmosphere of tolerance and plurality of agendas, will ever be repeated. A dialogue is, first and foremost, an acknowledgement of the interlocutor, but the motives for this may be merely circumstantial. Whatever the case, the meeting demonstrated the importance that *Vitral* has attained as a medium of communication. It demonstrated that not only did it have the capacity to influence public opinion in a way that the official media felt was dangerous but also that that power of small things, based on the idea of everyone freely stating what they think and acting in accordance, can bring about some measure of change.

Change

There is a ghost haunting Cuba. It is the spectre of change, awakened to a large extent by the visit of the pope during 21-25 January 1998, an event preceded by an intense journalistic blitz.[7] At that time, the journal was consolidating something it had been doing sporadically since late 1996: one-off issues, monographs and special publications. The latter is now being developed and will be published under the name of *Ediciones Vitral*. At present there are four series: *Huellas* [Traces], which follows ecclesiastical events in our country and the current challenges facing the church in a global sense, with a marked emphasis on social doctrine and the roots of Cuban Roman

 Catholicism; *Memoria* [Memory], devoted to relevant figures from our culture and other aspects of our cultural heritage, with an exhaustive bibliography and iconography; *Más Luz* [More Light], consisting of the winning books from the Annual Competition for Literature, organised by the journal since 1998, and *Puentes* [Bridges], containing work by foreign writers little-known in Cuba and by Cubans from the diaspora.

For many people HH John Paul II could be considered a regular collaborator of *Vitral*. The agreement between his message in Cuba and what the journal had been weaving together for a number of years was transparently clear. The journal had been establishing a form of humanism rooted in Christianity, in which man would not have to be afraid to open his doors to the truth – 'And the truth will set you free' – and also where a person does not have to be the instrument of totalitarian power, but a protagonist in his own personal and social history. Embracing the call of the pope for Cuba to open its doors to the world, on 22 February 1999 *Vitral* became the first Roman Catholic Cuban publication to have a site on the internet, www.vitral.org, without, of course, being connected to the net, due to governmental restrictions.

A year after the pope's visit, the view of many Cubans is that 'nothing is going on here'. However, in one of its most recent editorials, entitled 'Resistance to Change: a Cul-de-sac with No Way Out', the journal continues to rouse a sense of responsibility in each individual, in order to steer change along the path of dialogue and reconciliation. 'It is essential to continue to talk about this while injustice is present in the world, no matter how insignificant it may be, because if this was not the case the church would not be fulfilling the mission which Jesus Christ entrusted to it. In this sense it is man and humanity that is at stake.'[8]

Cultural diversity

Vitral, as an alternative contemporary Cuban cultural proposition, places itself within a journalistic tradition in which the written word is intimately intertwined with political developments. This is because it also wishes to create space for thought within the difficult present-day circumstances, fomenting reflection on the historic destiny upon which the nation is forged. This implies, essentially, an open, dynamic, comprehensive assessment of culture.

Even though *Vitral* seeks to emphasise the Christian values that a militant atheism has tried to obstruct within our culture – a culture, which is nonetheless eminently rooted in Roman Catholicism – the journal also knows that diversity is enriching. We are a mixture of cuisines, races and cultures, the result of cross-cultural fertilisation, synthesis and syncretism, an open bridge that links the outside world and our own culture. It is only in a large clay pot that the ingredients of 'Cubanness' can be stewed. A metaphor for the current state of our culture is made in a tasty editorial comparing the *criollo ajiaco* with the *caldosa*.[9] In the former, the original flavour and identity of each ingredient is conserved, whereas in the latter everything is reduced to a soup, a uniform mass, lacking individuality in terms of its ingredients, diluted into a liquid that is uniform in colour, with the various flavours indistinguishable. The *caldosa* has been turned into the official symbol, a national 'medium' widely recommended by television as a basis for 'activities' or 'mass-movement' rallies or celebrations.

The progressive loss of apprehension on the part of intellectuals to make their views known to ministry officials, this willingness to accept the new values and spectrum of opinions – because we all fashion culture together as a whole – reflects a level of maturity within which the aims of *Vitral* are clearly evident. Unfortunately, there is much prejudice, much mistrust, many threats

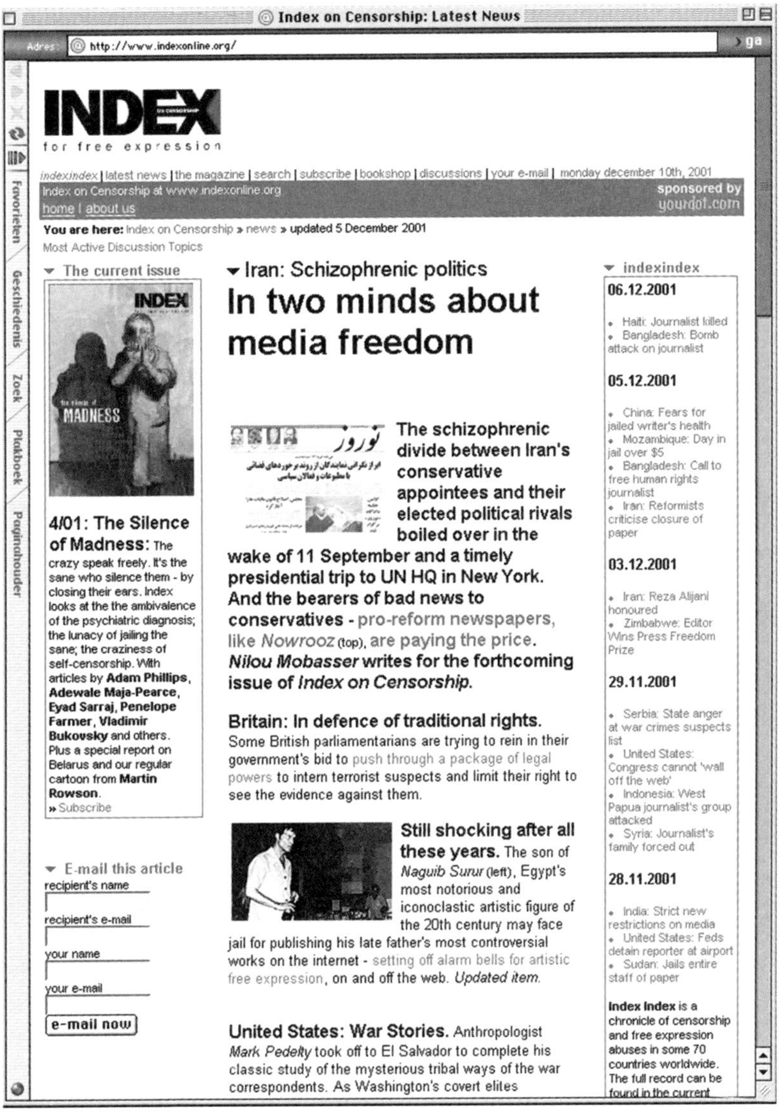

Index on Censorship: Latest News

http://www.indexonline.org/

INDEX

for free expression

indexindex | latest news | the magazine | search | subscribe | bookshop | discussions | your e-mail | monday december 10th, 2001

Index on Censorship at www.indexonline.org

home | about us

sponsored by yourdot.com

You are here: Index on Censorship » news » updated 5 December 2001

Most Active Discussion Topics

The current issue

4/01: The Silence of Madness: The crazy speak freely. It's the sane who silence them - by closing their ears. Index looks at the the ambivalence of the psychiatric diagnosis; the lunacy of jailing the sane; the craziness of self-censorship. With articles by **Adam Phillips, Adewale Maja-Pearce, Eyad Sarraj, Penelope Farmer, Vladimir Bukovsky** and others. Plus a special report on Belarus and our regular cartoon from **Martin Rowson**.

» Subscribe

E-mail this article

recipient's name

recipient's e-mail

your name

your e-mail

e-mail now

Iran: Schizophrenic politics

In two minds about media freedom

The schizophrenic divide between Iran's conservative appointees and their elected political rivals boiled over in the wake of 11 September and a timely presidential trip to UN HQ in New York. And the bearers of bad news to conservatives - pro-reform newspapers, like *Nowrooz* (top), are paying the price. *Nilou Mobasser* writes for the forthcoming issue of *Index on Censorship*.

Britain: In defence of traditional rights. Some British parliamentarians are trying to rein in their government's bid to push through a package of legal powers to intern terrorist suspects and limit their right to see the evidence against them.

Still shocking after all these years. The son of *Naguib Surur* (left), Egypt's most notorious and iconoclastic artistic figure of the 20th century may face jail for publishing his late father's most controversial works on the internet - setting off alarm bells for artistic free expression, on and off the web. *Updated item.*

United States: War Stories. Anthropologist *Mark Pedelty* took off to El Salvador to complete his classic study of the mysterious tribal ways of the war correspondents. As Washington's covert elites

indexindex

06.12.2001

- Haiti: Journalist killed
- Bangladesh: Bomb attack on journalist

05.12.2001

- China: Fears for jailed writer's health
- Mozambique: Day in jail over $5
- Bangladesh: Call to free human rights journalist
- Iran: Reformists criticise closure of paper

03.12.2001

- Iran: Reza Alijani honoured
- Zimbabwe: Editor Wins Press Freedom Prize

29.11.2001

- Serbia: State anger at war crimes suspects list
- United States: Congress cannot 'wall off the web'
- Indonesia: West Papua journalist's group attacked
- Syria: Journalist's family forced out

28.11.2001

- India: Strict new restrictions on media
- United States: Feds detain reporter at airport
- Sudan: Jails entire staff of paper

Index Index is a chronicle of censorship and free expression abuses in some 70 countries worldwide. The full record can be found in the current

Index on Censorship – www.indexoncensorship.org

Nineteen-ninety-seven Prince Claus laureate *Index on Censorship* is a quarterly magazine which 'widens the debates on freedom of expression with some of the world's best writers. Through interviews, reportage, banned literature and polemic, *Index* shows how free speech affects the issues of the moment'. The magazine was started 1972. Its website includes Human Rights Watch reports on imprisoned poets and RealAudio and Virtual TV debates on a range of timely issues, from censored Sri Lankan papers to a free Iranian press. *Index* also lists country-by-country free speech abuses, while the magazine's international cartoon archive speaks volumes about censorship in a few choice words and drawings.

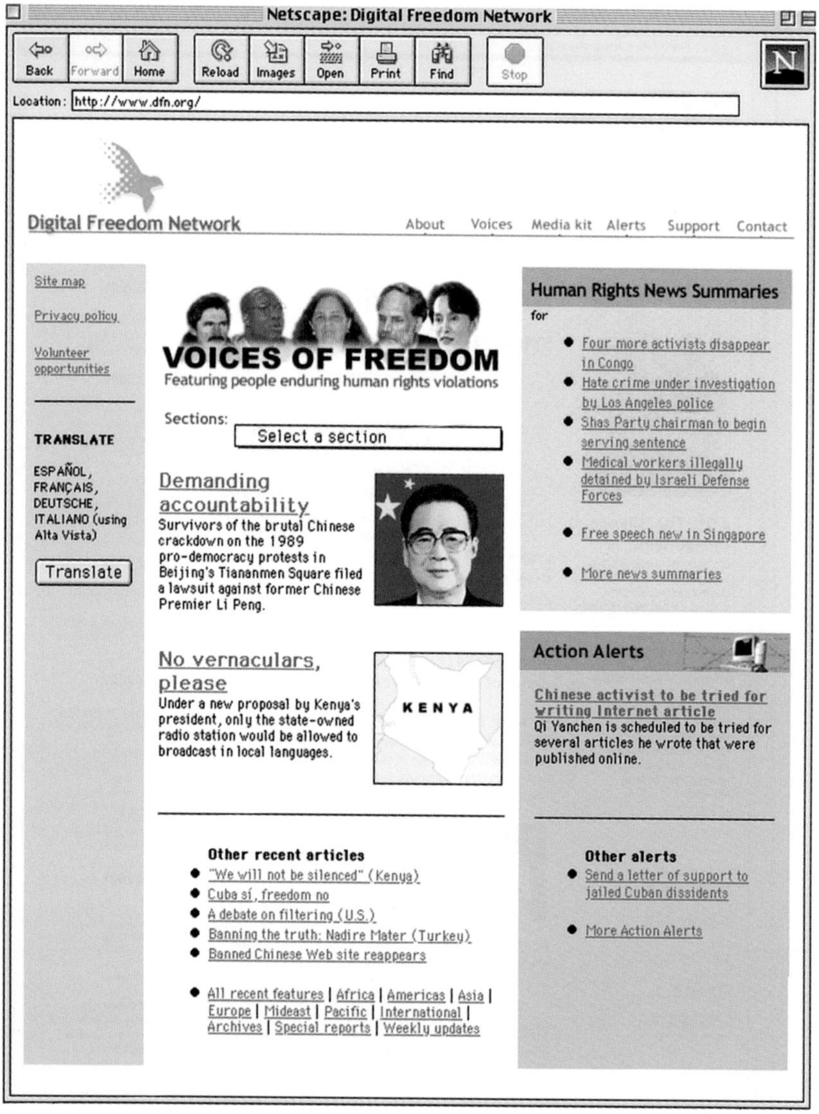

Digital Freedom Network – www.dfn.org

Suppression of free speech now stops at national borders. Covering censorship news from around the world, Digital Freedom Network's groundbreaking website has given a voice back to silenced writers, journalists and dissidents by publishing their threatened work. Materials including political cartoons, documents and song lyrics are available often for the first time in their uncensored form. 'People can decide for themselves whether these individuals are "dangerous traitors", as oppressive governments often call them, or peaceful advocates of freedom and democracy, as we believe,' writes DFN's Executive Director Bobson Wong on the website. Alongside editorials and freedom of expression campaigns, activist letters are also published.

from the political powers, which prevent more people from collaborating with *Vitral* and making a spontaneous contribution to culture.

Vitral does not want to be reduced by the mechanisms of cultural control, by officials, censors and people who 'look after' this area to a homogenous cream soup. In part, the journal's popularity among creative youth is because it offers alternative spaces to accommodate their works – amidst the inefficiency, disinterest or censorship of official culture. More importantly it introduces them to the natural dynamics of the cultural reality, stimulating the initiative and creativity so commonly found in Cubans. As Mons. Beniamino Stella, the former Papal Nuncio in Cuba, said, 'A nation is more than an ideological trench or a potential market: people wish to be considered as a community of values, as a sovereign and integrated identity, but above all, as a community of people with an inexorable and undying spirituality.'[10]

This is what the country requires and this has been the greatest contribution of *Vitral*. By including everybody, the journal shows the possibility of transforming an impoverished culture of exclusion into one that welcomes, vivifies and spawns new opportunities.

Translated from the Spanish by Jaime Flórez

1. 'Palabras para una Presentación', in *Vitral*, No. 32, July-August 1999
2. Also director of the Catholic Commission for Culture in the diocese
3. 'Declaración del Comité Permanente de la Conferencia de Obispos Católicos de Cuba', 7 October 1993, *La Voz de la Iglesia en Cuba*. 100 Documentos Episcopales, Mexico, 1995
4. There was a great lay presence at the congress and it invited the expression of the concerns, problems and hopes of Roman Catholics on the island. It was inspired not only by the Third General Latin American Episcopal Conference but also by a previous gathering in Medellín and by the texts of the Second Vatican Council. Its final document was prophetic in more senses than one and it is undoubtedly of historical significance.
5. 'Editorial', *Vitral*, No. 3, September-October 1994.
6. '¿Por qué la Iglesia se Mete en Política?', *Vitral*, No.15, September-October 1996
7. Montalban, Vázquez: *Y Dios Entró en La Habana* (Ediciones El País, S.A.) 1998, pp. 594-595
8. Paul II, John, *Homilía en la Plaza José Martí*, 25 January 1998
9. 'Cultura: ¿Ajiaco o Caldosa?', *Vitral*, No. 14, July-August 1996
10. *Para Cuba: Tiempo de Siembra y Esperanza, Ediciones Vitral*, April 1999, p. 150

Richard Eisendorf and Jens Robinson

Grey Lines and Red Lines: Editorial Cartoons in Freedom, Repression and Crisis

Editorial cartoons have a vital role in societies – to criticise, humour and judge. At their best, they have a lasting quality reflecting insight into the human condition. As both artist and journalist, the cartoonist has long served as a window into societies, striving to maintain an independent voice, especially in countries where freedoms are restricted.

With their language of pictures and words, editorial cartoonists have a unique tool for expression against injustice and inhumanity. 'By freeing the imagination, challenging the intellect, and resisting tyranny', political cartoons have the potential to generate positive change.[1] They can sometimes mobilise public opinion in support of a common cause, be a force of tolerance in society, and show the common humanity in all. As journalists who employ humour and art, cartoonists have been, over time, suppressed by the state and have occasionally liberated themselves through their creativity.

In the early nineteenth century, Henri Daumier drew a devastating series of drawings on the French monarchy, including one savaging King Louis Philippe as Gargantua gorging himself on the working class. Daumier's editor, Charles Philipon, metamorphosed the royal visage into a pear. The drawings landed both the artist and the editor in jail – resulting in the pear forever gaining a double-meaning in the French lexicon and demonstrating that the political cartoon is not only a powerful instrument in marshalling public opinion, but also can be a dangerous profession for the practitioner.

Times of crises are shots of adrenaline to cartoonists. For Daumier, it was the horror of war; for the great English artist William Hogarth, it was the alcoholism and class divide of urban degradation. The art of the classic cartoonists in the German magazine *Simplissimus*, George Grosz, Heinrich Kley and Olaf Gulbranson, focused on greed, sex and religion. These artists/activists were the precursors of the British cartoonist David Low, whose bold cartoons helped to alert a complacent world to burgeoning fascism. The first cartoonist in a British daily newspaper, Francis Carruthers, was a radical who fought the policies of British statesman, Joseph Chamberlain. The tradition of advocacy in the cause of justice continued with cartooning legend Thomas Nast, who popularised the elephant and the donkey as symbols of the American Republican and Democratic political parties respectively.

Even in this world of diverse cultures and demographic divisions, it is an axiom of humour that people in different countries tend to laugh at the same situations. By disrespecting authority figures and being critical of how they rule or govern, cartoonists worldwide find common cause. Yet, when it comes to drawing political leaders from around the world, cartoonists operate with

Protest'96 – www.galeb.etf.bg.ac.yu/~protest96/

The information blockade in Serbia was neatly curbed in 1996 when students from the University of Belgrade took to the internet with their campaign. It was a simple one: a fight for their constitutional rights after president Slobodan Milosevic annulled the municipal elections. Students demonstrated peacefully on campus with banners outside university halls, calling for the restoration of democracy. But while local media censored the protest, students continued to transmit their news through the only independent media left. Three months later, Milosevic relented and the elected mayor resumed power. It was the first time that a net student protest resulted in government change. Website © Protest96, 1998

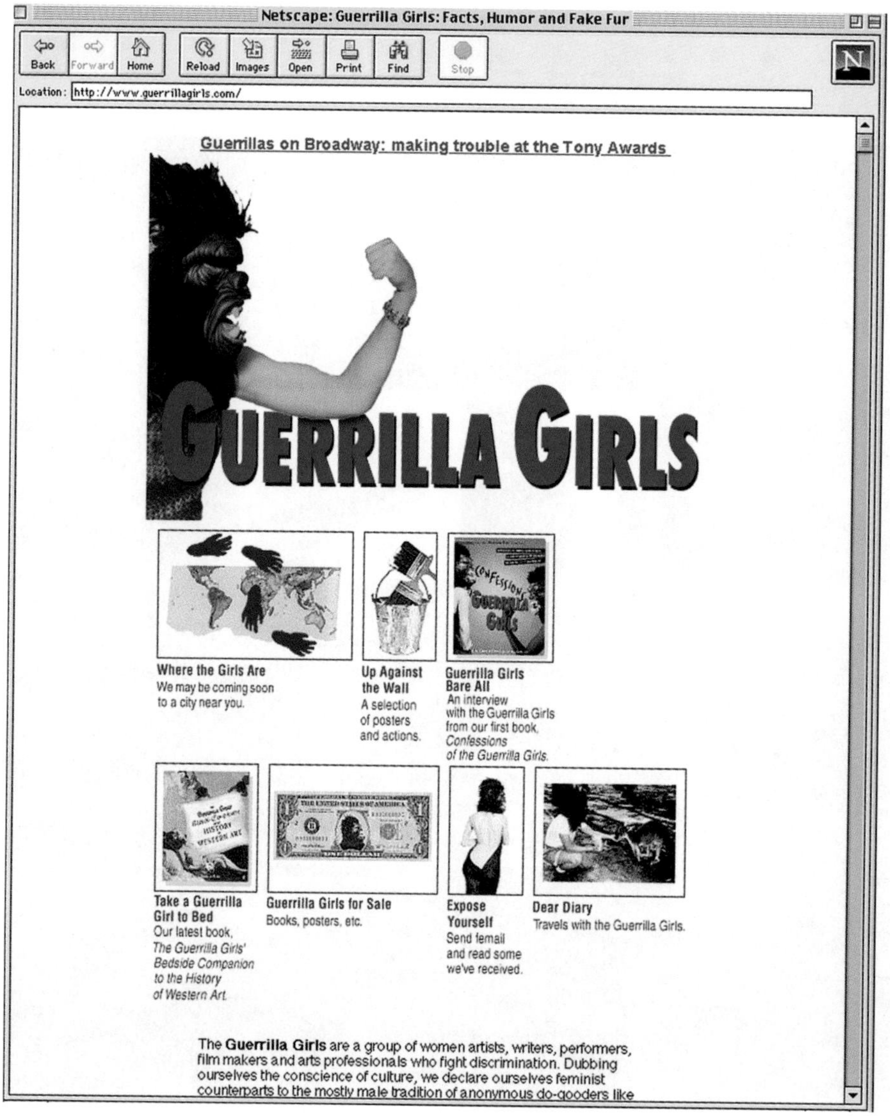

Guerrilla Girls – www.guerrillagirls.com

Their posters say it all. Confrontational, concise, and often well-placed sarcasm make the Guerrilla Girls difficult to miss. They started in 1985 to protest against an exhibition at New York's Museum of Modern Art which represented 169 artists of which only thirteen were women. Their cause is the championing of women and artists of colour in the art world. While they claim to have famous women in their group, identities are well protected and they use pseudonyms of dead artists like Frida Kahlo and Tina Modotti. Their recent expansions include publication of two books, while addressing current issues like environmentalism.
(See page 146)

differing amounts of freedom. Some cartoonists believe that one of their primary roles is to caricature. Satirising politicians keeps them humble and aware of their limitations. However, in many countries, cartoonists are not able to directly caricature or criticise those in authority. According to the Lebanese cartoonist Mahmoud Kahil, who works for the London-based *Al-Hayat* newspaper, 'Cartoonists are oppressed in the Arab world. Sometimes we have to be ambiguous to avoid censorship and other dangers.'[2]

When the Arab League sought to create a pan-Arab law abolishing the cartooning of Arab leaders in the 1970s, cartoonists found creative ways of getting their message across to their readers. A character for all occasions has been a regional favourite. Palestinian cartoonist Baha Boukhari, for example, created a single character, Abu Arab, who has enabled him to characterise all Arab leaders without actually drawing them distinctly. Egyptian caricaturist Bahgat drew the dictator Bahgatos in a multitude of guises, while Hanzala, the barefoot boy who represents the Palestinian people, appeared in the drawings of the assassinated cartoonist Naji Al-Ali.

In certain societies there are rules – written or unwritten – prescribing what cartoonists can and cannot portray. In some instances, those who step over the line are punished and this has a stifling effect on the creativity of others. After the sentencing and release of Egyptian cartoonist Essam Hanafy, Robert Russell, director of the Cartoonists Rights Network, reflected, 'Cartooning is being "dumbed down" all over Egypt and hard-hitting sharp cartoons are quickly becoming a thing of the past.'[3]

When cartoonists can be threatened, imprisoned – or worse – for their work, self-censorship becomes the policeman of each artist's freedom. 'Self-censorship is much worse than censorship,' said former Egyptian spokesman Tahseen Basheer. 'The censor protected the journalist from the government. Self-censorship … is very powerful. [It makes] *you* responsible.'[4] This situation is not unique to Egypt.

For the cartoonist, censorship (and press laws) also has another side. 'On the one hand, it imposed restrictions,' writes *Baltimore Sun* and *Economist* cartoonist Kevin 'Kal' Kallaugher, 'but on the other, it forced cartoonists to be more creative and subtle in getting their messages across.'[5] In a 1998 workshop for cartoonists from the Mediterranean and Middle Eastern regions, co-sponsored by Search for Common Ground and Cartoon Arts International, a Tunisian cartoonist told of his experiences trying to make a living as a cartoonist in France. In Tunisia, he was always conscious of the 'red lines' beyond which he knew he could not go. Yet in France, he had no limits on his freedom. Ironically, without any boundaries, he lost his creative edge.[6] Conversely, the experience of living and working in exile in the west has only sharpened the resolve of Algerian cartoonists Chawki Amari and Sid Ali Melouah to influence political change back home.

Grey lines

By necessity, cartoonists have developed a unique style, adapting to the limitations governments and societies place upon them. The craft has endured and even thrived in difficult circumstances because of this resilience. 'The immense social impact of the political cartoon derives from its simultaneous appeal to the intellect, conscience, and emotion,' writes Fatma Müge Göçekin in *Political Cartoons in the Middle East*. 'This rich representation is also able to resist control because of the ambiguities in the message that result from the multiple levels of meaning.'[7]

In so-called 'symbolic' cartoons, general themes are commented on metaphorically through the use of a symbol which represents a person or a policy. In the Soviet Union, the roots of this cartooning style began during the 1917 Russian revolution – a watershed for political visual material after many dormant years under the czars. The Bolsheviks favoured propagandist iconography by putting political art on posters and banners as well as in newspapers and leaflets. State restrictions after the Second World War rendered Russian politics off-limits to commentary by Russian artists and journalists, and when they ventured to speak their minds, there were severe repercussions. Viatcheslav Syssoyev was sent to the gulag after his work was smuggled out of Russia and delivered to the U.S. based Cartoonists & Writers Syndicate, which introduced it to the op-ed page of *The New York Times*.

Although cartoonists in the former Soviet Union and Eastern Europe were able to lampoon the west as well as their own society's bureaucracy and apparatchiks, prior to glasnost they were never able to criticise their top echelon of leaders directly. Cartoonists were forced to adapt. Yugoslavian cartoonist Yugoslav Vlahovic explains, 'We are used to expressing ourselves metaphorically, not by satirical directness. We used symbols a lot.'[8] It is a tradition still employed today by the Bulgarian cartoonist Ni©ky who excoriates human rights abuses with a symbol of the guillotine giving a press conference.

In some totalitarian regimes, the appearance of unlimited freedom of expression can be tantamount to propaganda. Before the fall of Slobodan Milosevic in Serbia, Koraksic 'Corax' was known for his bold, direct cartoons. An exception in this era of symbolic art, he expressed himself freely. But Corax was acutely aware of the complexity of his situation. He said, 'People here think that President Milosevic doesn't make any trouble [for] me because in that way he can show the west that [an] independent press exists [in Serbia].'[9]

No matter what the language – whether direct or symbolic – dissent can often be dangerous. Iranian Ardeshir Mohassess was forced to leave his country for his opposition to the Shah and later, ironically, prevented from returning because of his unwillingness to bend to Ayatollah Khomeini's rule. In Iran today cartoonists – like so many other journalists – are a visible part of the reformist 'revolution'. In early 1999, cartoonist Nikahang Kowsar, featured in the pro-reform daily *Azad*, drew cartoons critical of conservative clerics. Nearly costing him his life, these cartoons marked the first time since the 1979 Islamic revolution that a publication had criticised the clergy so directly.

Freedom of expression denied

The human rights abuses facing some cartoonists have strengthened the commitment of others to free expression. American syndicated cartoonist and historian Jerry Robinson observes that, 'It is increasingly important, and technically feasible, for western cartoonists to take activist roles in freedom of expression and human rights cases on behalf of persecuted colleagues worldwide.' The timely response to censorship, jailing, torture, and even murder can be crucial. In the 1980s, as president of the National Cartoonists Society, and later, the Association of American Editorial Cartoonists, Robinson and others mobilised artists and writers throughout the U.S., as well as in Canada, Mexico, and western Europe, on behalf of cartoonists in trouble. A successful two-year campaign was waged to free Uruguayan cartoonist Francisco Laurenzo Pons who was jailed and tortured by the then military junta for his cartoons advocating democracy. The concerted action of the cartoonists was a powerful tool in focusing public and press attention, which in turn generated the governmental and professional pressure necessary for action.
In the case of Nigeria, no international campaign was going to change the situation. Under

Radio Free Burma – www.fastnet.au/rfb/

With the Burmese military government regulating domestic media, locals have turned to the airwaves to hear about what's happening in their country from radio stations outside. Radio Free Burma, transmitting from Sydney, Australia and recently accessible from around the world via the internet, is the first international all-Burmese radio station. Their website, launched in October 1996, continues their campaign for democracy and human rights. Still under surveillance by Burma's State Peace and Development Council (SPDC), which censors foreign press interference, the site publishes only in Burmese. The archives include transcripts of interviews with opposition leader and 1995 Nobel Peace Prize laureate Daw Aung San Suu Kyi. Photo and website © Radio Free Burma, 2000, www.fastnet.au/rfb

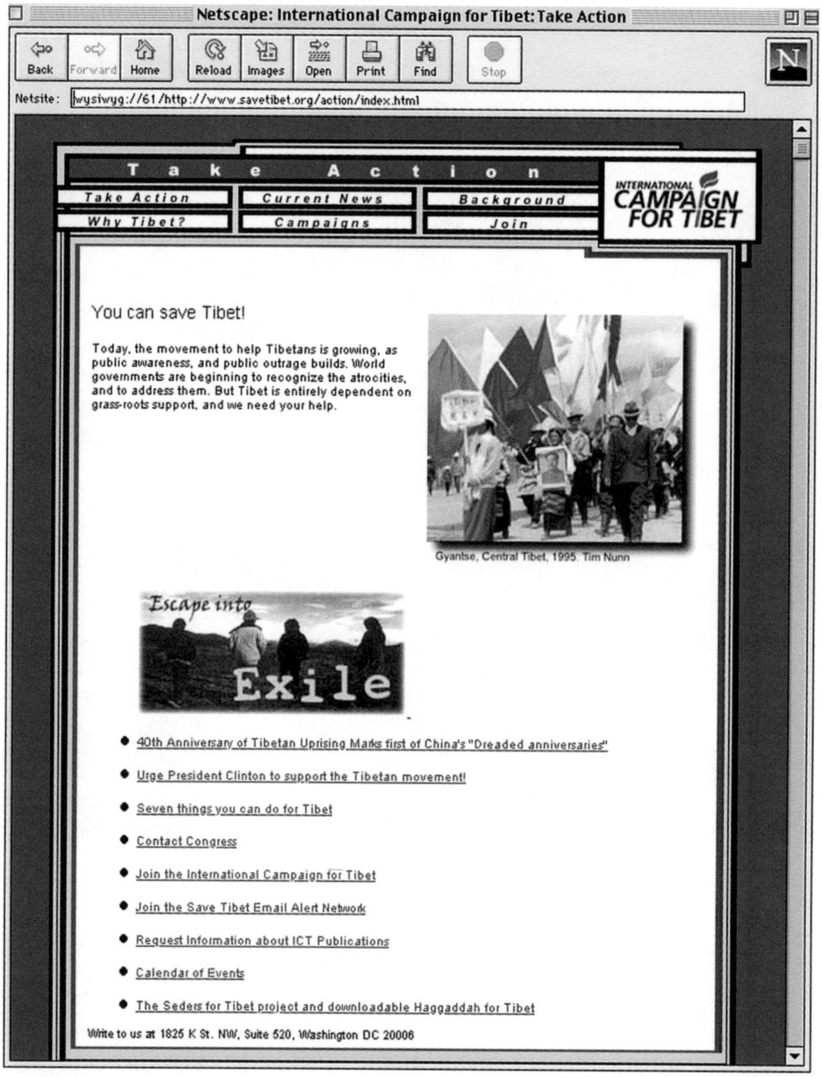

International Campaign for Tibet – www.savetibet.org

There is no shortage of organisations concerned with Chinese-occupied Tibet. The International Campaign for Tibet (ICT), however, is the most prolific. Its high visibility, since its inception in 1988, has made human rights the concern of governments everywhere. Based in Washington, D.C., it co-ordinated the first ever meeting between the Dalai Lama and a U.S. president in 1991 and has hosted major visits by the Dalai Lama over the years. ICT's Action Alerts and international campaigns have prompted unprecedented progress for the Tibetan Government-in-exile. Its recent campaigns include the suspension of World Bank-funded Chinese settlement in traditional Tibetan and Mongolian areas. Website © International Campaign for Tibet, 2000

General Sani Abacha, the country had one of the worst records for human rights and for freedom of the press, with more journalists in prison than in any other country in the world. When cartoonist Adenle Adewale substituted 'daft constitution' for 'draft constitution' in a cartoon critical of the political parties, he received threats from one of the many arms of the Nigerian security service. Only after Abacha died in 1998 did the press in Nigeria begin to resume its role of the pre-dictator days as a lively guardian against excessive governmental control.

Since then, editorial cartoons have achieved a great popularity in Nigeria, due in part to the multiparty system, which has brought into the marketplace new newspapers and magazines. According to Nigerian-born, London-based cartoonist Tayo Fatunla, 'Cartoons are used to educate and inform about the awareness of AIDS, immunisation and human rights issues … Cartoonists may not necessarily change things with their cartoons but they do express the general opinion of the masses through their pens, brushes and paper.' In a society such as Nigeria where illiteracy is high, such images can have great importance.

Black lines of division and reconciliation

In times of international conflict, cartoons can demonise the enemy and yet show remarkable insight into societies' prejudices. In the Middle East, as elsewhere, editorial cartoons do both. Unfortunately, it is the offensive images that are remembered and come to taint the genre.

In 1997, Israel and Egypt traded barbs on the images that appeared in editorial cartoons in both countries. Israelis were being portrayed in Egyptian cartoons with Nazi swastikas, tails and pointed ears, and in ugly depictions of stereotyped Jews. Meanwhile, stereotyped images of Arabs as terrorists appeared in the Israeli press. Unfortunately, this dehumanisation is repeating itself again in Middle Eastern cartoons today in light of the continuing crisis.

While both sides had shown evidence of how the other had offended them, the debates that ensued took on a purely political nature, involving Egyptian president Hosni Mubarak and the former Israeli Prime Minister Benjamin Netanyahu. The offences of each were well documented:

> The Anti-Defamation League in New York published a report on anti-Semitic cartoons in the Egyptian press and took out a full-page advertisement in *The New York Times* calling on President Hosni Mubarak to stop the 'anti-Semitic hate in Egypt'. The protest coincided with the Egyptian president's visit to Washington … Mubarak countered with a report from his Ministry of Information detailing attacks on Egyptian policy in the Israeli press. He publicly took particular exception to articles and cartoons in the *Jerusalem Post*: the newspaper was banned in Egypt [in 1996] when it was still edited by David Bar Illan, [then] one of Netanyahu's closest aides.[10]

The impression one gets from this and other such exchanges is that the press is filled with overwhelmingly vicious images of the 'other', and that this situation is inevitably much worse during times of war and conflict.

In *Faces of the Enemy*, Sam Keen writes, 'The object of warfare is to destroy or kill the enemy. But who is this enemy? Almost all works on war refer to the enemy obliquely. A strange silence pervades political, military, and popular thought on this matter. Our reluctance to think clearly about the enemy appears to be an unconscious conspiracy. We … insist that the enemy remain faceless …'[11] The more stereotyped, impersonal and demonising the images become, the less people have to think about the reality of war – and so violence becomes acceptable.

However, editorial cartoons at their best also communicate enduring images of the tragedy of war, the senseless loss of life, and can point to opportunities for reconciliation and healing.

In an exchange that typified the 1998 Malta workshop for Mediterranean and Middle Eastern cartoonists, the Egyptian Gomaa Farhat drew an example of the offensive stereotyped image of Arabs still portrayed in the western press today – with beards, *keffiyas*, robes and a dagger, implying a barbaric and violent nature. Israeli Yaakov 'Dry Bones' Kirschen considered the image. Then, with a few pen strokes (colouring in the traditional dress, adding a hat, a machine gun, and so on), he transformed the drawing into an equally offensive depiction of a stereotyped Israeli. This exercise demonstrated the common offence that is felt when negative stereotypes are reinforced in editorial cartoons.

It is clear, too, that stereotypes are an issue both within societies as well as between them. In Malta, Israeli cartoonist Yaacov 'Ze'ev' Farkas told of an experience he had in which he was accused of drawing anti-Semitic representations of religious Jews. Ze'ev was confronted by someone who was unhappy with the cartoonist's representation of religious elements in Israeli society as being politically powerful and clad totally in black. He then drew the same figure in another context, celebrating a holiday. It became clear that it was not the representation that was offensive, but the context of the representation.

A difficult task for cartoonists is how to use stereotypes and symbols essential for communication in this unique visual art and still avoid the danger of blanket condemnation and guilt by association. Jerry Robinson believes that 'The iconography of stereotypes used by cartoonists are symbols of society's perceived evils – the inhumane, unattractive, offensive – that can be attributed to the opposition. Caricature and stereotypes used to justify the dehumanisation of the enemy can be an easy substitute for insight.'

Red lines

Successful cartoonists of all stripes can recite a litany of those who have been offended by their cartoons. This is seen as a sign of success in this profession. When a society is offended, however, another question arises. Do cartoonists operate by any code of ethics to distinguish between what is acceptable and what is not?

While most cartoonists can easily identify the 'red lines' that may exist for them as a Palestinian, a Nigerian or a Turk, there are no universal principles. It was once commonplace for cartoonists in the U.S. to portray African Americans in ways that would now be recognised as racist and demeaning. Today, while individuals are lampooned daily in cartoons, to present a whole race in a stereotypical way crosses the line – and thus violates an unwritten code of conduct.

This happens within a society, but different rules apply when the 'other' is another people in another country, and especially a country with which one is at war. In those cases, there may be no red lines at all. And what is acceptable in one country may be highly offensive in another.

Turkish cartoonist Behiç Ak notes that editorial cartoonists do not necessarily want their work to be seen in a moral framework, but they are cautious about ethnic, racial, and sexist jokes. Ak believes that good cartooning is about creating new views and perspectives rather than re-creating old jokes. He would like editorial cartoons to avoid stereotypes and typologies. Cartoons, he believes, have a responsibility to avoid prejudice, sexism and the provocation of nationalism and racism.

Netscape: PEN American Center - Home Page
Back
Forward
Home
Reload
Images
Open
Print
Find
Stop
Location: http://www.pen.org/
PEN
AMERICAN CENTER
A fellowship of writers working for more than seventy-five years to advance literature, to promote a culture of reading, and to defend free expression.
Announcements
Upcoming Events
PEN News
General Information
Membership
Friends of PEN
2000 Literary Awards Announced
Dr. William Holda
Winner of the 2000 PEN / Newman's Own Award
Flora Brovina
Winner of the PEN / Barbara Goldsmith Freedom-to-Write Award
Freedom-to-Write - On behalf of writers and journalists everywhere, the Freedom-to-Write Program works to defend freedom of expression and to resist censorship worldwide.
Readers and Writers - PEN sends writers and their books to literacy programs, community centers, schools, prisons, and other sites across the U.S., reaching adults and children who have learned to read but have never read for pleasure.
Forums - Regularly scheduled public programs present contemporary and classic literature and explore the state of literary culture and of free expression.
Literary Awards - PEN American Center recognizes the excellence among American authors at work in a variety of genres, honors the art of literary translation, and highlights the distinctive contribution of literary editors.
Open Book - This program works to increase the participation of ethnic minorities within PEN, the literary culture at large, and the publishing industry.
Prison Writing Program - By providing information on writing and publishing, and by making referrals to other organizations, the Prison Writing Program advises inmate writers throughout the United States.
Writers Fund - Emergency funds, in the form of grants and interest-free loans of up to $1000, are given each year to more than 100 professional literary writers facing financial crisis.
Translation - The Translation Committee upholds the rights of American translators, and furthers the art of literary translation through annual awards and the month-long "World-in-Translation" celebration each May.
Children's Books - This committee promotes the interest in and recognition of children's book authors and organizes panels, readings, and forums.
Grants and Awards - Published by PEN American Center, the newest edition of this book lists a total of more than 1,000 American and international grants available to writers through 2001.

PEN – www.pen.org

When PEN published the first volume of *Threatened Literatures* on Burmese writers and their endangered freedom of expression, copies were smuggled into Myanma (Burma) and distributed across the country. As the only worldwide organisation for literary writers and contributors, PEN has been an active campaigner against censorship and the persecution of authors. Arthur Koestler and Wole Soyinka are two of many writers who have been released from prison with the aid of its Freedom to Write Committee. Teachers sacked for promoting gay literature in class-rooms and libraries attacked for stocking banned books have received legal advice and support. PEN also hosts literary awards and outreach projects. Website © PEN American Centre, 2000

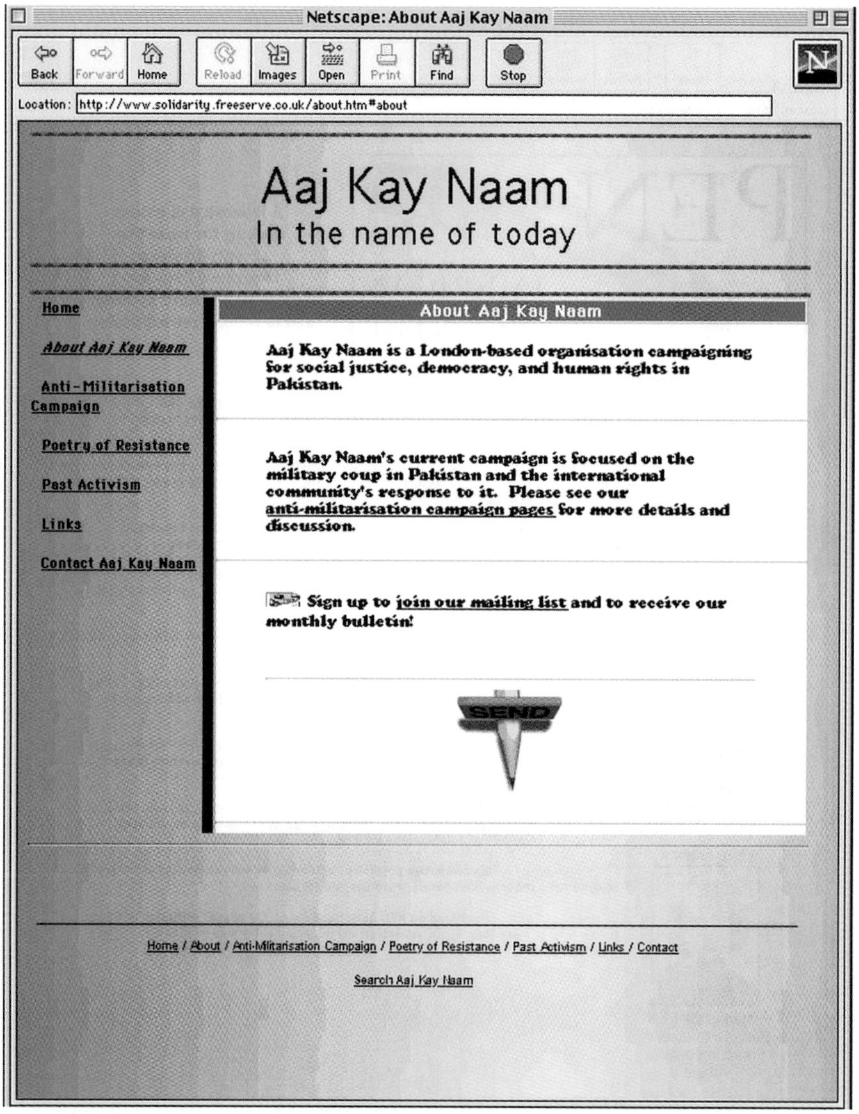

Aaj Kay Naam – www.solidarity.freeserve.co.uk

Pro-democracy organisations campaigned for social justice when the Pakistani army staged its fourth military coup. Under the guise of an anti-corruption investigation martial law has banned political activities, detained politicians without charge and excluded the military from this scrutiny. London-based Aaj Kay Naam [In Today's Name] has demonstrated for the return of constitutional rule through election and civil society movements. Aaj Kay Naam's visible presence has received the backing of international human rights organisations and the British parliament. Their website lists news reports on Pakistan as well as social commentary on censorship and anti-democracy movements around the world. Website © Aaj Kay Naam, 2000

Successful political cartooning also depends on the environment of creator freedom and, where freedom is scarce, on the creator's ability to adapt. Like a columnist, the cartoonist responds to a situation with a mixture of emotions, a sense of justice, an assessment of politics – yet unlike text journalists, he often adds wit and colour, which can defuse the tension. On the front page of *Sabah*, Istanbul's largest daily newspaper, Salih Memecan draws the characters and iconography of the American Wild West to represent Turkish politics and society in the comic strip 'Biximcity', an animated version of which appears daily on the television news.

Another Turkish cartoonist, Tan Oral, stresses, 'In making fun of things, [cartoonists] give rise to a tolerant environment,' an ingredient he sees as necessary for democratisation.[12] By finding humour in otherwise grave situations, political cartoons can be an engine for tolerance and an important element in social change.

1. Göçekin, Fatma Müge, ed., 'Political Cartoons as a Site of Representation and Resistance in the Middle East,' *Political Cartoons in the Middle East* (Markus Wiener Publishers, Princeton, 1998)
2. *The Observer*, London, 5 May 1996
3. Cartoonists Rights Network (CRN) Alert, 29 October 2000, www.cagle.com/crn. Started in 1991 by Robert Russell in the U.S. and Giffry Yoonoos in Sri Lanka, CRN is the only organisation concerned specifically with the rights of cartoonists. Its Alerts notify the cartooning and human rights communities of cartoonists under threat. The CRN has conducted workshops in cartooning for the Freedom Forum, published the world's first journal using editorial cartoons for lobbying, and compiled an archive of 'Art to Die for' – cartoons that precipitated the human rights abuses suffered by individual cartoonists from around the world.
4. Ambassador Tahseen Basheer in Istanbul, Turkey (September 2000) at a roundtable meeting of the Media Working Group of Search for Common Ground in the Middle East. Sponsored by UNESCO and the Umut Foundation, this group of influential media professionals has met annually since 1995 to develop activities around the role of the media in conflict and peace-building. It was one such meeting that gave rise to Search for Common Ground's work with editorial cartoonists in the Middle East. See www.sfcg.org for more information and meeting reports.
5. Kallaugher, Kevin, 'Drawing Conclusions in Malta', *The Baltimore Sun*, 8 January, 1999, p.15A
6. Portions of this article have been adapted from the report of Masterclass for Editorial Cartoonists, which took place in Malta, between 30 October and 2 November 1998. The workshop was co-sponsored by Search for Common Ground and the international cartoon syndicator Cartoon Arts International, in partnership with the Mediterranean Academy of Diplomatic Studies, the Swiss Government, and the journalism training institute, Jemstone. Well-known cartoonists from across the Mediterranean and Middle East regions and the U.S. discussed artistic styles, working conditions, stereotyping, and the ethics of cartooning. The exercise both opened cartoonists' eyes to the working realities of their counterparts across the region and laid the groundwork for subsequent projects. Among them are a Middle Eastern cartoon festival, travelling exhibits, and an ongoing exchange of editorial cartoons. For the complete report, see www.sfcg.org
7. Göçekin.
8. Lent, John, 'East European Cartooning: Differences over Time and Space', *International Journal of Cartoon Art* (Spring 2000), p. 103
9. Cartoonists Rights Network website, www.cagle.com/crn
10. Glanville, Jo, 'Lines of Attack', *Index on Censorship*, 5/98
11. Sam Keen, *Faces of the Enemy* (Harper & Row, 1986), p.24
12. Tan Oral in a paper presented in the Masterclass for Editorial Cartoonists from the Mediterranean and Middle Eastern regions, 1998

Laura Graziela Gomes

The Case of Brazilian *Telenovelas*

In the spectacular development of television in Brazil, media pundits regard *telenovelas,* or soap operas, as an authentic product of mass popular culture. For the Brazilian population, *telenovelas* have illustrated and disseminated the urban and industrial changes that have taken place in their country since the Fifties. However, this is not the sole reason for *telenovelas*' enormous success. These dramas and mini-series have also been politically effective. From the Sixties to the Eighties, *telenovelas* provided one of the few forums for cultural expression at a time when Brazil underwent one of its harshest authoritative and anti-democratic periods.

For a long time, many left-leaning Brazilian intellectuals attributed the success of TV Globo and its *telenovelas* to the network's monopolistic status and to the Machiavellian ties its owner Robert Marinho had with the military regime, rather than the quality of the *telenovelas* themselves. It was a perception that was repeated abroad, until TV Globo's soap operas were exported and broadcast in foreign territories. The programmes' sophisticated presentation of complex social and cultural themes stood out even to critics in countries with more political freedom than Brazil.

The heroic years

The 'heroic' years of the Brazilian teledrama, spanning from the Sixties to the early Eighties, are marked by experiments featuring formal innovations in the *telenovela* series and mini-series genres and ideas that challenged censorship and political repression. In the late Sixties and throughout the Seventies, TV Globo *telenovelas* in the 10pm evening prime-time schedule used language that mixed fiction with investigative journalism, resulting in an agile teledrama style that conformed to the colloquial language and everyday life in Brazilian cities. An important milestone was the soap opera *Beto Rockefeller*, produced and transmitted by the now extinct TV Tupi in 1968. Other TV Globo *telenovelas* dealing with themes that were, apart from their controversial nature, socially significant for the time included *O Espigão*, broadcast in 1974, about unbridled real estate speculation prevalent in Rio de Janeiro, and *Sinal de Alerta*, about pollution and environmental degradation – the awareness of which was just beginning – produced and transmitted in 1978-79.

Needless to say, these soap operas, and many others, provoked the ire of military and political authorities and led to TV censorship. It is important to emphasise that although the spectacular development of television in Brazil was an undertaking supported by the military regime, as was all the country's telecommunications, the television programmes that were broadcast were not always under the control of the regime or in accordance with its ideology. This was confirmed by the countless soap operas and programmes that criticised the regime and were censored, even though they were produced by a network whose owner unquestionably had strong connections with the military dictatorship. Since TV Globo's creation in 1965, this fact never prevented the network from working with executives, directors, writers, producers and actors who were opposed to the military and were militant leftists or political activists. One of the best examples was the most successful and prolific *telenovela* playwright Dias Gomes who wrote *O Espigão* and *Sinal de Alerta*. He and his wife, the dramatist Janete Clair – now both deceased –

Frantz Fanon, Martinique / Algeria
***Wretched of the Earth*, 1961**

After fighting with the French resistance in World War II, Martinique-born Frantz Fanon studied medicine and psychiatry in France. He was working in Blida-Joinville Hospital in Algeria when the war of independence broke out. His patients' stories about torture solidified his abhorrence of colonialism. He became a passionate spokesman and organiser for the rebels and wrote *L'An V de la Révolution Algérienne* [Year Five of the Algerian Revolution], and *Les Damnés de la Terre* [The Wretched of the Earth], which was published by Sartre in 1961 – the year Fanon died from leukaemia at the age of 36. Book cover courtesy of Penguin Books, photo courtesy of Paul Strand Archive

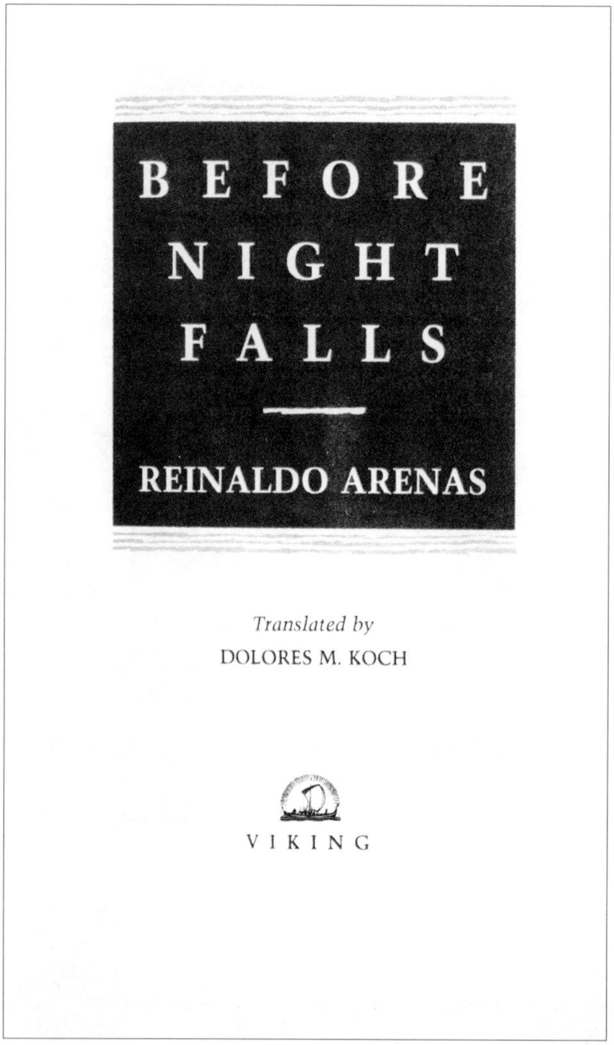
BEFORE NIGHT FALLS

REINALDO ARENAS

Translated by

DOLORES M. KOCH

VIKING

Dear friends:

Due to my delicate state of health and to the terrible emotional depression it causes me not to be able to continue writing and struggling for the freedom of Cuba, I am ending my life. During the past few years, even though I felt very ill, I have been able to finish my literary work, to which I have devoted almost 30 years. You are the heirs of all my terrors, but also of my hope that Cuba will soon be free. I am satisfied to have contributed, though in a very small way, to the triumph of this freedom. I end my life voluntarily because I cannot continue working. Persons near me are in no way responsible for my decision. There is only one person I hold accountable: Fidel Castro. The sufferings of exile, the pain of being banished from my country, the loneliness, and the diseases contracted in exile would probably never have happened if I had been able to enjoy freedom in my country.

I want to encourage the Cuban people out of the country as well as on the island to continue fighting for freedom. I do not want to convey to you a message of defeat but of continued struggle and of hope.

Cuba will be free. I already am.

(signed)
Reinaldo Arenas

Reinaldo Arenas, Cuba
***Before Night Falls*, 1993**

Born in Oriente, Cuba, the home province of Batista and Castro, Reinaldo Arenas was a teenage communist guerrilla. The Writers' Union published his first novel *Celestino Before Dawn* in 1967. His rejected second novel, *Hallucinations*, was smuggled off the island, along with other manuscripts. Both his writing and his homosexuality resulted in Arenas' imprisonment among Cuba's hardcore criminals. In his memoir, *Before Night Falls*, Arenas confesses to sleeping with 5,000 men. Eventually, he was expelled from Cuba. In 1990, he committed suicide. The book concludes with his suicide note. Title page and suicide note, above right, from *Before Night Falls: A Memoir* by Reinaldo Arenas. Translated by Dolores M. Koch © 1993 by the Estate of Reinaldo Arenas and Dolores M. Koch. English translation used by permission of Viking Penguin, a division of Penguin Putnam Inc.

were responsible for recreating the Brazilian social universe with countless character roles.

Another teledrama that caused repercussions in the country, as well as being awarded numerous international awards for the Globo network, was *Malu Mulher*. This Seventies series aimed at women presented a cast of feminist issues: separation, extramarital sex, relationships, career/profession, financial independence, political activism, single parenthood, children's upbringing, abortion, among other themes. However, the series' approach was less radical than American feminism, and consequently more attractive and palatable to Brazilian, other Latin American, and even European women who found in Malu – and not in Betty Friedan – a model on which they could base change in their lives.

Women's increasing social freedoms in Brazil were influenced not by intellectual or even political women, but by media entertainers who had little in common with American intellectual feminists. It was through actors like Leila Diniz, a theatre, cinema and TV star, and Regina Duarte who played the character Malu, that a grassroots feminism became influential in Brazil, along the lines of Che Guevara's famous motto: *'Hay que luchar pero jamás perder la ternura'* [One must fight, but never relinquish tenderness]. Leila Diniz and Regina Duarte influenced a whole generation of young Brazilian women without resorting to the clichés and aggressive stereotypes of feminist activists in other countries.

In the Eighties, Brazilian *telenovelas* matured and consolidated a totally unique style of addressing diverse themes and issues by dynamically incorporating problems inherent to Brazilian society into their plots. One that remains significant until today is the soap opera *Vale Tudo* [Anything Goes], broadcast by TV Globo, in 1988, which dealt with corruption, a serious national problem. Many Brazilians consider *Vale Tudo* vital to discussions about citizenship due to the way the series portrayed the political motivations behind corruption, as well as its cultural and sociological implications. The soap opera showed the underlying psychological tensions, which lead countless people into a life of corruption. Through the characters Maria de Fátima and Odete Roitman, among others, viewers were provided with a critical inside view. Coinciding as it did with the end of censorship and the dictatorship, *Vale Tudo* was seen as a 'virtual' forum for most Brazilians.

Through the discussion and analysis of these societal themes, TV Globo became one of the most important channels of expression for millions of Brazilians regardless of race, religion, gender or economic and social group. In the network's mini-series and soap operas, their problems and anxieties, along with prospects for the future, were examined and debated. In this sense, TV Globo's *telenovelas* constituted an important device for simultaneously viewing global and national perspectives, questioning and playing out conventional and modern roles, at the same time producing new forms of patriotism and different senses of locality, according to anthropologist Arjun Appadurai[1] and Latin American scholar Nestor Garcia Canclini.[2] Finally, to borrow from Clifford Geertz[3] and his ideas on cockfighting in Bali, *telenovelas* are stories about us, told by us, and made exclusively by us. As a result, Brazil is one of the few developing societies – along with India and Mexico – which produces its own powerful and rich audio-visual repository.

Intimacy

Following the heroic years when, to a certain extent, not only TV, but also all the mass communications media in Brazil became freedom-promoting spaces, the return to political normalcy did not signify abandoning the forms of struggle. It was an opportunity for new forms of expression. If, from the point of view of its political institutions, the country seemed to regain normalcy, from the cultural, social, and personal viewpoints there were a great number of unpaid debts stemming from the high price of anti-dictatorship activism. Suddenly there was an urgency to discuss issues, which for a long time had been relegated to a secondary position or were even considered superfluous by the leaderships of leftist movements for so long in opposition to the military.

It was at this point that TV networks produced *telenovelas* that showed the great transformations which were taking place from 1960 to 1980 in the arena of personal relations – changes that had been overshadowed by the political situation. With their sensibilities attuned to this phenomenon, *telenovela* dramatists were able to ensure that television – better than any other vehicle – illustrated this silent revolution in the models of personal, amorous and sexual relations; in other words, intimacy according to Anthony Giddens.[4]

These transformations were taking place in a television universe, which up until then had been dominated by macho representations of male role models. The first themes of the new individualism and subjectivity began in soap operas showing homosexuality. Previously, the few times gays were featured in comedic or amorous *telenovela* intrigues, they were nearly always depicted as exaggerated queens. Their transformation into 'normal' people with their own feelings and concerns suggested that there might be some change of attitude on the part of viewers due to the institutional and educational nature of Brazilian *telenovelas*.

Soap operas such as *Vale Tudo*, from 1988, and *A Próxima Vítima* [The Next Victim] (TV Globo, 1996) introduced a new approach to gays on television, precisely because these gay characters were so different from previous stereotypes. Another departure was that these soap operas sought to emphasise not only gays' sexual preferences, but at the same time, their dilemmas and conflicts stemming from these preferences. In short, for the first time *telenovelas* showed the consequences of sexual choices in characters' day-to-day lives.

Vale Tudo featured lesbian relationships which, although socially more tolerated, continue to be less 'visible' than masculine homoerotic relationships. Besides, the two women featured in *Vale Tudo* were sophisticated people from the urban middle classes who were also members of socially prestigious families. This whole set of factors suggested to viewers that this amorous relationship was part of a particular lifestyle, and therefore much more related to patterns of choice than to 'deviant behaviour'. It was in this context that Brazilians were able to view the first discussions regarding the issue of inheritance in homosexual couples, when one of the women died in an automobile accident. Because of the *telenovela*, a controversial topic relating to gay life stirred public opinion.

A Próxima Vítima was also innovative. The two young men Sandro and Jefferson – one white and the other black – were still virtually adolescents, as well as also being members of socially prominent, upper middle-class families. In this case, the characters' youth and positive physical attributes, plus the fact that both boys belonged to an organised family, contributed to the changing image of blacks and gays on television. Once again, it allowed gays to be seen not only from the viewpoint of 'deviant behaviour', but from an individual and existential angle, signalling to viewers the emergence of another dimension of Brazilian social life that television had not yet explored to any extent: intimacy – which must not be confused with private life in domestic and family terms.

In the case of the black youth, viewers were also given the opportunity of entering the home of a black, middle-class Brazilian family, one that enjoys a standard of living and consumption equivalent to whites of the same class. From the sociological viewpoint, this was a major fact in the story. Immediately afterwards, there was a rush on the part of the printed media to feature

Pramoedya Ananta Toer, Indonesia
House of Glass, 1982

Many of Pramoedya Ananta Toer's novels were written in prison. First imprisoned by the Dutch, he was later jailed by the Indonesian government for being a member of the Communist Party's cultural association. In 1965, he was imprisoned without being charged, along with 250,000 Indonesians. In 1973, when prisoners were allowed retraining opportunities, he chose to write. When his originals were confiscated, he replaced them with carbon copies, which he traded with fellow inmates. He was released in 1979. A year later, according to *Index on Censorship*, 10,000 copies of his novels had been burned by the authorities. While General Suharto was in power, Toer was not allowed to leave Jakarta. Book cover © Penguin Books Australia Ltd., illustration by Stephan Daigle

Duong Thu Huong, Vietnam
***Novel Without a Name*, 1995**

During the Vietnam War, Duong Thu Huong led a Communist Youth Brigade and was one of three survivors in a unit of 40 men and women who fought alongside the Viet Cong. In 1980, she started criticising the party. By 1989, she was expelled for advocating democracy and human rights. Arrested and sentenced without a trial in 1991, she spent seven months in jail on false charges of sending 'state secrets' abroad. Her four novels sold thousands of copies in Vietnam before they were withdrawn by the authorities. Smuggled into the country, foreign language editions are widely read. Duong received a Prince Claus Award in 2001. (See page 14) Book cover © Picador 1995, photograph courtesy of the Indochina Centre at U.C. Berkeley, original photograph from Vietnam News Agency of Hanoi articles portraying individuals from the black middle classes. In 1996, *Raça Brasil*, a monthly magazine dedicated to the Brazilian black middle-class, city dwellers, was launched and gained a high circulation.

Xica da Silva (TV Manchete, 1996) is another Brazilian *telenovela* that showed a different side of Brazilian homosexuality. Through the life of the character Zé Mulher, an in-depth historical view of sexual habits in Brazilian colonial life was revealed, based on the works of Gilberto Freyre, one of the most important twentieth century, Brazilian social thinkers. In the Thirties, Freyre drafted the first 'intimate' history of early Brazilian society in his groundbreaking book *Casa Grande & Senzala*[5] [Lords and Slaves], that showed the extent to which homoerotic relationships were present between whites and blacks, masters and slaves. For a long time Freyre, little known outside of academia, was criticised by the left and by the black Brazilian movement for idealising racial relations. His research, and the arguments against it, stimulate a media that has been building an audio-visual image of Brazil from the sixteenth century, which already includes seminal work by Brazilian authors and essayists: Jorge Amado, Nelson Rodrigues, João Guimarães Rosa, Érico Veríssimo, among others.

Xica da Silva poses the question: how does discussion about identities considered controversial in Brazilian history illustrate other social dimensions scantly valued by television and culture? The attempt to imprint dignity on identities traditionally considered 'deviant' or 'morally condemnable', such as gays, has made the work of dramatists such as Gilberto Braga and Aguinaldo Silva essential to modern Brazilian television.

The 8pm soap opera, *Suave Veneno* [Tender Poison] featured two gay men, Uálber and Edilberto. Uálber was a highly respected 'paranormal sensitive' – a clairvoyant and shell reader – with a large clientele. Interestingly, from the point of view of reality, the soap opera merely brought to the screen what all Brazilians already know but, for various cultural and social reasons, was never made explicit on television: a large number of *pais de santo*, Afro-Brazilian cult leaders, soothsayers, faith healers, and 'sensitives' – the very people who boast spiritual authority and ascendancy in the country – are gay. This fact, previously denied due to social prejudice, was made explicit in *Suave Veneno*. The story-line related the character's sexual preference to his mystic vocation in a positive manner. Uálber was presented as one of the most ethical and dignified characters in the plot, the character most conscientious in regard to his moral principles, and because of this, most closely aligned to traditional family values.

Another novelty in the *telenovela* was when Uálber reveals his true sexual orientation to his mother and states that his being homosexual does not prevent him from loving and respecting other people and their values. Uálber's conversation with his mother was responsible for one of the highest viewer ratings ever obtained by *Suave Veneno*. This fact indicated the episode's importance to the Brazilian public in general, and the discussions sparked by the episode continued in other social forums, at school and at work.

The third novelty of this soap opera was its ending, when Edilberto, Uálber's secretary, was finally adopted by Uálber's mother, and everyone lives together in Uálber's house. In the meantime, Uálber, in front of all the family members, happy with his new boyfriend, sponsors a gala family dinner during which his mother declares him 'head of the family' and he makes a speech ratifying traditional Brazilian family values. In the final scenes of the soap opera, another character, Nana, follows a much less conventional course than the one chosen by Uálber.
The inversion between Uálber and Nana indicates the extent to which *telenovelas* function as an agent of change, as well as a laboratory for experiencing these emerging identities and their

lifestyles. In this regard, Nana was an equally interesting and relatively new female character in Brazilian *telenovelas*. A mature, fiftyish loner, she was the pretext for another issue that is beginning to register in Brazilian television: intimacy in the course of the life of older and independent women. Traditionally, *telenovelas* always focused on young women about to be married, or even young married women, and when older women were featured, it was always in the role of the grandmother. In the case of recent teledramas, this attitude has changed significantly. It has now become quite commonplace to see older female characters like Nana who prefer independence and the freedom to enjoy their sexuality instead of marrying again. In the case of Nana, she chose an unprecedented course: to keep both of her suitors, Alceste and Gato, as lovers while maintaining her independence.

Brazilian teledramas have shown remarkable advances, since *Malu Mulher* from the Seventies, in which feminine issues were discussed in more combative terms based on the activist discourse characteristic of that time, and by a character who embodied all of the feminine demands, and precisely for this reason, had to assume a heroic and epic posture because she was living in a situation that had little to do with the majority of Brazil's female population. The series *Mulher* from 1997 presented many important changes. To begin with, there were two main characters, Dr Martha and Dr Cris, both of whom are more realistic in their portrayal of women in contemporary Brazilian society than Malu from the Seventies. *Mulher* has been a great success exactly because it manages to present a much more complex panorama of the female condition in the Brazil of today, showing how much this has changed for the better since *Malu Mulher*. At the same time, *Mulher* signals to viewers how much the female condition in Brazil demands change and attention on the part of social and political institutions. To achieve this end, the strategy used in the *telenovela* was to introduce two female characters of different generations who have contrasting outlooks on the world, but who are linked together by their profession, as well as by a solid friendship and mutual admiration. They also share the same feelings of compassion and solidarity in regard to the needy people who come to them as patients in the clinic where they work as gynaecologists. Because they are gynaecologists, they are privy to problems and dilemmas, questions and misgivings of other women. In *Mulher* we have 'new women' who emerge from these episodes on the one hand less activist than the feminist character of the Seventies, and on the other, more generous and open in regards to life.

Brazil's complex ethnic and labour history: *Terra Nostra*

In April 2000, Brazil commemorated the 500th anniversary of its discovery and to celebrate TV Globo, one of the largest television networks in the world, produced a new 8pm *telenovela*. *Terra Nostra* is the saga of the first Italian immigrants to Brazil, which, at the same time, poses the question: why highlight the end of one century and the beginning of another by producing a soap opera featuring Italian immigrants?

Although immigrants and their descendents – especially Italians – are featured as characters in countless soap operas and series, there has never been a *telenovela* that concentrated specifically on the arrival of any one group of immigrants in Brazil, and showed their expectations, dreams and difficulties in adjusting, as well as the conflicts and personal tragedies of the original group members. Actually, the presentation of this theme is new, and reveals an approach to the formation of Brazil more in line with contemporary multicultural perspectives, which emphasise the heterogeneity of ethnic composition in many modern societies as one of the most important

Chinua Achebe, Nigeria
Anthills of the Savannah, 1987

In his essay 'Morning Yet on Creation Day', Chinua Achebe writes, 'Art is, and always was, at the service of man. Our ancestors created their myths and told their stories for a human purpose ... any good novel should have a message, should have a purpose.' Achebe's own purpose has been 'to help my society regain belief in itself and put away the complexes of the years of denigration and self-abasement'. His first novel, *Things Fall Apart* (1958) was written in response to western characterisations of Africans. His fifth, *Anthills of the Savannah* (1987) depicted the struggle of Africans to free themselves from the European inheritance.

WOLE
SOYINKA
PLAYS: 1
THE TRIALS OF BROTHER JERO
JERO'S METAMORPHOSIS • CAMWOOD ON THE LEAVES
DEATH AND THE KING'S HORSEMAN
MADMEN AND SPECIALISTS • OPERA WONYOSI

Wole Soyinka, Nigeria
***Collected Plays: Soyinka*, 1984**

Wole Soyinka's 1986 Nobel Prize for Literature – the first to be given to an African – was in recognition of his plays. His best known pieces, *Death and the King's Horseman* and the satirical *A Play of Giants* show the difficulties of everyday African life. A novelist and prolific essayist, Soyinka was arrested and imprisoned during Nigeria's civil war, during which time he wrote his prison notes, *The Man Died*. In 1996, threatened by the military dictatorship of General Abacha, he fled the country. In 1997, he was tried *in absentia* on charges of treason. In 1998, after Abacha's death, Soyinka returned to Nigeria. His play *King Baabu*, which had its première in Lagos in 2001, critically analysed dictators in African countries. (See page 25) Book cover courtesy of Methuen Publishing Ltd.

assets. This means Brazilians are finally breaking away from the traditional view of the 'myth of the three races' and forming a more complex perspective of their country's inception. In this sense, *Terra Nostra* is another landmark in Brazilian television which helps to replace, perhaps once and for all, traditional representations of Brazilian national identity, focused on the ideology of 'racial miscegenation' – the mixture of whites (Portuguese colonisers), blacks (African slaves) and Indians (native Brazilians) – with more complex themes of ethnicity based on the inclusion of a variety of groups. It is this identity which is contributing to the new image of Brazil that is plural, complex and modern.

Terra Nostra also shows that the immigrant theme is not being introduced merely to show Brazilian society's multi-ethnic make-up in a positive light. Historically, the Italians' arrival in Brazil related to the beginning of a new cycle in the Brazilian economy, the growing and production of coffee and its attendant forms of labour relations. This soap opera shows another important change of the paradigm regarding conventional Brazilian television images. Depicting a self-sustaining Brazilian economy depends on replacing very persistent images of the slave labour that existed under the colonial regime, something that still produces many negative associations concerning the idea of work, as well as management-labour relations in Brazil.

Therefore, a story that dramatises the arrival of the Italian immigrants in Brazil could not fail to illuminate the work ethic and the civic culture that these immigrants brought with them. It also shows the immigrants' will to fight for their human and political rights in the new nation they themselves are helping to build, and it is this concept that collides headlong with another view of political rights and responsibilities in Brazil, that is human rights are not gifts granted by the state and the leading élite, they are earned by means of struggle, and above all, the development of a civic culture. Italian immigrants were chosen instead of German, Japanese or Jewish immigrants – groups who also gave shape to a modern Brazil – because the Italians contributed the most in terms of political leadership and ideologies to the organisation of labour unions, co-operative movements and many of the country's other social struggles. Santa Cecilia, the first anarchist colony in the world, was created in Brazil after the arrival of the first group of Italian immigrants and Emperor Dom Pedro II granted them land to settle.

Brazilian teledrama, especially the *telenovelas*, with their issues and themes of general interest to the population, make explicit and accessible the whole cast of a society's inherent problems. The major difference between *telenovelas* and other vehicles, which also deal with these same issues, is that soap operas and mini-series carry out this task in a language accessible to all, therefore including all categories of people who see themselves represented in the characters and in the plots. This is the most democratic aspect of Brazilian *telenovelas*: the fact that they seek to feature all the characters and social dramas present in society, and do so in a way in which both – characters and dramas – are recognised and identified by the general population. This also explains the great passion aroused by *telenovelas*. They are our stories, told by us, about us …

In a country where the majority of the population is not yet part of a lettered or even illustrated culture, these stories are the main means of access for people to become aware of national issues, and in some way, take part in the sociopolitical processes that are shaping the country.

Translated from the Portuguese by Doris Hefti

1. Appadurai, Arjun; *Modernity at Large: Cultural Dimensions of Globalization* (Minneapolis: University of Minnesota Press, 1997)
2. Canclini, Nestor Garcia; *Culturas Híbridas: estratégias para entrar e sair da modernidade* (São Paulo: EDUSP, 1997)
3. Geertz, Clifford; *The Interpretation of Cultures* (New York: Basic Books, 1973)
4. Giddens, Anthony; *Tradução brasileira: A Transformação da Intimidade:sexualidade, amor e erotismo nas sociedades modernas.* [The Transformation of Intimacy: Sexuality, Love and Eroticism in Modern Societies] (São Paulo: Editora UNESP, 1992)
5. Freyre, Gilberto; *Casa Grande & Senzala: Formação da Família Brasileira sob o regime patriarcal* (Rio de Janeiro, Livraria José Olympio Editora, 1981); the first edition of *Casa Grande & Senzala* was published in 1933

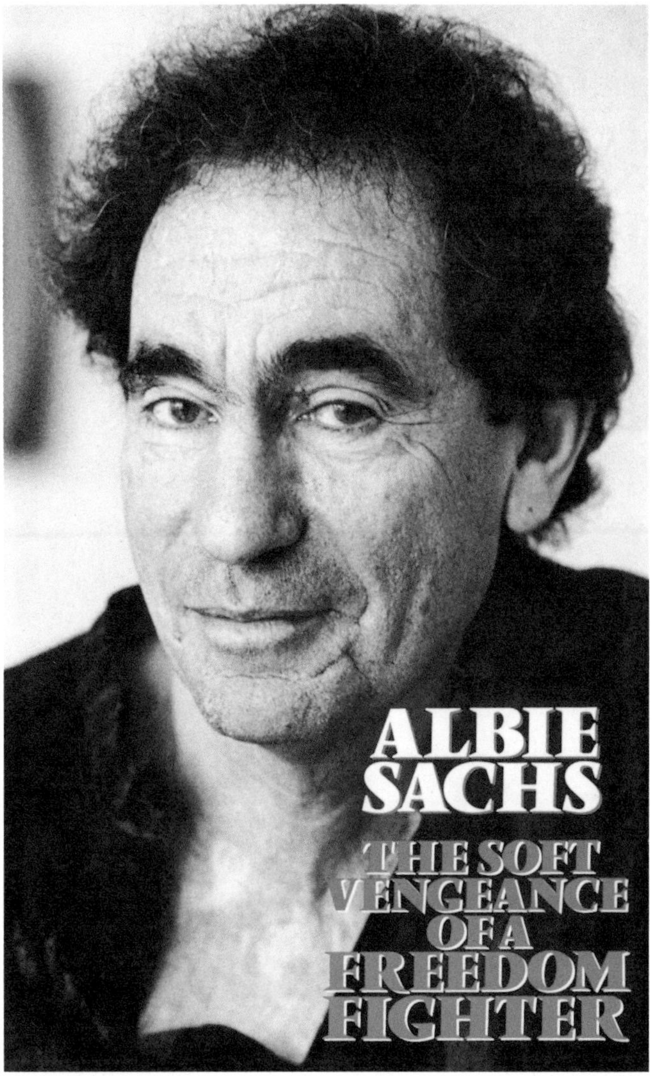

Albie Sachs, South Africa
***The Soft Vengeance of a Freedom Fighter*, 1990**

Albie Sachs joined the ANC as a law student in the early Fifties and defended anti-apartheid activists. He was imprisoned and kept in solitary confinement for 168 days. After leaving South Africa in 1966, he lost an arm and the sight in one eye from a car bomb planted by South African security forces in Mozambique. In *The Soft Vengeance of a Freedom Fighter*, he details the rigours of recovery. 'This is where a certain measure of courage comes in perhaps. Not physical bravery but the courage of conception.' In 1991, he returned to South Africa and, under Nelson Mandela, helped to draft the country's constitution. Sachs is a constitutional court justice in South Africa. (See page 73) (Louis Freeberg, 'White Exile Returns to South Africa', *San Francisco Chronicle*, 9 May 1999, p. A2) Book cover courtesy of Albie Sachs

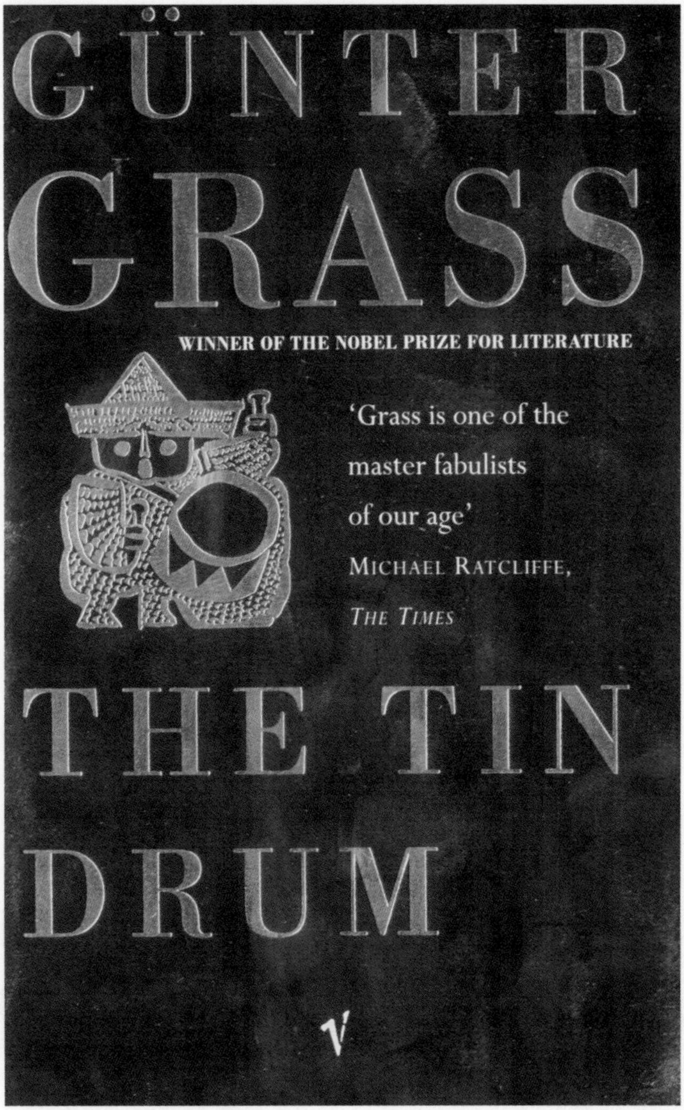

Günter Grass, Germany
***The Tin Drum*, 1959**

Günter Grass' first novel, *The Tin Drum*, caused a uproar in Germany with its depiction of the Nazis. Set during the rise of the Third Reich, the book is the autobiography of Oskar, who arrests his growth to avoid his inevitable adult fate. Remaining in a child's body, he beats his drum. *The Tin Drum* is still hailed by international critics as one of the most powerful novels of last century. However, the controversy continued with the 1979 Oscar-winning film adaptation by Volker Schlöndorff, which was banned by the Oklahoma Library Association in the U.S. on grounds of 'child pornography'. Book cover courtesy of Vintage Books, a division of Random House Inc.

Edmundo Paz-Soldán

Latin American Literature: The New Map

The publication in Spain of the 1999 anthology *Líneas aéreas*[1] [Air Lines] served to introduce a new generation of Latin American writers: those born around 1960, who began publishing their works in the last decade of the century. Even though attempts had been made to bring together the most prominent writers of the new generation before the arrival of this anthology – notably in the provocative and vilified *McOndo*[2] – none rival the all-encompassing work of Eduardo Becerra, the anthologist of *Líneas aéreas*. Indeed, if the *McOndo* anthology, compiled by the Chilean writers Alberto Fuguet and Sergio Gómez, was criticised for grouping together seventeen writers – not a single woman among them – who seemed (only *seemed*) to share more ideological and aesthetic similarities than differences, *Líneas aéreas* is guilty of being overgenerous: with 60 writers from twenty different countries, it is difficult to find a consistent level of quality. In the prologue, Becerra mentions that the 'principle of quality' was just as important as the 'principle of representation' in the process of selection.[3] But should not the 'principle of quality' be the only decisive factor?

McOndo was an important work because the editors broke with the closed national circles in which, despite many editorial efforts, the Latin American cultural markets operate. Fuguet and Gómez decided to look beyond Chile and encountered in the process many writers who found themselves on the same *rupturista* [favouring a break or a rupture] wavelength with respect to certain issues: on the one hand, on an aesthetic level, the abandonment of magical realism, the narrative form which had so prominently characterised Latin American literature during the last 30 years (and which, in an indirect way, has served to 'exoticise' representations of the continent); on the other hand, in terms of attitude, the desire that the writer should withdraw from public life and dedicate himself to writing in his own 'private quarters'. In a rather naïve way, in a continent with a long tradition of relating the world of politics to the literary world and of viewing writers as symbolic figures in the public sphere, Fuguet and Gómez pointed out that, 'If, a few years ago, a young writer's alternatives consisted of taking up either the pen or the sword it would now appear that what they find most agonising is whether to choose Windows 95 or Macintosh.'[4] Fuguet and Gómez linked this attitude to the neo-liberal wave sweeping the continent and the world at the beginning of the Nineties: a Latin American *McOndo* of shopping malls, cable television, suburbs and pollution was positioning itself, half-seriously and half-jokingly, against García Márquez's *Macondo*. In this way, the new writers were regarded as the Latin American version of Generation x, a band of cynical, trendy pseudo-intellectual youths who were incapable of contemplating important social and political issues in Latin America and who viewed with mockery the grandiose and utopian proposals for social change put forward by previous generations.

Over the years this image has become more nuanced. The excesses of *McOndo* have given way to the vision of an eclectic new generation, a vision in which dissimilar proposals and influences co-exist, but which is generally characterised by its desire to engage literarily with problematic and controversial issues affecting Latin American societies. This is corroborated as much by a reading of

 Líneas aéreas as by a brief examination of some of the most outstanding works of these young writers. Literature in Latin America has always worked as a test laboratory for new subjective perceptions and forms of social interaction. The use of literature has been accompanied on many occasions by a self-legitimisation on the part of the author to act as a kind of moral conscience for the country, the intellectual capable of diagnosing the national ills: the solemn voice of those without a voice, the individual that speaks, in the classic Nerudian formulation of 'Alturas de Macchu Picchu' [Heights of Macchu Picchu], with his 'words' and his 'blood' through 'the defunct mouth' of the people.

The attitude of the new writers finds itself, with a certain irreverence, within the tradition of using artistic space to intervene in the public debate and to liberate certain issues from their heavy load of orthodoxy and repression. At the same time, this form of participation is not accompanied by the presumption that the writer is in possession of any particular capability to resolve the crises at hand. The new writers want to place themselves within the context of the Latin American literary tradition of combating certain traditional ways of thinking and of being, but they want to do this on their own terms, in a more modest way than before but, in some cases, no less ambitiously.

In the following sections I will concentrate on three of the most important themes for the new generation: the relationship between literature and politics; the exploration of forms of identity that are not solidly linked to the nation state; and the representation of alternative sexual orientations which question the orthodox vision of a continent characterised by strong heterosexual norms. My analysis of the works of the Costa Rican Carlos Cortés, the Peruvian Iván Thays and the Mexican-Peruvian Mario Bellatín demonstrate how literature is used by the new Latin American writers as a vehicle for challenging established truths, making possible different modes of expression for conflicts that societies have invariably attempted to silence or erase from the national imagination.

Literature and politics

To express no explicit political commitment to a specific ideology does not necessarily entail an indifference towards politics and history as such. This preoccupation arises continually in the works of the new generation, although in a more allegorical and in a less direct form than it had in the works of the writers of previous generations, and which nevertheless manifests the will to intervene in the processes of sociopolitical change in their respective countries.

The Costa Rican Carlos Cortés (b. 1962) is one of the few who has dared, in *Cruz de olvido*[5] [Cross of the Forgotten], to deal head on with the cost of political instability and of the revolutionary movements in Central America. This striking novel provides Cortés with the opportunity to engage forcefully in the debate about the future of post-revolutionary Central America: this intervention suggests that solutions to the crisis can only be found by discussing it frankly, ignoring the inveterate continental custom of throwing the pious *cruz de olvido* on conflicts, thus allowing the nation to continue as if nothing had happened. Literature is, for Cortés, an instrument that impedes our tendency to forget and invites us to confront the magnitude of the crisis of individual and social values.

Cortés' style has a tendency towards the hyperbolic and the grotesque, though always in the most carefully measured way, without fully abandoning its real point of reference. He makes use of sophisticated and diverse narrative strategies in order to descend into the purgatory of a society

ff
BREYTEN
BREYTENBACH
The True Confessions
of an Albino Terrorist
'A classic of prison writing.' Financial Times

Breyten Breytenbach, South Africa
***The True Confessions of an Albino Terrorist*, 1985**

From a prominent South African family, Breyten Breytenbach is considered the foremost Afrikaans poet. At 24, he was already living in exile in Paris. In the Seventies, he decided that cultural activities weren't effective against apartheid and became politically active. During a clandestine visit to his country in 1975, he was betrayed, arrested and charged with terrorism. A harrowing seven-year imprisonment in the Pretoria Central Prison was the basis for *The True Confessions of an Albino Terrorist*. Afterwards, Breytenbach was instrumental in arranging the first meeting between Afrikaans leaders and ANC officials on Gorée Island in Senegal. Book cover courtesy of Faber & Faber

FATIMA MERNISSI
BEYOND THE VEIL
MALE-FEMALE DYNAMICS IN MUSLIM SOCIETY

Fatima Mernissi, Morocco
***Beyond the Veil*, 1975**

Sociologist Fatima Mernissi grew up in one of the last harems in Morocco and is widely regarded as the leading feminist Islamic scholar in the Arab world. Her thesis is based on women's equality as expressed in the Quran, a text which, according to her, has been repeatedly misinterpreted by male religious leaders. Despite her books being banned in her own country, the public seek out copies. Her popularity in the west applies equally in North Africa and the Middle East. Her acclaimed 1975 publication *Beyond the Veil*, reprinted in 1987, analyses the 'unveiling' of women's sexual identity and social role through educational equality. Book cover courtesy of Saqi Books in which the state of ideological crisis is accompanied by the most rampant moral and material decomposition. 'We live in crisis,' says Martín, the Sandinista revolutionary of Costa Rican origin who, at the beginning of the novel, returns to Costa Rica after the handing over of power by the Sandinistas to Violeta Chamorro:

> The Institutional Crisis. The customs crisis. The fiscal crisis. The industrial crisis. The social crisis. The parliamentary crisis. The food crisis. The ideological crisis. The constitutional crisis. The governmental crisis. The general crisis. The crisis crisis.[6]

The crisis, however, is not due to the failure of the revolution in Nicaragua, but rather its roots are buried deep in a certain inferiority complex which seeks to overcome itself in a grandiloquent participation in history. The devotion to the Revolution has been little more than a devotion to the idea of the Revolution: 'And I later discovered, perhaps too late, that I didn't love the Revolution either ... I was really in love with a scenario in which I could be able to walk around.'[7] Martín has devoted himself to the Revolution, amongst other things, in order to liberate himself from an insignificant national identity, his status as a civilian in a country like Costa Rica, in which one feels like 'an orphan of things that are on a big scale, an orphan of power, an orphan of history and of the ideas that destroyed this pointless century'.[8]

If the lack of a 'strong' national identity is that which leads Martín to embrace the Sandinista struggle, what really enters into crisis in Cortés' novel is a subjectivity linked to the nation itself. If it is the nations that have historically appealed to individuals and have taken them to war, in *Cruz de olvido*, this is inverted and the individual enters into a state of crisis due to a lack of national interpellation: the State leaves the individual in a state of symbolic orphanhood but is nevertheless always present in the making of the parameters of his destiny. In a perverse kind of way, it seems that a 'weak' national identity configures the individual's freedom and determines to a great extent his actions in much the same way as a 'strong' one.

In *Cruz de olvido*, the failure of the Sandinista revolution and the return of Martín to civilian life can be read in a paradigmatic way: like Martín (although with greater political indifference) many of the central figures in the new literature are individuals under the age of 40, belonging to a disenchanted generation that, after the failure of the utopian proposals for social change of the previous generations, seek, often without luck, to take refuge in their alienation or in a pragmatic way of viewing reality. The 'incurable emptiness' remains[9] the 'mediocre security',[10] 'the fact of knowing that you don't belong to anyone, you don't have any ties to this world and that you only survive caught up in a few frayed threads of time lost in the memory'.[11]

New identities: between the local and the global

Many of the protagonists of the new narrative seek in one way or another to insert themselves into an increasingly strange society in which they have difficulty recognising themselves. The predominant attitude among the new writers is not one of disdain towards the public sphere but the majority have no confidence in their capacity to transform society through literature. However, this does not necessarily lead to a sense of resignation or desperation. Rather, there is a renewed confidence in literature's capacity for narrating the divergence between reality and desire, in stating that which the prevailing mass media – radio, television, film – do not dare to say straight out. The new writers have accepted a certain marginalisation of literature when it comes to public debate, but not the irrelevance that could accompany this. From the margins, they can concentrate better on the development of their aesthetic project and explore with greater freedom the polemical issues that need to be discussed by society.

One of the most interesting explorations carried out by new writers has to do with the formation of more flexible identities, less fixed on both political and civilian identities (the point of reference which brings about the crisis of the protagonist in *Cruz de olvido*). The representation of these new subjectivities is tied to the historic moment of cultural and economic globalisation, and to the erosion of the frontiers of the nation state. Today, a local sense of identity is necessarily permeated by networks of a transnational sense of identity. In a continent in which the symbolic power of artists and intellectuals has traditionally been derived from their engagement in the sociopolitical issues arising from a broad variety of national realities, the tendency on the part of some writers to detach themselves from this type of engagement has been viewed as a clear example of their own alienation and superficiality. However, perhaps this behaviour can be understood as the impossibility to speak today of 'clear-cut' identities for which national citizenship is the main reference point. Literature in this way would once again be fulfilling its purpose as a test site for new and future identities, for new and future forms of social and gender interrelationships, for new and future forms of understanding the local, national, and global spheres.

There are abundant examples today of a Latin American literature not necessarily tied to a national or continental point of reference. This does not imply, as Iván Thays states in his essay 'La edad de la inocencia' [The Age of Innocence], that this should be automatically construed as 'stateless' or 'cosmopolitan', but that literary reality does not have to conform to a civil framework: 'real literature is a globe that is reconstructed by our own tastes, our ideas, our affinities, our kindred spirits, our teachers ...'[12]

In the work of Thays and that of the new generation one can perceive a certain tendency to freely assimilate elements of other traditions. This tendency was already (and best) exemplified by the Argentine writer Jorge Luis Borges. In his essay 'The Argentinean Writer and Tradition', Borges pointed out that Argentinean tradition incorporates 'the whole of western culture' and went on to assert, in a provocative way, that the right to that tradition 'was greater than the right of any inhabitant of any western nation'.[13] That 'greater' right is due to the lack of any 'special devotion' to western culture on the part of the Argentineans: 'I believe that Argentineans, all South Americans ... are able to handle all European cultural themes and handle them in a practical and objective way, with an irreverence that can have, and has already had, fortunate consequences.'[14]

The master's disciples have learned this lesson. The Mexican Jorge Volpi (b. 1968) situates his novel *En busca de Klingsor*[15] [In Search of Klingsor], winner of the prestigious Biblioteca Breve Prize 1999, in post-war Germany: the plot is centred on the efforts of a U.S. Army lieutenant to find, during the Nuremburg Trials, the German scientist in charge of the nuclear tests carried out during the Third Reich. The Argentine Federico Andahazi (b. 1963) situates his book *El Anatomista*[16] [The Anatomist] in the Venice of the Renaissance, where a scientist with the surname Colombus struggles against medieval science in his quest to discover the clitoris, thereby demonstrating that women are able to experience pleasure during sex. Iván Thays' melancholic work *El viaje interior*[17] [The Voyage to the Interior] takes place in Busardo, a Mediterranean city full of ruins visited by tourists, in which the protagonist ends up with his lover Kaas. Faced with the prospect of Kaas abandoning him, the protagonist increasingly finds himself settling in Busardo 'without feeling the terrible burden of being in exile since, could exile perchance exist for someone who never had for a homeland anything more than a fleeting encounter with a woman?'[18]

Salman Rushdie, India / UK
***The Satanic Verses*, 1988**

Within a month of the publication of *The Satanic Verses*, Salman Rushdie was receiving death threats at his British home. India was the first country to ban the novel. Saudi Arabia, Egypt, Somalia, Pakistan, Bangladesh, Sudan, Malaysia, Indonesia and Qatar followed. In January 1989, Muslims in Bradford burned the book and riots in Islamabad left six people dead. In February, after the Ayatollah Khomeini issued his fatwa against the author – offering a reward that eventually rose to $2.5 million – Rushdie went into hiding. Violent riots ensued worldwide. Belgian Muslim leaders opposed to the fatwa were murdered, as was the book's Japanese translator Hitoshi Igarashi. Under Iran's President Khatami, the fatwa has been lifted.
Book cover courtesy of Penguin Books. Image of 'Rustam Killing the White Demon' from the *Shahnama (The Book of Kings)* from the Large Clive Album, Mughal, Seventeenth Century, (illustrated text). Victoria & Albert Museum, London, UK/Bridgeman Art Library

Taslima Nasrin, India
***Lajja*, 1993**

Taslima Nasrin wrote her novel *Lajja* [Shame] seven days after the destruction of the Babri mosque in Ayodha, India, an incident that ignited ethnic violence against Indian and Bangladeshi Hindus. In 1993, *Lajja* sold 60,000 copies before it was banned in Bangladesh. In September, a daily newspaper ad called for Nasrin's death. A fatwa and reward for her death soon followed. After rioting in Bangladesh, the government charged her on a British colonial statute for writings that insult religion and religious believers. An international campaign insured Nasrin's bail and she went into exile. In 1988, she returned to Bangladesh and went into hiding. Book cover: courtesy of Penguin Books, design by Sunil Sil, photograph by Shyamal Chakraborti

For Thays, the homeland is not necessarily related to the public sphere of the nation or to the idea of citizenship. The narrator of *El viaje interior* contemptuously describes his country as 'a bunch of unpresentable savages excessively steeped in folklore who live in mud-brick houses full of fleas.'[19] The narrator rebels against a public identity, against the nationality imposed upon him by his homeland. The end-of-century globalised citizens are able to choose whichever homeland takes their fancy, and they may find it as much in another country as in another literary tradition – in Thays' case, Durrel and Nabokov – or in another individual, or in the very spaces found within the 'voyage to the interior'. The homeland is, rather, one's hometown: 'memories ... people that we love ... books that we read and characters that we admire'.[20]

One of the fundamental questions of the novel involves private and public loyalties: 'What common spirit drives those who are united to remain united?'[21] The narrator relates this question as much to his private life (his love for Kaas) as to his public life (the fragile sense of identification with his homeland). There are no easy answers to this question: his love for Kaas lacked that 'common spirit' and seems to have been sustained by a blind narcissism; in terms of his country, this 'common spirit' was upheld by the values of the '*patria chica*' [one's small town], not by a nationalist pride. But this bond is so tenuous that it threatens to break at any moment. A character in the novel says: 'There are those who choose their own homeland, and they are well within their rights to do so.'[22]

At the end of *El viaje interior* when the narrator defends Busardo, something he never did with London, where he studied, or with his never mentioned country of origin, it is suggested that the narrator has chosen, finally, a city as his homeland. There is a 'common spirit' between the narrator and Busardo, something that the narrator never had with his geographically and emotionally remote country of origin.

The question of sexuality

One of the most important features of the new narrative concerns an explicit representation of sexuality, markedly different to the orthodox vision of a Latin American culture divided into closed heterosexual circles. There is a more frank discussion of bi/homosexual issues, an important issue in a continent that still does not tolerate easily those sexual orientations that deviate from the norms of supposedly proud heterosexuality (and machismo and sexism). Despite the fact that we can find in our history numerous examples of writers with an 'alternative' vision to heterosexuality, homosexual issues had generally been discussed using codified procedures which have only in the last few decades received the attention of the critics.

Some examples of this tendency of a more explicit dealing of sexuality can be found in the novels of the Peruvian Jaime Bayly which deal with the bi/homosexual worlds of certain sections of the well-to-do classes in Lima. Another example is *La nada cotidiana*[23] [Yocandra in the Paradise of Nada], the novel by the Cuban Zoé Valdés about a young woman in Havana, who, during the days of the Special Period, is more interested in giving a free rein to her sexual desire than being a good revolutionary, and the erotic tales of the Puerto Rican Mayra Santos and the Argentine Cristina Civale.

One of the most radical projects is that of Bellatín (b. 1960). In his work, geography, characters, and dramatic situations are developed on an abstract level: the true point of reference is barely more than a departure point for the creation of an autonomous narrative world. This can provoke a distancing effect, the sensation of finding oneself within a cold universe of narrative, which lacks materiality as in the case of the *Poeta ciego*[24] [Blind Poet], his unsuccessful 1998 novel. In this novel many atrocities take place, but they are dealt with in such a dispassionate way that they do not affect the reader. However, when Bellatín manages to find the appropriate metaphors to describe his abstractions, as in the case of *Salón de belleza* [Beauty Salon] from 1994, his literature reaches some of the greatest heights attained by the new generation.

Salón de belleza is the story of a gay hairdresser who, in response to the calamity of a plague that ravages the city, decides to turn his beauty salon into a medieval style *moridero* [hospice]. This is where the men who have been given their final rites – women and children are not admitted – go to receive the final offerings of hospitality before they die. The beauty salon is full of aquariums with multicoloured fish. When it catered to women, the hairdresser wanted his 'female clients to have the sensation of being submerged in crystal waters while they were being treated so as to subsequently be able to return to the surface rejuvenated'.[25] The aquariums acquire increasing splendour as the beauty salon grows and falls into decay as it is turned into a *moridero*. The collection of escalaris, goldfish and pencil fish slowly diminishes and finally only one aquarium is left. The others are used to store the personal belongings of the dying patients. The designated space for beauty is transformed into a space designated for death.

The transformation of the beauty salon into a *moridero* has obvious parallels with the transformation of the aquariums into small tombs that allude to those who have fallen ill with the plague. The narrative axis of the novel rests in this parallelism and is its mechanism for producing images and ideas. One of these ideas compares, without the idea itself becoming an automatic rule, the world of animal behaviour to that of human beings. The fish eat one another and 'nobody cares about the disappearance of a fish'.[26] When one of the residents, a lad with whom the hairdresser had intimate contact, dies, three fish also die. In the baths, a place of homosexual promiscuity, where anything can happen, the protagonist feels 'as if I were in one of my aquariums',[27] something to which the rarified atmosphere of the place contributes as well as 'the strange sensation produced by the large fish's pursuit of the smaller fish that they wished to eat'.[28] The world in which the protagonist operates is very similar to the Darwinian world of the fish. The naturalism of the end of the nineteenth century vigorously reappears in this disturbing end of the twentieth century.

In this novel, the true-life point of reference for the plague would appear to be AIDS, but Bellatín never actually mentions it, and the way in which the theme is dealt with invites an allegorical reading. The narrative evokes a certain climate of biblical punishment surrounding the dissolute life of the homosexual protagonist: 'With all the excesses of my street adventures my life began to lose its sense of balance.'[29] The life that the patients had led before arriving at the *moridero* also affects the more or less rapid way with which the plague exterminates them. The administration of the *moridero* will lead the protagonist to a more responsible and unselfish way of life, although this does not imply the adoption of a more religious attitude:

> No one here is a convert to priesthood. The efforts that are made in this respect comply with a more human, more practical and more real sentiment. There is another rule which I have not mentioned through fear that they might censor me, and it is that crucifixes, religious images, and prayers of any type are prohibited in the *moridero*.[30]

If a corrupt lifestyle implies a punishment in the form of the plague, the protagonist is unrepentant: in this way, the narrative does not slip into a banal moralising didacticism. Illness and

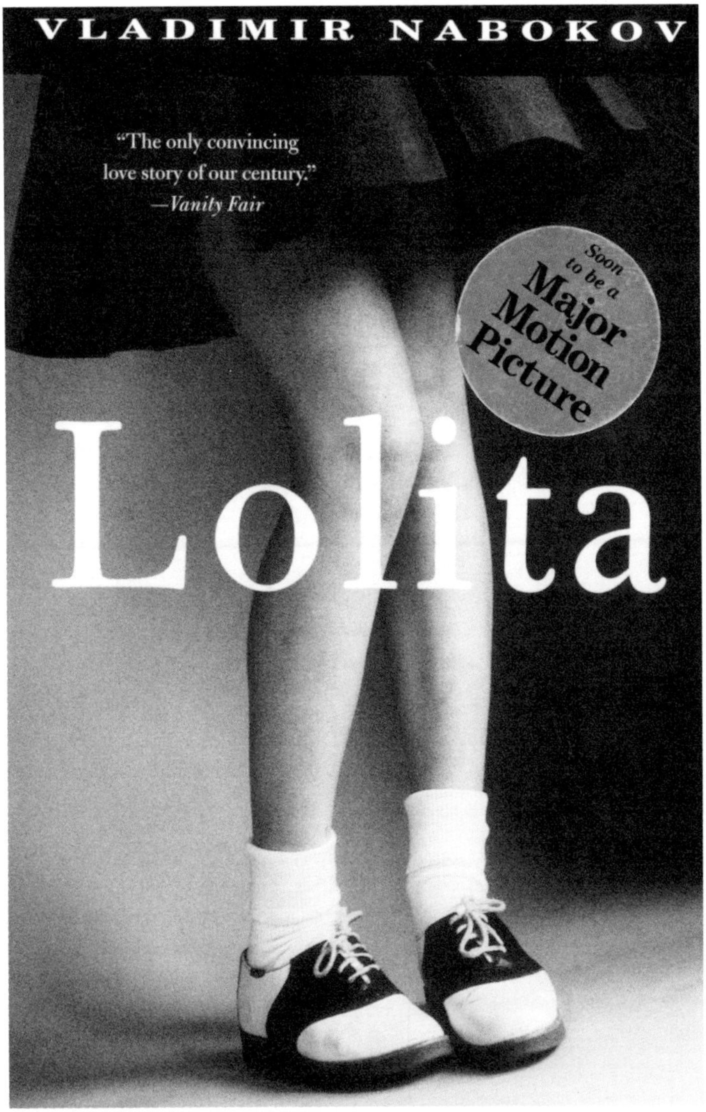

Vladimir Nabokov, Russia / U.S.
Lolita, 1955

Unable to find a U.S. publisher, *Lolita*, by Vladimir Nabokov, was sent to Olympia Press in Paris. *Lolita*, about an older man's sexual obsession with a young girl, was published in English and then banned in Britain in 1955 and in France in 1956. In 1957, the U.S. allowed *Lolita* into the country, although it still could not be legally imported. By 1959, it was available in French, British and U.S. bookstores. As late as 1974, South Africa banned the novel, but lifted the ban eight years later. (Nicholas Karolides, Margaret Bald and Dawn Sova, eds., *100 Banned Books: Censorship Histories of World Literature*, New York: Checkmark Books, p. 304). Book cover courtesy of Vintage Books, a Division of Random House Inc.

الخرطوم

يومية مستقلة تصدرها دار الخرطوم للصحافة

AL - Khartoum • Thursday • 4 May 2000 • No. (2404)

الميرغني يبحث مع المسئولين المصريين خطوات تفعيل المبادرة المشتركة ويرأس في القاهرة اجتماع الأمانة التنفيذية للتجمع الوطني

اجتماع لتذليل عقبات إطلاق سراح الأسرى

بين الحركة والمجموعة السودانية لحقوق الإنسان

بنك السودان يصدر منشوره المرتقب حول الهيكلة:

دمج البنوك اختياري.. ويُستكمل قبل يونيو ٢٠٠١ في حدود ٦ مجموعات

أو رفع رأس مال كل بنك إلى ثلاثة مليارات دينار بنهاية ٢٠٠٢

ابراهيم مادبو يرحب بدعوة قرنق لعقد مؤتمر قبائل التماس

بعد استنكارها الاتهام برعاية الارهاب:

الحكومة السودانية تستنكر الاتهام الأمريكي لها بممارسة التمييز الديني

جنود على ظهور الابل يطاردون المشتبه فيهم:

خبير عسكري ينتقد التدابير الأمنية لحماية خط أنابيب البترول

آدم مادبو يردّ على البشير

اليونان وباكستان ترفضان الاتهامات الأمريكية حول الإرهاب

عنان يشيد بوقف إطلاق النار في السودان

الخرطوم اليوم

التفجير الثالث

قيادات في النظام تحذر من مغبة الخلافات على مستقبل الحركة الإسلامية

تأبين فقيد الوطن ربيع حسنين بلندن ١٤ مايو

العاملون ببنك فيصل يرفعون إضرابهم

***Al-Khartoum*, Sudan / Egypt**
4 May 2000

On 17 April 1993, the first issue of the independent daily *Al-Khartoum* appeared in Cairo, a city hosting over two million Sudanese refugees. For them, the primarily political newspaper has become an important and reliable source of information about events in Sudan. Moreover, *Al-Khartoum's* insightful reports and politically active discussions serve a growing readership around the world. (See page 61) (Ahmed Al-Mukarram, 'Sudanese Culture', *Cairene Exile*, 21 October 1999) Newspaper front page courtesy of *Al-Khartoum* imminent death do not worry the hairdresser as much as the fact of dying alone. The idea of living life to the full so as to take advantage of one's youth prevents him from thinking about the future: 'I am afraid that at some point I felt myself to be immortal … This feeling perhaps stopped me from allowing myself time to be alone with myself. I find no other way of explaining to myself why I am so alone in this period of my life.'[31]

Salón de belleza suggests and condenses in an apocalyptic way two themes that are dear to the new generation: on the one hand, the forgetting of transcendental projects in order to devote oneself to taking advantage of one's fleeting youth while one is still able; on the other hand, the existential anguish brought about by orphanhood in a chaotic world devoid of love and affection. It is a vicious circle – a lack of love leads to a hedonistic attitude of indulgence; but at the same time, this desire to take advantage of the present stands in the way of the creation of a social space governed by love.

Bellatín emerges gracefully from such a difficult task as the one of giving voice, subjectivity and representation to a homosexual character in Latin American literature, while at the same time avoiding Manichaean moralisms and convenient piety, victimisation or stigmatisation. Though Bellatín's aesthetic proposal is very different to that of Cortés and Thays, these writers, and others that the scope of this brief work cannot encompass, create a literary space that does not shy away from complex issues and avoids the temptation of offering simple solutions.

Translated from the Spanish by Shirin Shenassa

1. Becerra, Eduardo, ed.; *Líneas aéreas* (Madrid: Lengua de Trapo, 1999)
2. Fuguet, Alberto and Gómez, Sergio, eds.; *McOndo* (Barcelona/Santiago: Mondadori, 1996)
3. *Lineas*, p. XIII
4. *McOndo*, p. 15
5. Cortés, Carlos; *Cruz de olvido* (Mexico: Alfaguara, 1999)
6. Ibid., p. 66
7. Ibid., p. 41
8. Ibid., p. 310
9. Ibid., p. 140
10. Ibid., p. 2
11. Ibid., p. 18
12. Thays, Iván; 'La edad de la inocencia'. *Vórtice* (Lima, June 1999), p. 54
13. Borges, Jorges Luis; 'The Argentinean Writer and Tradition', *Discusión, Obras completas* (Buenos Aires: Emecé, 1974), p. 272
14. Ibid., p. 273
15. Volpi, Jorge; *En busca de Klingsor* (Barcelona: Seix Barral, 1999)
16. Andahazi, Federico; *El Anatomista* (Buenos Aires: Planeta, 1996)
17. Thays, Iván; *El viaje interior* (Lima: Peisa, 1999)
18. Ibid., p. 272
19. Ibid., p. 226
20. Ibid., p. 41
21. Ibid., p. 256
22. Ibid., p. 226
23. Valdés, Zoé; *La Nada Cotidiana* (Buenos Aires: Emecé, 1996)
24. Bellatín, Mario; *Poeta ciego* (Mexico: Tusquets, 1998)
25. Bellatín, Mario; *Salón de belleza* (México: Tusquets, 1999)
26. Ibid., p. 65
27. Ibid., p. 19
28. Ibid., p. 19-20
29. Ibid., p. 47
30. Ibid., p. 61
31. Ibid., p. 72

Kiran Karnik

Cyberia: True Freedom?

Outer space has long been considered the 'final frontier'. However, it would seem that the true final frontier is space of a different kind: cyberspace. If the word 'frontier' evokes images of the American Wild West, of a pioneering spirit, of battles and conquest, of *laissez-faire* and no authorities; then, doubtless, it is cyberspace that best matches these features. 'Cyberia' may well be the ultimate word for freedom.

Cyberia, or cyberspace, is concretised in the internet. This is, basically, a meta-network, a network of networks. Like outer space, the oceans or celestial bodies, it is a new territory, one that will hopefully not see the kinds of past battles that were waged over seas and shipping lanes. Like the Moon Treaty, cyberspace could be declared 'the heritage of all mankind'. Yet, nations – and corporate entities – are already battling for ownership of the conduit, dominance over the content, and control of the key software and portals. Meanwhile, the internet grows exponentially.

At the end of 1984, there were 1,000 hosts (computers with a registered IP address). In early 1987, the number crossed 10,000, and two years later it was over 100,000. The million mark was hit in 1992 and the 10 million point was reached in 1996. A mid-1999 estimate put the figure at 56 million.[1] The number of users is obviously far greater: not only do many addresses have multiple users from the same household, but there has also been an explosion of cyber-cafés, which provide access (at rapidly decreasing costs) to the internet. These public access facilities are of particular importance in developing countries, where only a small proportion of the population can afford to buy a computer. (However, the rapidly decreasing price of computers is noteworthy. This is thanks both to technological advances and economies of scale in production. The price of accessing the internet has been decreasing even more dramatically. For example, in India, 500 hours of internet access cost Rs.15,000 in 1998; it now costs just Rs.2,750. In some countries, access is now free. This is bound to lead to even greater growth in the number of internet users.)

Despite its growing popularity, governments around the world seem to be ambivalent about the internet. On the one hand, they see it as an essential and dynamic part of the new economy that will drive growth, create employment and propel the country forward. On the other hand, governments – and all forms of authority – also recognise the internet's potential to completely erode traditional concepts of boundaries, controls, hierarchy and sovereignty. Ironically, this amorphous entity, which has created new space outside any form of rigid control, owes its development – and, substantially, its genesis – to the most rigidly organised and controlled arm of the state: the military.

The development of the internet was driven by the need of the U.S. defence establishment for a survivable, war-proof communications network. This led to the concept of multiple, independent networks, autonomous but interconnected, with no single control centre, so that the network could continue to function even if any node was incapacitated. This non-hierarchical network topography has been the internet's most outstanding feature. In simplistic terms, therefore,

AÑO 1. No. 1.
Vitral
MAYO - JUNIO, 1994.
REVISTA DEL CENTRO CATÓLICO DE FORMACIÓN CÍVICA Y RELIGIOSA DE PINAR DEL RÍO
LA LIBERTAD DE LA LUZ
Encuentro con...:
Obispo de Pinar del Río.
GALERÍA: Pedro Pablo Oliva.
"JARDÍN" Realidad y fantasía de Dulce María Loynaz

***Vitral*, Cuba**
No. 1, 1994

'Cultural freedom can be found locally, in cultural margins, creating a free space from within. The Cuban magazine *Vitral* enjoys the protection of its small scale. In co-operation with the Roman Catholic Church in its hometown Pinar del Río, it has founded a journal in which intellectuals, artists and philosophers can speak out. Stimulated by a growing readership, *Vitral* gives the floor to a number of different voices in Cuba.' *Vitral* was one of the recipients of the Principal 1999 Prince Claus Award. (See page 94) (Prince Claus, 'Address to the Recipients of the Principal 1999 Prince Claus Award: Mohamed Fellag, *Vitral* and Al-Jazeera', *1999 Prince Claus Awards*, The Hague: Prince Claus Fund, p. 8) Magazine cover courtesy of *Vitral*

Vitral, Cuba
No. 24, 1998

In 1994, the Cuban sociopolitical cultural journal *Vitral* defined its purpose as 'a space for transparency and the multicoloured light of our society' which seeks 'to contemplate the limits of our current co-existence in order to emerge, collectively, from this state of prostration through the pathway of creativity.' Five years later, *Vitral* has become an arts powerhouse publishing rock fanzines, literary magazines, special editions and one-off publications, all to show that Cuba is 'a mixture of cuisines, races and cultures, the result of cross-cultural fertilisation, synthesis and syncretism, an open bridge that links the outside world and our own culture.' (See page 94) (Ernesto Ortiz Hernández, 'The Cuban Sociocultural Journal *Vitral*') Magazine cover courtesy of *Vitral* no one person or organisation 'owns' or controls the internet. Out of the needs of war has emerged a unique tool for freedom.

From its early days, when it was used by the U.S. research community to exchange findings and material, mainly on projects funded by various defence agencies, the internet has evolved and grown at a phenomenal rate. Today, a user located anywhere on earth can send a message to any one or more of the millions of other users. Messages may be routed through a variety of alternative pathways, going through a large number of different nodes or servers, before reaching their ultimate destination. The 'message' can comprise text, audio, graphics, pictures or even video and also any combinations of these. The limiting factor is basically the bandwidth, or the carrying capacity of the communication links that are involved.

With regard to the further evolution of internet, it would be best to quote those who were instrumental in creating it. According to 'A Brief History of the Internet', a document which is, quite appropriately, on the internet, at www.isoc.org:

> One should not conclude that the internet has now finished changing. The internet, although a network in name and geography, is a creature of the computer, not the traditional network of the telephone or television industry. It will, indeed it must, continue to change and evolve at the speed of the computer industry if it is to remain relevant.[2]

The internet and free expression

Widespread access to the internet has spawned a variety of applications. It gave rise to e-commerce and created dot com mania, with new websites being created by the million – a new one every five seconds, by one estimate – as quickly as it became responsible for the current bust. Despite the failing e-commerce climate, anyone can start a new site with relative ease. All that is required is a small amount of money to formally register the site, and space on a server to host the site. It is this freedom of creation, coupled with the freedom of access, which is of great significance to individuals or groups whose freedom of expression is muzzled by their situation or society. In many societies, alternative, dissenting or radical views are not permitted space. Even where formal censorship is not practised, various forms of self-censorship exist. These controls are exercised in direct or indirect ways by the owners or controllers of media. The victims of such censorship are those whose opinions differ from the mainstream view in politics, economics, social issues or art. For all such individuals and groups, the internet provides a platform through which they can offer access to their views and work to millions of people around the world.

This possibility has become known now to many groups and they have moved quickly to take advantage of it. This includes those fighting wars of liberation, ethnic groups or other minorities who feel oppressed, writers whose views and work are not acceptable to the traditional media and artists whose creative endeavours are not given space because of political, economic or censorship issues. Such groups – sometimes even individuals – have established websites for the dissemination of their viewpoints. In addition, the internet enables such individuals or groups to send out information to specific individuals through email.

Malaysia is an example. A government ruling forbids party newsletters from being sold to non-party members. On the basis of this, authorities confiscated copies of *Harakah* (an opposition party newsletter) early this year, because it was being sold on news-stands. Another Malay-language magazine, *Detik*, which has been critical of the government, is now banned. A weekly tabloid, *Eksklusif*, has not been able to get its publishing permit renewed. Partly as a result of such moves, the opposition is making full use of the internet as an alternative medium for dissemination. Websites critical of the government were set up and an online newspaper was established. Online newscasts are poised to follow. In May 2000, the opposition PAS (Malaysian Islamic Party) launched its web TV channel on www.harakahdaily.com. As the media analyst, Dr Mustafa Anuar has noted, 'It's an attempt to find ways and means of using information and communication technology to reach out to people and to provide a platform for them to express their views.'[3]

At the height of the rebellion in the state of Chiapas in Mexico, the rebel leader Subcomandante Marcos was quoted as saying that his internet connectivity was of greater importance to him than guns. The reason was that the rebels could reach out – via cyberspace – to influence people and policy-makers around the world, who would then pressurise the Mexican government to hold back its troops and eventually come to the negotiating table.

For separatist movements, the internet is an extremely potent means of spreading information – or, sometimes, disinformation. The Liberation Tigers of Tamil Eelam have been using the internet, and their site, www.eelamweb.com, as a source to cross-check statements put out by the government about the military situation in the embattled Jaffna peninsula in Sri Lanka. With the government clamping censorship on news reports from Jaffna, the LTTE site has become essential. Similarly, Kashmir militants too have been putting out their viewpoints on the internet from sites like www.jklf.com.

With powerful search engines, it is now easy to find dozens of sites that have been set up by (or provide details of) separatist movements. Although some countries are able to prevent access to some sites by firewalls, generally governments find themselves in an insolvable dilemma. They want to push forward the idea of technology, but technology itself is individually empowering. Once people experience the borderless state of the internet – whether politics or porn – they start to question fundamental issues of state control.

Cultural expression and the net

Control, like freedom, can come in many guises. A consumer-based, free speech revolution has been taking place in the U.S. among the under-30s, primarily at college campuses. The freshman Shawn Fanning established the Napster internet music community in 1999. Napster had 58 million users who were able to download digital music files from other members' hard drives. The widespread access to free music – often before it has been officially released – nearly succeeded in loosening the financial and creative stranglehold record companies and retailers have over the music industry.

Although Napster maintained that the sharing of computer files, whatever their content, was legal, the RIAA (Recording Industry Association of America) filed a lawsuit against them on 6 December 1999 for infringement of copyright. Napster was made to sign a deal with Bertelsmann (who own BMG, one of the five record companies represented by the RIAA) in October 2000. A subscription-based membership and distribution system that will guarantee payments to artists (and to the record companies) will soon be in place at www.napster.com. In the meantime the site has been voluntarily shut down and Shawn Fanning has been replaced as CEO by Konrad Hilbers, who has vowed to reinvigorate the Napster brand while ensuring protection for copyright holders.

His language here is significant: Napster is no longer a renegade youth movement, but a 'brand'. It is unlikely that he will be able to revive the excitement that surrounded Napster's phenomenal

Chris Ofili, Nigeria / UK
The Holy Virgin Mary, mixed media, 1996

The exhibition, *SENSATION: Young British Art from the Saatchi Collection*, at the Brooklyn Museum of Art, from October 1999 to January 2000, included Chris Ofili's *The Holy Virgin Mary*, a paper collage of pornographic images, oil paint, glitter, polyester resin, map pins on linen and elephant dung. Offended, New York City's Mayor Rudolph Giuliani attempted to freeze the museum's $7 million city subsidy. The museum countersued and, in a letter written in December 1999, museum director Arnold L. Lehman states that the preliminary injunction ruling 'powerfully reaffirmed that our First Amendment freedoms are indeed inviolable and cannot be abridged through political intimidation'. (www.brooklynart.org/sensation/letterdef.html)
Photo: Stephen White, courtesy of the Saatchi Gallery, London

Shirin Neshat, Iran / U.S.
***Turbulent*, video installation, 1998**

Turbulent **by Iranian artist Shirin Neshat shows two films which appear opposite each other. Above, Iranian-Kurdish singer Shahran Nazereri performs a thirteenth century Rumi poem in front of a male-only audience. Below, avant-garde vocalist Sussan Deyhim sings guttural and meaningless sounds to an empty auditorium. After Ayatollah Khomeini banned women singers from performing in public, Islamic militants destroyed records and cassettes by female recording artists. Under President Khatami, female singers Pari Zangeneh and Khatereh Parvaneh perform to women-only audiences. Some women have been able to perform on stage with male family members or have appeared by themselves on the covers of women's magazines.** Videostills courtesy of the artist growth before it was cut back by the majors. When the site comes back up, its music library will be strictly limited to artists already on the Bertelsmann label. Major record labels are hijacking Napster's innovation and then stultifying its liberating potential in order to monopolise the commercial gains: Universal and Sony are setting up a file-swapping site called PressPlay; BMG, EMI and Warner have set up MusicNet. None of the sites will offer universal access to music from each other's labels and probably none will feature the rarities and bootlegs that made Napster so vital.

However, in Napster's absence, new free file-swapping sites have sprung up, such as Gnutella, Audiogalaxy, BearShare, and LimeWire – proof that the internet is almost impossible to police; no amount of corporate weedkiller can kill off its burgeoning growth.

For many musicians, non-acceptance in the commercial marketplace is the equivalent of censorship – despite it being unspoken and, often times, unofficial. In the case of Napster and the new underground sites which are replacing it, it is the consumers who are waging war against the blandness of commercial tyranny. The musicians themselves are divided. Some, such as the San Francisco-based rock group Metallica, who filed a suit against Napster in April 2000, are vocal about protecting their copyright interests; others are more interested in harnessing the net as a new way of making and spreading their music. If any one sure conclusion can be drawn from the argument, it is that the internet gives artists the facility to bypass gatekeepers of all kinds, whether art critics, moral censors or powerful commercial interests.

For fine artists, the inability to secure an association with a gallery can result in near invisibility. Even exhibited painters and sculptors who rely on shows and catalogue publications are caught in a double bind, since both venues are limited and normally accessible only at a high cost. Fledgling artists face great problems, and even well-known artists have difficulty in taking their work beyond a limited geographic scope. The internet offers an alternative: a free and freely accessible exhibition space. The artists can also control the context in which their art is viewed. As a result, the internet has become important for artists inside and outside the critical art establishment, as well as for artists residing in societies where cultural expression has been curbed.

Previously, any discussion of art and politics was confined to academic or critical journals, unless the international press picked up a human interest arts story. Now, lengthy analysis can be found at the touch of a button. When art has been born out of a political struggle like South Africa's, sites such as www.one.people.com and SARA (South African Resistance Art) at www.library.thinkquest.org, which include artists' interviews or biographical information, examples of their work and political analysis, convey not only the art itself, but the social climate in which the art was created. Even internationally renowned, primarily non-western, artists benefit from web exposure, and sometimes not on art-related sites. Community Aid Oxfam Australia, www.caa.org.au/horizons/h12/alders.html, is one of the most visited sites, according to the popular search engine www.google.com, for information about the Mozambique artist Malangatana Ngwenya.

Artists themselves have also been using the internet to air their views, critical and otherwise. On Art on the Net, only artists critique art. Webpages on www.art.net are devoted to 'Keeping Free Speech' and artists' reactions to New York Mayor Rudolph Giuliani's 1999 court case brought against the Brooklyn Museum of Art for exhibiting Chris Ofili's elephant dung splattered collage, *The Holy Virgin Mary*, in *SENSATION: Young British Art from the Saatchi Collection*. In addition, Art on the Net provides a facility for web rings, making it easier for someone to find a particular artist in a crowd of websites.

For some artists, the internet also provides an opportunity – much like a coffee shop or a living-room – where they can meet informally on a regular basis. In 1993, the Hereford Salon at www.ourworld.compuserve.com/homepages/HerefordSalon/ began 'with the objective of providing an informal environment in which artists could discuss their work in progress'. Their home-page continues, 'We are concerned with the relationship between artists and the multitude of intermediaries who separate them from the public and each other. We are especially interested in how to help artists communicate and cooperate among themselves.' Hereford Salon's Lauren Bon has expanded her artistic involvement with the net, by showing pieces of virtual work to interested galleries before presenting real ones.

Ironically, both the internet's accessibility and chaos have made it ideal for buying and selling – in short, shopping – a service provided by a plethora of art sites. At the high end of the connoisseur market, the famous auction house Sotheby's at www.sothebys.com includes a section featuring online auctions. In the U.S., www.globalart.net allows artists to submit their work and a brief write-up for display and sale, all for a small fee. Recently, NuCent Technologies has launched an art portal. Artsall at www.artsall.com holds some 750 paintings and sculptures, the numbers of which are expected to increase to 5,000.

Despite the growing volume of art on the internet, a single picture can still focus a thousand minds. In repressive societies, art and photography – any kind of cross-cultural communication – can make a huge impact. This was brought home by the famous image of a terror-stricken, nine-year-old Vietnamese child who had been burnt by U.S. napalm,[4] or more recently, the lone figure of a Chinese protestor standing in front of a tank during the 1989 pro-democracy demonstrations in Beijing's Tiananmen Square. For creative artists, whether painters or photographers, the internet can act as both a space for increased free expression, and a force for change.

The regulatory framework

> India rushes in from every direction … Buy Chilly cockroach traps! Drink Hello mineral water! Speed Thrills But Kills! shout the hoardings. There are new kinds of message, too. Enroll for Oracle 81. Graduate with Java.
>
> Salman Rushdie on returning home[5]

My country, India, has been successfully riding the IT wave, and reaping considerable economic rewards. It has also become one of the first countries to pass e-commerce legislation. In May 2000, just a few days after the huge international outcry about the 'Love Bug' virus,[6] the Indian Information Technology Act, which includes clauses related to obscenity, cyber-crime and detention powers, was approved by parliament. Given the speed of actions on the net, the act allows for immediate as well as anticipatory action; a senior police officer can enter any public place and 'search and arrest without warrant any person found therein who is reasonably suspected of having committed or of committing or of being about to commit any offence under this act'.

Despite considerable public consternation, this draconian provision has been retained in the act. The government's defence is that it is no different from what already exists as a general law; in fact, the safeguard in the act is that only a specified, high ranking police officer has the power to search and arrest without a warrant. Apart from broader civil liberties issues, there is concern that such a law provides the scope for undue harassment. Fortunately, a provision that would have required all cyber-café owners to maintain a record – or face imprisonment – of the customers'

Dinh Q. Lê, Vietnam
***Lotusland*, installation, 1999**

The Lotusland installation is the second project by the Vietnamese artist Dinh Q. Lê on the continuing effects of the chemical herbicide Agent Orange. His country experienced prolonged exposure to the toxic pesticide during the Vietnam war. This has resulted in a high incidence of birth defects, including an unprecedented rate of conjoined (Siamese) twins, the majority of whom die at birth. Some Vietnamese believe that the twins, after death, become Buddhist deities and spirits. Lê has great difficulty exhibiting his work at home. A Prince Claus Fund grant enabled him to attend the London opening of *Lotusland* at the *Rich Mix Slow Release* exhibition. Photo courtesy of the artist

William Kentridge, South Africa
Overvloed, film, 1999

From animated films, opera and theatre productions, South African artist and filmmaker William Kentridge examines the personal within the context of his country's politics and history. His film *Overvloed* was projected onto the ceiling of the Royal Palace in Amsterdam during the 1999 Prince Claus Awards ceremony. According to the presentation, 'With every ceiling painting ... one struggles to find a point ... from which it makes sense ... The building of the Royal Palace (1648) coincides with the Dutch colonisation of southern Africa (1652). What ... was the pinnacle of the Dutch Golden Era was the start of an extremely complicated chapter in South African history.' The artist addressed this issue openly at this prestigious event in a building that was constructed during that golden age. Film still courtesy of the Prince Claus Fund identities and the websites they visited was ultimately dropped. However, a clause that makes applicable existing obscenity laws to 'transmitting or publishing' material in electronic form has been included. Many critics worry that the interpretation of this could result in prosecution of not only the individual accessing any 'obscene' material, but also the owner of a cyber-café (from where this is done), or the search engine provider, or the portal through which access is obtained.

The ease with which information can be put on the net, and its worldwide reach, are issues of grave concern to many governments. There is now wide recognition that, no longer does 'power flow from a barrel of a gun' (as Mao Tse Tung stated), or even from a barrel of oil – as seemed to be the case for some years – but from a computer monitor. Given this power of information – its ability to influence commodity and share prices, to affect currency exchange rates, and to expose the misdeeds of authorities – it is inevitable that many countries are wary of the effects. This concern is amplified by the fact that the internet makes it so easy to send information to anyone, anywhere (as long as the person can access a computer and a telephone line).

As a result, there have been many attempts to impose some form of control, if not censorship. Of course, this is not a recent phenomenon. As Germany's Culture Minister, Michael Naumann, points out, the printing press – like each subsequent new medium – aroused the mistrust of authorities: within 30 years after Gutenberg's invention, the first censors were appointed. Yet, Naumann feels, 'The epoch of unequivocal power ended in 1455. No one can control the information channels any longer.'[7]

Such optimism would seem justified in the internet age. After all, here is a 'medium', an invention, that no one person owns or effectively controls; anyone can put out information or views, at little or no cost; and these are accessible to millions of internet users around the world. Therefore, any form of censorship seems difficult, if not infeasible. However, governments and authorities may not be as powerless as they seem. Censorship is yet possible at two levels: the pre-emptive and the post-publication. The former is exercised through laws relating to sedition, obscenity or even 'public interest'. These act as a deterrent; further, laws are sometimes pre-emptive – as in India's IT Act. At the post-publication stage, governments that control the telecommunication networks are able to block access to certain sites, through firewalls. However, with increasing privatisation of communication networks, and the downloading of internet data via direct-to-home (DTH) satellite broadcasting, such control is becoming increasingly difficult. Also, the fact that the creators of such sites (namely, separatist organisations) often operate from outside their 'home' country – for example, from exile – reduces fear and the possibility of legal actions.

While censorship poses a serious challenge to free expression, and dilutes – even negates – the very philosophy of the internet, there is also a threat of a different nature: the violation of personal privacy. The fact is that databases about individuals (for example, health records or credit card expenses) can provide a lot of guarded, personal information. Therefore, in many countries there are privacy laws that limit access to such data. Now, some internet advertising companies are seeking to get information about individuals through their activity on the internet, so as to better target their advertisements. Last year, Jodie Bernstein, Director of the Bureau of Consumer Protection at the U.S. Federal Trade Commission, showed senators how websites and advertising companies track users through so-called 'cookies' – small text files stored and read on a user's hard disk drive. Through these files, which generally contain an identification number, ad companies can see where users 'travel' on the internet. As one senator commented: 'If local shops did things like this, we'd be outraged.'[8] Like an inverted form of censorship, the excessive and intrusive collecting and divulging of personal information is also an infringement of personal liberty and freedom.

A digital speakers' corner

The topography of the internet is radically different from that of the conventional media. Print, radio, television, or even cinema, theatre and folk forms, all operate in a regulated arena, with a 'star' topology. Unlike other mass media, there is little or no scope for a gatekeeper function in the internet. These unique characteristics make the internet the ideal medium for true free expression, providing an arena for complete freedom of views and enabling vast reach at a very low cost. It is, in effect, an enlarged and electronic version of Hyde Park's Speakers' Corner – a place where anyone can give vent to their views, without restraints or constraints – or a large scale graffiti wall, where anyone can express an opinion or thought. With recent technological advances, this new medium can now carry a variety of material: text, audio, graphics, animation and even video.

Ironically, however, it is this extremely low-cost freedom – the immense and unique strength of the internet – that is likely to constrain it. The very fact that there are hundreds of thousands of sites on the internet *requires* that there be search engines that help users locate specific information or sites. Saturation of information necessitates a filter, a degree of control. The sophistication and size of these result in only a limited number existing. Over time, one may well see more and more sites, the entry to which is accessed (i.e. controlled) through fewer and fewer portals or search engines. Commercialisation and competition will lead to attrition and a further concentration. Finally, search engines may well act as gatekeepers, not unlike the gatekeeper function in traditional media.

Another concerning trend is the mergers amongst media entities, resulting in a concentration of media power in a very few media/infocom mega-corporations. Today, less than a dozen such companies completely dominate the media scene, not unlike the time when a few wire services enjoyed a virtual monopoly over news dissemination. The mergers between already massive media companies (for example, AT&T with TCI and then with Media One; AOL with Time-Warner and the Vivendi-Seagram deal) is creating monoliths of unimaginable power. These few companies may soon completely determine what we see, hear or read – whether in print, TV or radio. Their portals and search engines may determine which sites we can access. The potential of the internet, the hope of letting 'a thousand flowers bloom', may well be nipped in the bud. Commercialisation, censorship and control – each one the very anti-thesis of the structure and philosophy of the internet – may end up getting the upper hand.

This rather unfortunate scenario is not an unlikely one, given present trends. Guarding against such a development, by preventing monopolies of power – through portals, search engines and massive infocom companies – is a necessary step for ensuring that the internet remains a truly free space, a vital component of civil society, a tool for freedom, free expression and democracy. It must play the pivotal role in enlarging the public sphere, and it is for each enlightened citizen to ensure that there is no question about the unique and special role of the internet in promoting freedom.

Additional research by Ketaki Karnik and James Westcott

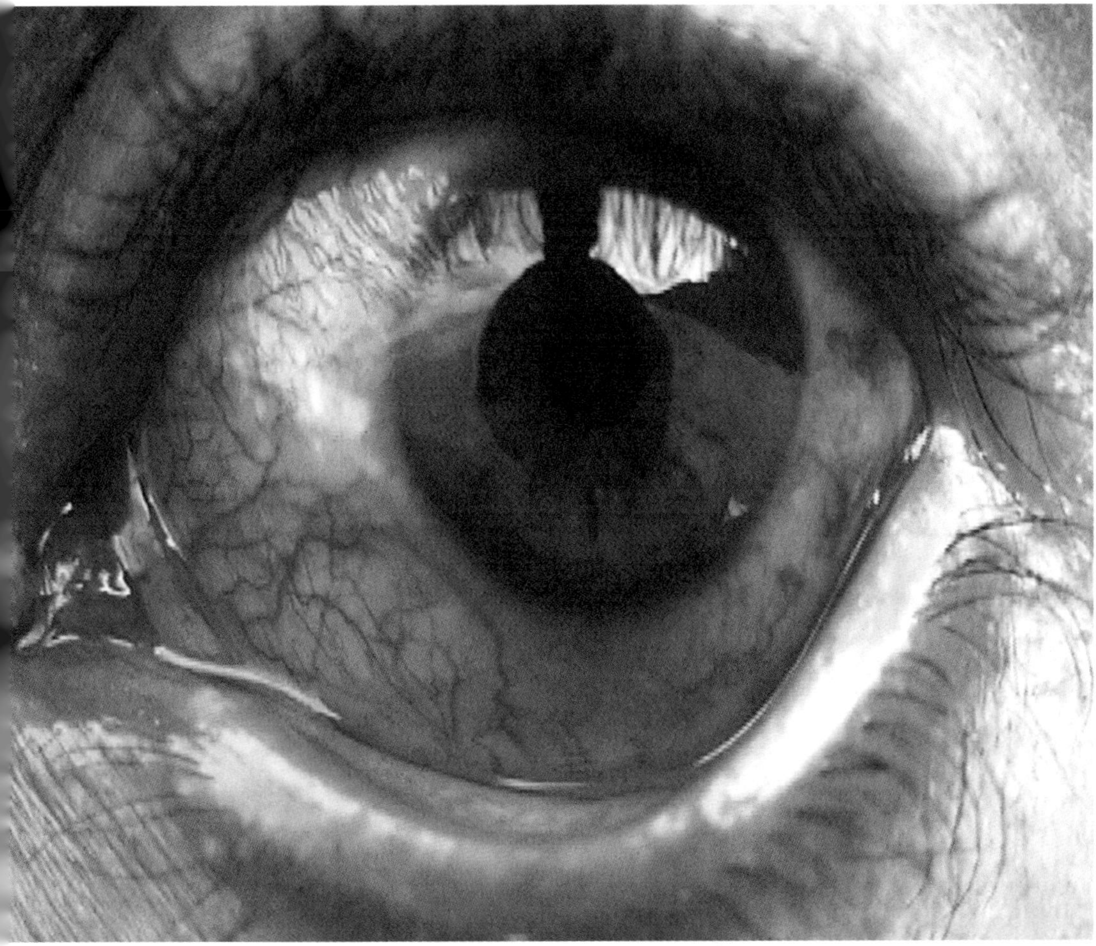

Fernando Arias, Colombia
Shot on Location, video installation, 2001

Shot on Location 'tells explicitly of the seeming madness and inverted morality which is taking place in war-torn Colombia today. Madness, because the representatives of power within the so-called state apparatus all too often behave like the heinous beings they claim to condemn and pursue. While the poor, trapped by the circumstances of their material dependency, fall victim to drug criminality on the one hand, and forms of overt social repression and victimisation on the other ... The bloodshot condition of the artist's eye [is] an appropriate metaphor ... ' (Mark Gisbourne, 9 September 2001) Videostill courtesy of the artist

>>

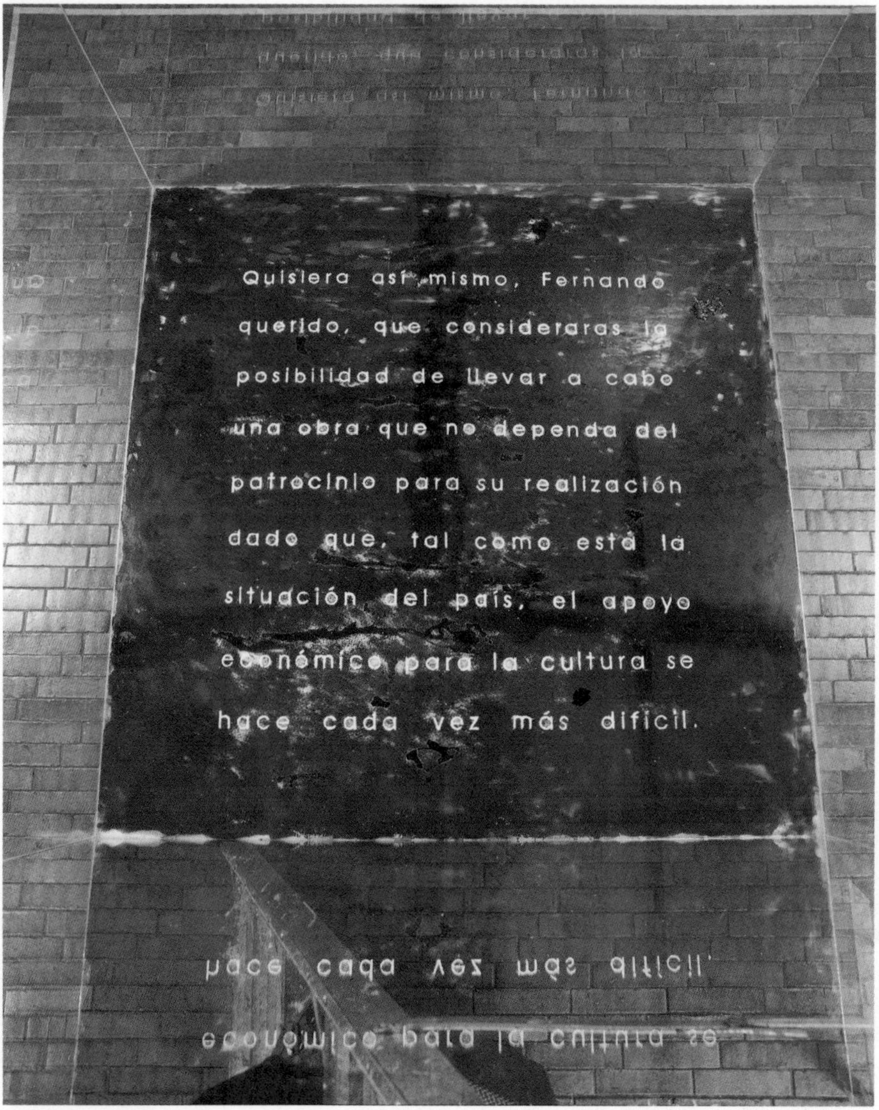

Fernando Arias, Colombia
Unititled, installation with cocaine, 1996

'I would like to ask you, my dear Fernando, to consider the possibility of making a piece that would not require sponsorship because, given the bad situation of the country, finding economic assistance for cultural projects is more difficult each day,' writes a museum director in a rejection letter to Fernando Arias. The director is complaining of dwindling sponsorship for the arts, despite the wealth cocaine generates as Colombia's main cash crop. In response, Arias wrote these words from the letter in cocaine on his own blood to protest the continuing devastation of his country by drugs and civil strife. Photo: Julian Vélasquez, courtesy of the artist

1. Leiner, Barry M., Vinton, G. Cerf, Clark, David D., Kahn, Robert E., Kleinrock, Leonard, Lynch, Daniel C., Postel, Jon, Roberts, Larry G. and Wolff, Stephen, 'A Brief History of the Internet', www.isoc.org
2. Ibid.
3. Netto, Anil, from Inter Press Service, reproduced in *The Asian Age* (Bombay) 5 May 2000
4. Phan Thi Kim Phuc is a goodwill ambassador for UNESCO
5. Rushdie, Salman, 'Letter from India: A Dream of Glorious Return,' *The New Yorker*, 19 & 26 June 2000, p. 96
6. The virus was named 'Love Bug' because it infected computers through an intriguing email entitled 'I Love You'.
7. Schmid, John, in the *International Herald Tribune*, reproduced as 'A Word of Praise for a Media Wizard' in *The Asian Age* (Bangalore) 7 June 2000
8. News item, 'They Know What You Are Doing on the Internet', *The Economics Times* (Delhi), 16 June 2000

Arif Azad

The Success of Junoon[1]

Pakistan:

> was a word born in exile which then went east, was borne across or translated, and imposed itself on history; a returning migrant, settling down on partitioned land, forming a palimpsest on the past. A palimpsest obscures what lies beneath. To build Pakistan it was necessary to cover up Indian history, to deny that Indian centuries lay just beneath the surface of Pakistani Standard Time. The past was rewritten; there was nothing else to be done.
>
> It is possible to see the subsequent history of Pakistan as a duel between two layers of time, the obscured world forcing its way back through what-had-been-imposed. It is the true desire of every artist to impose his or her version on the world; and Pakistan, the peeling, fragmenting palimpsest, increasingly at war with itself, may be described as a failure of the dreaming mind. Perhaps the pigments used were the wrong ones, impermanent, like Leonardo's; or perhaps the place was insufficiently imagined, a picture full of irreconcilable elements, midriffbaring immigrants' saris versus demure indigenous Sindhi *shalwar-kurtas*, Urdu versus Punjabi, now versus then: a miracle that went wrong.

This extract from Salman Rushdie's novel *Shame* hits on the fault lines running through Pakistan's history. Since the country's creation – which came into being on 14 August 1947 as a Muslim state, in consequence of the Partition of India – state managers have endeavoured to create a new ideological basis for Pakistan. This has inevitably involved the denial of Pakistan's shared roots with India, and instead nailed its ideological colour to the mast of Middle Eastern ideology. The upshot was the construction of patriotism based on anti-Indian identity and wrapping up the state in the flag of Islam. The battle for artistic expression thus involves a daily battle with the state definition of patriotism and religious identity. A state that chooses to base itself on such powder-fragile foundations tends to police the parameters of cultural and artistic tastes with clumsy ruthlessness. From day one, it is no wonder then that the Pakistani state has kept a vigilant watch over artists critical of official truths. In return, artists with critical sensibilities have sought ways of creating an alternative narrative to counter the inherent falsehood of state ideology. This gargantuan struggle, involving the saying of the unsayable and the thinking of the unthinkable, has taken on many forms and spans literature, the performing arts and music.

Literature and theatre

In the arena of literary suppression, the fiction of pre-eminent writer Sadat Hassan Manto (1912-1955) fell under official censorship, and subsequent court cases threw an interesting spotlight on the way the officers of literature worked in a theocratic state. Poets were more fortunate than fiction writers in the sense that *ghazal* (a metrical literary composition), which has for centuries provided great scope for social comment due to its well-known resources of indirectness, afforded

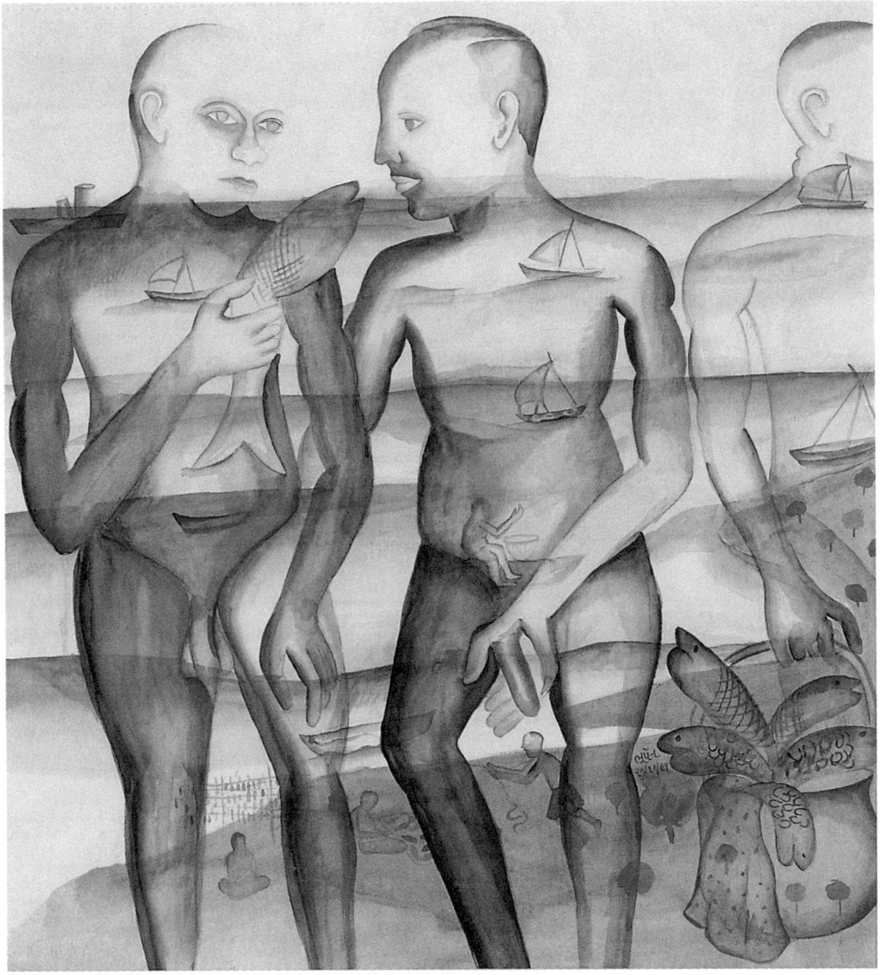

Bhupen Khakhar, India
***Figures on a Landscape*, acrylic on canvas, 1995**

Despite the sensuality of Indian art, homosexuality is rarely addressed in the country's modern art scene. The painter Bhupen Khakhar from Baroda has been influenced by his immediate environment. His work displays a candour about his own vulnerability, dreams and sexuality. There is 'a tension between naiveté and precision, between charm and pain, between autobiography and abstraction ... [Khakhar] acts as a "hinge" between east and west. He has found a language with which you can establish a dialogue between different cultures'. Khakhar was awarded a 2000 Prince Claus Award. (Jan Hoet, *2000 Prince Claus Awards*, The Hague: Prince Claus Fund) Photo: Gerry Hurkmans, courtesy of the Foundation for Indian Artists, Amsterdam

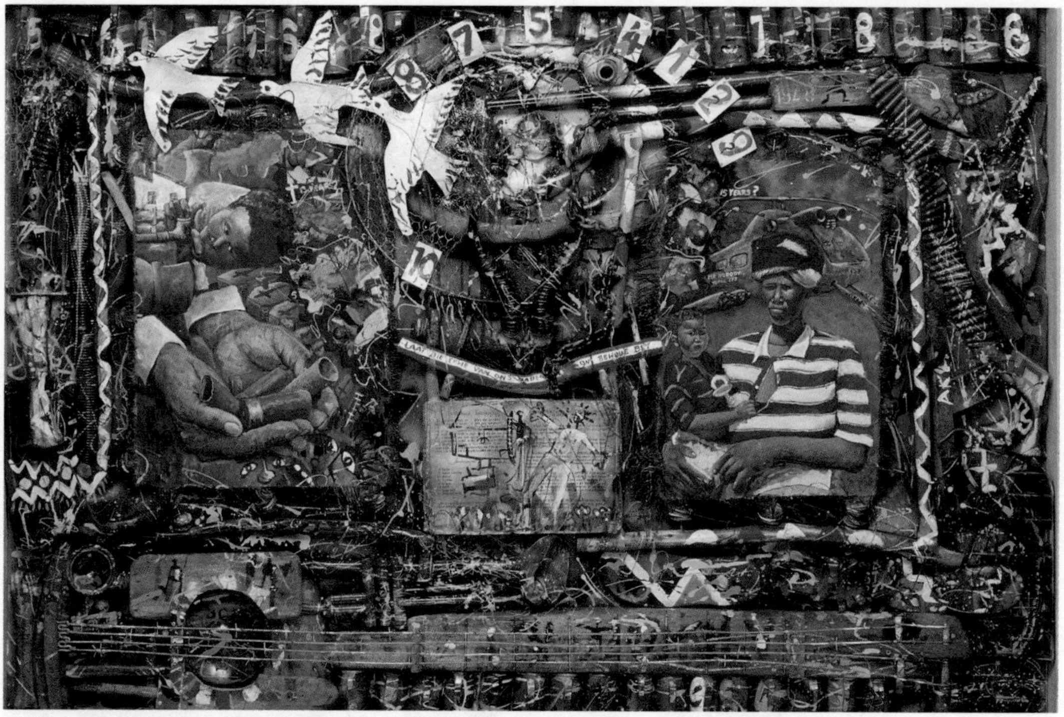

Willie Bester, South Africa
***Transition*, mixed media, 1994**

Willie Bester left school in the ninth grade and sold handmade crafts to avoid working for whites in apartheid South Africa. Later in Cape Town, he assisted a dental technician for fifteen years. Initially Bester wanted to keep his multimedia collages of newspaper cuttings, oil paint and found objects – discarded machine parts, sticks, tin cans and sheep bones – for himself. He maintains that his work 'depicts an era in our history that should be known by all. My art is a means to give a more reliable expression of living conditions in the townships.' (SARA (South Africa Resistance Art), http://library.thinkquest.org/18799/wbesgen.html)
Courtesy of Triangle Arts Trust, London

them a considerable leeway in encoding critical sensibility in metaphors and similes. In the course of time, *ghazal* acquired a permanent coded language that kept alive the circulation of dissident ideas. Pakistan's most famous poet, Faiz Ahmed Faiz (1911-1984), perfected the *ghazal* genre to spread his intensely private view of the rotten state of affairs in an increasingly theocratised state. Since then *ghazal* has become an established vehicle to convey critical and dissident voices.

In the performing arts, drama or theatre groups sought a space outside official avenues. During the time of military dictator General Zia-ul-Haq (1977-88), a heavy-handed suppression of the theatre, as indeed of any other artistic activity, was practised. A number of theatre groups emerged hand-in-hand with political opposition movements. In Pakistan, all theatre avenues are state-owned, and the scissors of censors operate with abandon. As a result, political theatre groups either took to the streets or performed in large, private homes – this avenue was soon blocked – or alternatively in German cultural centres in Karachi and Lahore, where the writ of censors was not enforced as rigidly as in state-owned venues. In those years when direct criticism of the martial law regime was considered a crime, the street theatre group Ajoka skirted around the authorities by performing Bertolt Brecht's plays to convey criticism of the repressive regime through adaptations relevant to the Pakistani situation.

Popular and devotional music

The ability of music to transmit critical sensibility has been recognised from time immemorial. From Nazi Germany to Soviet Russia, Kenya and Algeria, the state has resorted to heavy-handed suppression of politically charged music. In Pakistan, too, singers have sought to mount criticism of the deadening uniformity that the Pakistani state has sought to impose on music. The songs of the 'Melody Queen' Noor Jehan (1926-2000) remain hugely popular, despite the slings and arrows of religious zealots aimed at her music. Her songs carry a sense of the buoyant spirit of a woman fighting against the mighty institutional odds stacked against all women. Similar music based on politically charged poetry has remained off the air since the establishment of Pakistan. Musically rendered poetry by Faiz Ahmed Faiz is the clearest example of this. Only for brief spells during Pakistan's history, when left-of-centre governments of the Pakistan People's Party (PPP; 1971-77, 1988-90) were in office, was his poetry-based music permitted on the official airwaves. At all other times he has remained banned, although the immediacy of his poetry has earned him a lasting place in the hearts and minds of the people.

Even under General Zia's jackboots, musicians continued to create music that relieved the sorely distressed spirit of the nation. In an effort to impose official Islam, his dictatorial regime actively promoted devotional music as part of his larger aim of religionising society. Some musicians, however, chose to create and transmit a message of humanism, tolerance and diversity through Sufi music, as opposed to official monolithic Islam. Historically, tension has persisted between Sufi Islam and state-promoted Islam. While Sufi music spreads the message of brotherhood in its music, state-promoted Islam, on the other hand, abhors music and propagates soulless uniformity. The musical genius of Nusrat Fateh Ali Khan (1948-1997), the master who has done much to introduce the *Qawali* genre to the west, flowered as a result of creative tension between these two opposing forces.

Pop music and the rise of Junoon

Pop music generates responses different from local styles of music for reasons that have a lot do with Islam's strained dialogue with the west. Pop's western origin and the dance-related culture that it allegedly promotes are considered deeply subversive with regard to the official ideology that seeks to keep the country not only spiritually clean, but the bodies of its young people regulated and regimented – dance in all forms has remained banned from official channels since the days of General Zia. Indeed, the Muslim League administration headed by Prime Minister Nawaz Sharif (1997-99) made a great electoral play of the first pop concert broadcast live on Pakistan Television (PTV) where the long-suppressed youth mixed and danced ecstatically to welcome Benazir Bhutto's coming to power in 1988. This ingrained antipathy to pop music has remained a constant with the right-wing regime of Nawaz Sharif who has inherited conservative values from his one-time mentor General Zia. The principal reason why pop music has not received any official encouragement since independence can be found in the well-rooted conservative reflex in the psyche of the Pakistani establishment.

It was only under the first democratically elected government headed by the Pakistan People's Party (PPP) under Zulfikar Ali Bhutto (1971-77) that pop music made it onto the national television as a local ripple of the global rock wave. Alamgir and Mohammad Ali Shehki were the first pop singers to be broadcast nationally. This era of brief cultural openness was cruelly terminated when General Zia staged a right-wing military coup on 5 July 1977. Not surprisingly, pop music became the public enemy number one of the military dictator's constituency of right-wing zealots.

Despite official discouragement however, pop music continued to grow, thanks to mushrooming audio cassettes and the satellite music channels of the 1980s. This pop culture resulted from an interaction between the narrow music agenda pursued by the military dictator and the constant beaming of pop music from the satellite channels. In response to this new global youth culture, a plethora of pop groups burst onto the national scene in the early part of that decade. Most of the pop groups operated mainly underground, away from official scrutiny. By the end of the Eighties, it became necessary for liberal leaning politicians to make a nod in the direction of pop music in view of its popularity with Pakistani youth. After the long period of martial rule ended, Benazir Bhutto's PPP (1988-90) duly responded to young people's demands, and Pakistan Television invited all pop groups to perform live on television after long years in the underground wilderness. Predictably, the sight of long-suppressed youth dancing to the tune of pop music did not go down well with organised right-wing religious interests. The standard official reflex, formed during successive martial law regimes, has continued unchanged in respect to pop music despite brief spells of civilian rule. The story of the Pakistani rock trio, Junoon [Obsession], needs to be set against this backdrop.

The roots of Junoon began in another pop group, Vital Signs, whose first number 'Dil Dil Pakistan' [Pakistan Is Heart and Soul] was a great hit. Soon afterwards, guitarist and songwriter Salman Ahmed from Vital Signs teamed up with the wild boy of the Lahore underground pop scene, Ali Azmat, to form Junoon. Later, they were joined by Salman's childhood friend from the U.S., bass player Brian Thomas O'Connell. This powerful trio has catapulted the band to its current popularity. Junoon was quick to respond to the tastes and yearning of young people by soaking up the aspirations and frustrations of the generation reared under martial law, caught up in the pincer movement of repressive ideology at home and the liberalising influence of global rock music. Junoon's second album, *Talaash* [Quest], was a moderate success, but it set the tone for the

Heri Dono, Indonesia
Blooming in Arms, installation, 1996

When asked in 1996 what he looked forward to, Indonesian artist Heri Dono replied, 'To destroy the feelings of fear, to be able to talk freely, to develop individual opinion. This is dangerous to the [Suharto] Government, but I am optimistic. Information and human freedom cannot ultimately be stopped.' Dono's installation *Blooming in Arms* was an expression of this view. His use of objects like helmets and artificial limbs was politically loaded at that time. Dono's interview with Tim Martin was published in *Heri Dono*, a book that was banned in Indonesia because it included critical writings by the artist. Since Suharto's fall, it has now become available. (David Elliott and Gilane Tawadros, eds., *Heri Dono*, London: INIVA in collaboration with Museum of Modern Art Oxford, 1996, p. 41) Photograph courtesy of INIVA

Alfredo Jaar, Chile
***Rwanda Project*, 1994-2000**

After the artist Alfredo Jaar returned from Rwanda, he was invited to create a public project in Malmö, a small town in Sweden. He was offered 50 light boxes dispersed around the city. 'I was not yet ready to show the most horrifying images I had taken in my life, so I simply put up a sign which said Rwanda, Rwanda, Rwanda. I used the most common font, Helvetica Bold, and repeated the word as many times as I could. It was a kind of cry that no one was hearing. Because the light boxes had been offered to the institution sponsoring the art project, most of them were placed in marginal areas of the city. I actually liked that, the solitude of these cries lost in the city, it was a metaphor for the solitude of the Rwandan people during the killings. Rwanda, Rwanda.' (Alfredo Jaar, 'It Is Difficult', performance, 2001 New Delhi 'Truth and Reconciliation' conference organised by *Documenta 11* and the Prince Claus Fund) Photo courtesy of the artist

>>

incredibly popular third album, *Inquilaab* [Revolution]. Significantly, it featured three songs, 'Rooh Ki Pyas' [Quest of the Soul], 'Mein Kaun Hoon' [Who I Am] and 'Iltija' [Request] that abstractly hinted at political alienation and the identity crisis afflicting young people. It also included 'Jazba-e-Junoon' a song that became the signature tune of the 1996 Cricket World Cup. Musically, the band evolved a new vocabulary that is simple but indirect, like Urdu *ghazal*. They also incorporated Sufi music into a modern pop sound. The combination of the local and global hit a responsive chord with the young.

While Junoon grounded itself in the national imagination, there were also many sociopolitical changes occurring in the background. The decade-long iron rule of the military dictator General Zia, actively aided by the western powers and by religious zealots, had winnowed out any political or cultural opposition. Junoon's music was greatly appealing to the whole new generation of depoliticised youth that had meanwhile grown to adulthood. At the same time, the Pakistani political élite, after having been schooled by the military dictator, had solidified into a right-wing theocratic mould. Junoon's case clearly illustrates how illiberal and ideologically regressive the political élite has become, so that even the voicing of minimal sociopolitical demands through music is not acceptable to them. Pakistan state managers' thick-fisted treatment of Junoon clearly illustrates this point.

Heartened by the success of *Inquilaab*, Junoon began to address sociopolitical themes in its lyrics, thus delivering a big boost to the sociopolitical movements that had sprung up around that time. Junoon first overtly addressed politics when it gave voice to the deeply felt resentment over the growing curse of corruption in high places. In 1996, the song 'Ehtessaab' [Accountability] and its accompanying video tapped into the national mood. The video featured a horse dining from a table in a five-star hotel – a dig at the polo-loving husband of Prime Minister Benazir Bhutto. The then caretaker Prime Minister, Mairaj Khalid, immediately banned the video and song from television as they were deemed likely to prejudice the verdict of the voters in the approaching elections. This open criticism of corruption in high places earned Junoon the lasting enmity of the ruling class.

From then onwards Junoon became the *bête noire* of the Pakistani state. The group's declaration of support for an opposition politician, Imran Khan, only added fuel to the official fire ready to engulf dissident singers. In 1997, Junoon released its fourth album, *Azadi* [Freedom], which included the song 'Sayonee' [Confidant]. Within days 'Sayonee' topped the charts in both Pakistan and India. Again, the video was considered controversial. This time round objection was raised to the inclusion of sacred shrines in the video. This footage, according to the powerful vocal conservative lobby, amounted to the desecration of religious sites. Now everything Junoon did was open to well-organised criticism from the right-wing press and politicians.

Next came criticism from the Muslim League government, which criticised Junoon's rendition of disparate verses by Pakistan's national poet, Allama Iqbal (b. 1938), in the form of one song titled 'Khudi' [Self-awareness]. The national poet Iqbal has been appropriated by the Pakistani establishment to enhance its right-wing agenda. Emphasising aspects of his religious poetry rather than his progressive poetry has become a standard method of advancing the right-wing agenda. Criticism by religious purists and the ruling Muslim League party rested on the grounds that the group had exceeded poetic licence by joining together different verses to create one song. But the real reason lay elsewhere. It was the state vendetta against a pop group that dared to challenge ordered bounds on freedom of expression, by making creative use of Iqbal's verses.

Junoon's daring acts in defence of the freedom of artistic expression earned the group the ire of no less a person than Prime Minister Nawaz Sharif, who personally intervened towards the end of 1997 to ban Junoon from the official media. He publicly declared that from now on young people with long hair and blue jeans – a reference to a westernised youth now uninfluenced by official ideology – would not be permitted on state-owned media.

Junoon's controversial tour of India

Junoon's long-troubled relations with official ideology came to a head when the group visited India to sing at the Cine-Film award ceremony in March 1998. This was followed by a series of concerts across India, where fans mobbed the band. On the day India detonated a nuclear bomb, Junoon was performing to a packed crowd in Chandigarh, and criticised the looming nuclearisation of South Asia. Their popularity and open advocacy of cultural links rang alarm bells in the corridors of power across the border.

This was in line with what is by now a well-established pattern, whereby artists and writers visiting India are dubbed as traitors working to undermine the Pakistani state's two nation theory – which states that religion was the sole basis for the creation of Pakistan. Anyone who strives to find cultural similarities between India and Pakistan cuts at the roots of this ideology. In line with the state ideology, intelligence agencies have been keeping a close watch on artists visiting India. The moment an artist or writer speaks of a shared cultural history, intelligence agencies and organised right-wing interests in the media go into overdrive, maligning cultural visits and visiting artists. It is invariably a concerted and organised affair. Before Junoon, the street theatre group Ajoka came under official and unofficial criticism for having toured India and maligned the name of the country through plays. On returning from India, Junoon was called before officials of the Information Ministry to answer charges of 'belittling the concept of the ideology of Pakistan', 'disagreeing with national opinion' regarding the country's nuclear testing and talking of 'cultural similarities and hoped-for reunification'. The sitting Muslim League government used the Indian visit as an excuse to ban pop music from the official airwaves. However, despite the governmental ban, Junoon has continued to grow in popularity.

Through innovation and a certain musical flare alongside sociopolitical themes, Junoon has gained a permanent place in the history of Pakistani music. It has tasted all the creative fruits forbidden by the Pakistani establishment, while working within a fine balance of tradition and modernity. Absolute freedom is a *sine qua non* if artists are to look at the world in new ways. As rightly expressed by Turgenev, 'Without freedom in the widest sense of the word, in relation to oneself … to one's people and one's history, a true artist is unthinkable; without that air, it is impossible to breathe.' Junoon, after the fashion of true artists, is continuing to roll back the boundaries of a power-serving ideology, which keeps people in permanent mental and cultural bunkers.

1. 'The Success of Junoon' was written before the seizure of power by the military on 12 October 1999. Arif Azad thanks Professor Amin Mughal, Hasan Zaidi and Robert Nieuwenhuijs for their assistance.

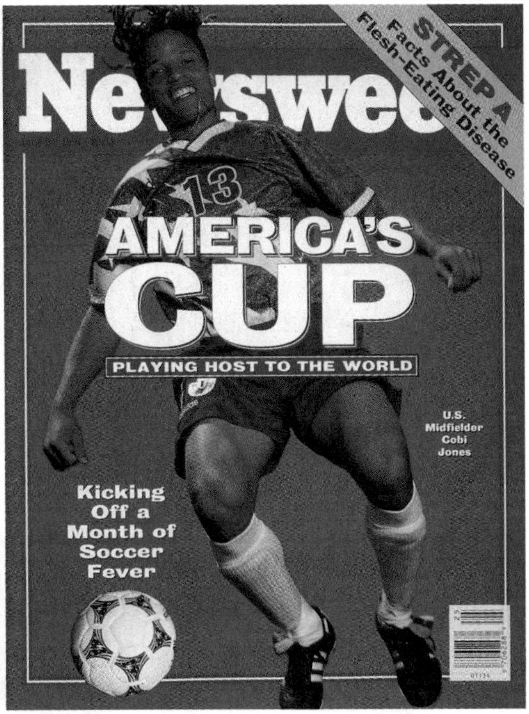

Alfredo Jaar, Chile
Rwanda Project, 1994-2000

As part of his *Rwanda Project*, Alfredo Jaar shows slides of *Newsweek* magazine covers at the same time reading facts about Rwanda. For the two covers, above, from 6 and 20 June 1994, the artist provides the following narrative: 'June 5, 1994: the U.S. argues with the UN over the cost of providing heavy armoured vehicles for the peacekeeping force. Five hundred thousand deaths. June 10, 1994: the killing of Tutsis and moderate Hutus continues, even in refugee camps. Six hundred thousand deaths. June 17, 1994: France announces its plan to send 2,500 troops to Rwanda as an interim peacekeeping force until the UN troops arrive. Seven hundred thousand deaths. June 22, 1994: with still no sign of UN deployment, the UN Security Council authorises the deployment of 2,500 French troops in south-west Rwanda. Eight hundred thousand deaths.' By the time *Newsweek* devoted its 1 August 1994 cover to the genocide in Rwanda, over three million people had been murdered. (Alfredo Jaar, 'It Is Difficult', performance, 2001 New Delhi 'Truth and Reconciliation' conference organised by *Documenta 11* and the Prince Claus Fund) Photos courtesy of the artist

>>

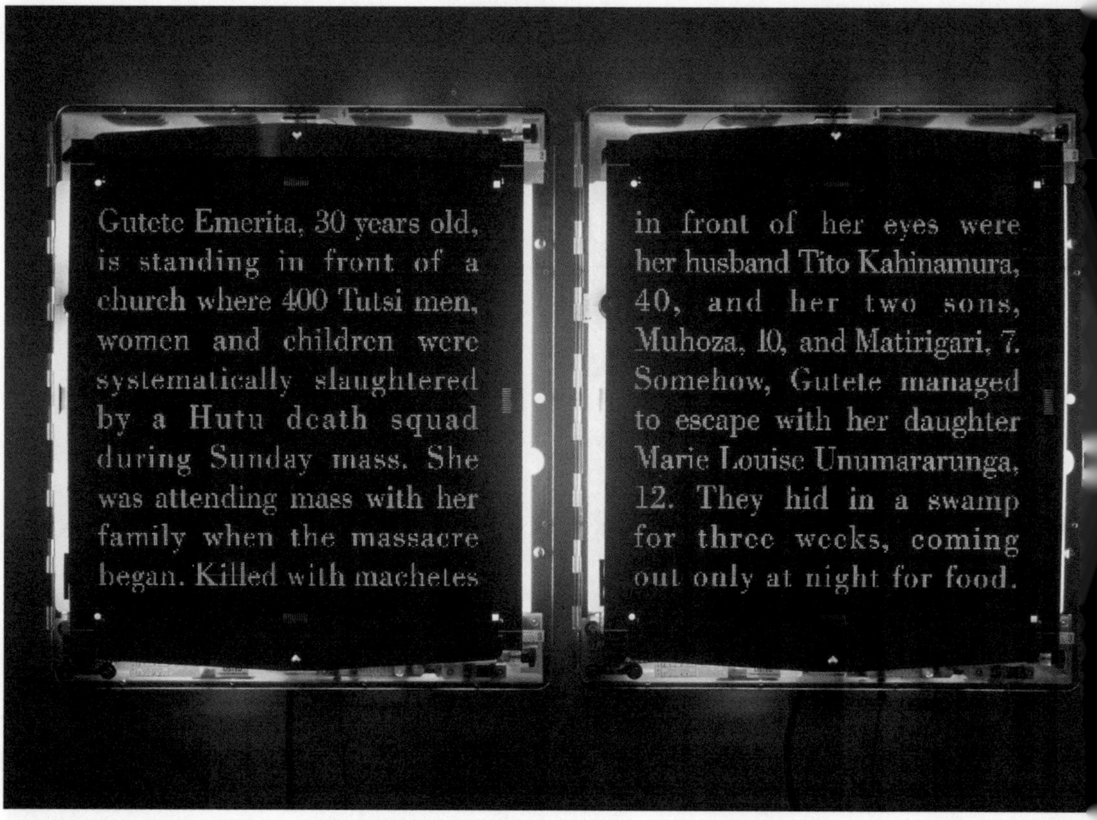

Alfredo Jaar, Chile
***Rwanda Project*, 1994-2000**

'This is another installation with two quadvision boxes. The text: "Gutete Emerita, 30 years old, is standing in front of a church where 400 Tutsi men, women and children were systematically slaughtered by a Hutu death squad during Sunday mass. She was attending mass with her family when the massacre began. Killed with machetes in front of her eyes were her husband Tito Kahinamura, 40, and her two sons, Muhoza, ten, and Matirigari, seven. Somehow, Gutete managed to escape with her daughter Marie Louise Unumararunga, twelve. They hid in a swamp for three weeks, coming out only at night for food." This text stays on the screen for 45 seconds. For those very few who are patient and stay here, they will see the next sequence: "Her eyes look lost and incredulous. Her face is the face of someone who has witnessed an unbelievable tragedy and now wears it. She has returned to this place in the woods because she has nowhere else to go. When she speaks about her lost family, she gestures to the corpses on the ground, rotting in the African sun." This text will last 30 seconds and move on.' (Alfredo Jaar, 'It Is Difficult', performance, 2001 New Delhi 'Truth and Reconciliation' conference organised by *Documenta 11* and the Prince Claus Fund) Photo courtesy of the artist

Ahmed Abdalla

The Arabic Satellite News Network: Al-Jazeera

When a videotape of Osama Bin Laden threatening the U.S. with more terror was delivered to Al-Jazeera's trusted Kabul correspondent Tayfeer Alouni shortly after 11 September 2001, he knew he was sitting on an incendiary world exclusive. He called Al-Jazeera's executives for advice. Without watching the footage, they told Alouni to broadcast it immediately. Al-Jazeera does not bury bad news. The tape was televised, unfiltered, uncensored, from the Middle East to the world, and Al-Jazeera created more news as a result: anti-American riots erupted in Gaza City and the cult of Bin Laden was strengthened; fear and loathing grew in the U.S., together with a certain bitterness that Bin Laden could win the propaganda war with one speech to one camera, and a mainline into the biggest, freest, most popular Arabic news station ever.

Al-Jazeera does not try to filter reality to create a perception of a restrained, diplomatic objectivity that tiptoes on the tightrope between opposing opinions. The Qatar-based station's concept of objectivity is to show 'the view and the other view' (a slogan it trumpets with pride), beaming both extremities around the world, and creating a new space of freedom in between.

Al-Jazeera's unflinching coverage of the attack on Afghanistan and the airtime it gave to Bin Laden epitomised the station's comfort with controversy – a price it willingly pays for its pioneering, fiercely independent style. Since Al-Jazeera's creation in 1996, every single country in the Arab League has taken offence at the station's brusque style and made a complaint; the U.S. joined the condemnation when they filed a formal diplomatic complaint with Qatar, criticising the station for being a conduit for al-Qaida, Bin Laden's terrorist network. 'At best, Osama Bin Laden's message is propaganda, calling on people to kill Americans,' the White House press secretary Ari Fleischer said. 'At worst, he could be issuing orders to his followers to initiate attacks.'[1] But for Al-Jazeera it is anathema to impose a no-platform policy. The liberal philosophy of their commentary programmes[2] suffuses their news coverage too.

Despite the official complaints and the reservations about Al-Jazeera, the network provides a unique window on the Arab world and its political sensibilities. A subtitle on the channel during the first night of the U.S. bombing of Kabul described the Taliban firing at 'the enemy's planes'. Interestingly, the U.S. had to depend on Al-Jazeera during the early days of the attack on Afghanistan for its exclusive pictures of the bombing – Al-Jazeera was the only news channel to have working offices in Kabul under the Taliban. The U.S. was forced into the rare position of being reliant on foreign media, even if the pictures it broadcast of civilian casualties were detrimental to the U.S. propaganda war. The U.S. government was also conscious of the massive popularity of Al-Jazeera in the Middle East and beyond: the station reaches more than 35 million Arabs, including 150,000 in the U.S. (At the height of the war, CNN only broadcast to three million.) Accordingly, cabinet members Colin Powell, Condoleezza Rice, and Donald Rumsfeld all appeared on Al-Jazeera to try to convince the Arab world that this was a war on terrorism, not a war on Islam. Charlotte Beers, the U.S. under secretary of state for public diplomacy, even considered buying advertising space on the channel to get the American message across.

But when western stations reopened their Kabul offices after the Taliban left town and the U.S. no longer had to rely on the controversial station for its gritty pictures of the bombing, the Al-Jazeera offices themselves were bombed. Al-Jazeera officials believed it was a deliberate strike, a U.S. conspiracy to win control of the propaganda campaign. The chief editor, Ibrahim Hilal, said: 'I still believe the decision to exclude our office from the coverage was taken weeks before the bombing. But I don't think they would do that while we were the only [news broadcasters] in Kabul.' The Pentagon dismissed Al-Jazeera's claims as just a conspiracy theory. U.S. military spokesman Colonel Hoey said the Pentagon did not have the location co-ordinates of the Al-Jazeera office in Kabul – even though the broadcaster said it had passed them on, several times, via its partner CNN in Washington, D.C. 'The U.S. military does not and will not target media,' Hoey said. 'We would not, as a policy, target news media organisations – it would not even begin to make sense.'[3]

Just as the Gulf War made CNN famous in the west and infamous in the east, the attack on Afghanistan gave Al-Jazeera the opposite standing – famous in the east and infamous in the west. A station almost unknown outside the Arab world before 11 September 2001, it has now become the focus of U.S. attention because of its perceived anti-American, pro-al-Qaida bias. The station was approached, together with CNN, by a man claiming to represent al-Qaida, asking them to submit questions to Bin Laden. The cautious reaction of CNN throws into sharp relief the gung-ho attitude of Al-Jazeera, which had already broadcast an interview with Bin Laden in 1998. Wolf Blitzer, the CNN anchorman, said: 'We want to stress that CNN has no information about Bin Laden or whether he is dead or alive. We do not know how al-Qaida communicates with Al-Jazeera or how Al-Jazeera plans to get the questions to Bin Laden.'[4] The implication is of a dubious connection between Al-Jazeera and al-Qaida – a significant mistrust of Al-Jazeera's professionalism which is entirely misplaced.

Professionalism

The channel may be immature and prone to a 'scoop' mentality – a willy-nilly attitude towards fast-breaking news that characterises less seasoned media organisations – but it is not naive. Long before Al-Jazeera aroused the suspicions of the west, its long-standing popularity in the Arab world came about as a result of its precise professionalism as well as its liberal principles. Al-Jazeera's professionalism began with the conscious realisation of this raison d'être. The managing director Mohamed Jasem Al-Ali explained, 'Arab viewers used to get their entertainment from local channels but relied on foreign channels for their "news and views". Based in the Arab world, we tried to fill that vacuum. We stormed a field from which others escaped. It was a risk, but the popularity of this type of programming by the BBC and CNN was an indication that we too might be successful.' A measure of Al-Jazeera's success is the fact that, with its new-found worldwide prominence, advertisers are now lining up – and just in time: the $130m grant from the Emir of Qatar, Sheikh Hamad Bin Khalifa al-Thani, which has been subsidising the station, runs out at the end of 2001.

Entry into the unmapped Arab world of independent news media was no guarantee of success, no matter how much courage or calculation was involved. Attracting viewers required a more cohesive philosophy. Al-Ali said, 'We began by addressing the problem of objectivity, impartiality and respect for the viewer's discretion. Thus precise information became our bridge to the viewer's trust.'

Precise information, however, does not completely account for the prestige attained by such a small channel over a relatively short period of time. Other dimensions of professionalism are no less important: charismatic broadcasters who are masters of classical Arabic, alert correspondents – like Tayfeer Alouni in Kabul – who quickly follow up events, and an impressive list of commentators and guests, including foreign analysts who speak Arabic – something quite fascinating to Arabic viewers.

Hélio Oiticica, Brazil
***Seja marginal, seja herói*, silkscreen on nylon, 1968 edition, replica 1992**

Wearable art, elaborate installations, paintings, drawings, sculptures and public events created by Brazilian artist Hélio Oiticica (1937-1980) explored the interior and exterior spaces of the body, all within the framework of modern Brazil. His ideas about society and the environment challenged viewers to participate with his interactive art through touch, taste, smell, even movement, during walks through Rio's shanty towns – all part of the 'experimental exercise of liberty', a phrase coined by Mario Pedrosa that was often used by Oiticica. (Simone Osthoff, 'Lygia Clark and Hélio Oiticica: A Legacy of Interactivity and Participation for a Telematic Future', *Leonardo On-line*, 20 August 1988, www.mitpress.com/e-journals/Leonardo/-isast/spec.projects/osthoff/osthoffpt2.html) Photo: B. Goedewaagen, courtesy of Witte de With, Rotterdam

David Koloane, South Africa
Untitled, pencil on paper, 1995

At a time when black South Africans had restricted access to art education, painter David Koloane was instrumental in setting up initiatives for black artists. Currently the chairman of the Bag Factory, the artists' studio complex in Johannesburg, he 'explored abstraction, which came to offer a powerful mode of resistance against the perceived dictates of a predominantly white, western-oriented market – a market which often still persists in viewing abstraction as an inauthentic idiom for black artists'. In 1998, Koloane received a Prince Claus Award. (Jennifer Law, 'Unleashing Energies', in *Cross Currents: Contemporary Art Practice in South Africa*, eds. John Picton and Jennifer Law, Somerset: Atkinson Gallery, 2000, p. 15) Courtesy of Robert Loder

These subjective features are enhanced by the more objective attractions of fast-breaking news, informative programmes, instructive documentaries – translated or tailored – and amusing talk shows.

To Al-Jazeera, talk shows are no less important than the news. Al-Jazeera walks on two legs, or rather flies with two wings – news and views. Illustrating this is a promotion spot with a broadcaster's voice referring to Al-Jazeera's 'journey behind events everywhere' while remaining true to its promise to show both sides of every story.

This brings Al-Jazeera more closely into the arena of freedom of expression, but Al-Ali still analysed it as a challenge of professionalism. 'There are demarcation lines for a professional operation: in order to present a view we must also present the other view. And if a representative of the other view is not present, the broadcaster himself should present it[5] or let viewers do so by telephone. The channel does not endorse a particular viewpoint or adopt a particular cause. But given enough space, just causes press their point and gain sympathy.'

Freedom

An efficient, professional media can be a catalyst for freedom in the political sense. However, freedom is not necessarily a by-product of professionalism, either in society in general or in the media in particular. Freedom is the one just cause that is served by an ardent and endless effort to deliberately realise it. Are Al-Jazeera's men (and, notably, women) unaware of a subconscious drive for freedom? On the contrary, freedom of debate is their totally conscious motivation and the yardstick of their professional performance.[6]

Al-Jazeera has served the cause of freedom in the Arab media by broadcasting political, on-air talk shows, discussing thorny issues, allowing unconventional views, hosting opposition politicians and intellectuals and by airing viewers' opinions received by telephone and fax.

In doing so, Al-Jazeera has become an initiator and an accelerator of competition in the Arab satellite media. This is positive feedback from its professional standards. The lesson here: not only does censorship curtail freedom, it is also responsible for bad journalism. This is an axiom Al-Jazeera has passed on to the bulk of the Arab media – which is free of freedom. Al-Jazeera's very creation was a reaction to censorship. The station replaced a BBC Arabic news channel which collapsed when its Saudi Arabian sponsors deemed it too liberal and pulled the plug. With the munificence of the Emir and the rehired BBC staff, Al-Jazeera was created to broadcast what censored stations would not be inclined to.

By combining a good news service and the free expression of views, Al-Jazeera has brought the Arab viewer to the qualitatively higher level of having informed views, rather than merely ending up with an expression of an impression. The channel's insistence on broadcasting the opposite poles of an emotive issue enhances the process of democratisation in the Arab world by presenting aspects of freedom of expression and acknowledging pluralism. As a result, this format of an audio-visual Athens – albeit by satellite – constitutes a socialisation process which teaches viewers how to debate (and not to listen unthinkingly to official clichés from other Arab channels).

The experience is enhanced by Al-Jazeera's participatory framework, which gives viewers airtime in talk shows. The demand from viewers who wish to have their say is astonishing; scores of them wait on the telephone and send faxes. The need and obvious enjoyment of expressing themselves is a reflection of the many grievances harboured by Arab citizens under stifling political systems in their own countries.

By addressing Arab viewers in the Middle East and North Africa and in the world at large, and by making a point of covering the affairs of all Arab countries, Al-Jazeera has established itself as a pan-Arab channel while other stations remain parochial, tied to a particular region and to a particular government. Al-Jazeera's diverse list of guests on both sides of programming – news and views – has influenced the formation of an Arab political and intellectual élite. Some of Al-Jazeera's guests, a number of whom made their first appearances on the channel, have become well-known figures at home and abroad.

By linking the global with the regional, Al-Jazeera has contributed to the ongoing debate about globalisation. As well as having grievances against the autocracy of their national systems, Arab citizens also have grievances against the imbalances and injustices of the global system – issues which have become even more urgent since 11 September 2001. Some would adopt isolationism, especially in reaction to the west, as a premise for attaining Arab independence and freedom. Al-Jazeera's broadcasting has prompted an alternative means of attaining Arab rights through the interactive process of engagement with the rest of the world – even if its relationship with the U.S. remains turbulent.

The channel takes pride in having replaced CNN and the BBC in providing Arab viewers with a good news service, with management and personnel almost exclusively Arab.

Critique

Al-Jazeera's trajectory to success was not smooth and its current authority and acceptability in the west is still tenuous.[7] Since the beginning it has provoked the animosity of many influential groups: Arab governments (literally all of them), political parties, other competing TV channels, writers and journalists. But the criticism is wide-ranging: there is a considerable distance between the accusations that Al-Jazeera is pro-Iraqi and that it is pro-Israeli.[8] This suggests that complaints arise out of a piqued pride; to Al-Jazeera complaints are therefore proof that they are doing something right:

> We do not exaggerate when we say Al-Jazeera is no more the channel of 'The View and the Other View', as it describes itself. It devotes itself to the release of the poison and malice of those anti-Iraqi trivial mercenaries.
>
> Director of Information, Iraqi Culture Ministry, *Al-Watan* (28 August 1999)

> While I welcome free dialogues, I am surprised that this freedom is meant to insult a particular state. In the Arab world there are ugly things from which Saudi Arabia stands aloof.
>
> Turki Al-Sedairi, *Al-Riyadh* (12 December 1998)

> Those in charge of this channel do not miss an opportunity to insult Egypt and attack it.
>
> Mohamed Al-Zahhar, *Al-Akhbar* (11 October 1997)

> A fierce war is being launched against Kuwait by satellites, headed by this evil channel that is born a bastard and will be buried with its staff of mercenaries.
>
> Rashed Al-Radaan, *Al-Watan* (18 December 1997)

> Al-Jazeera went too far in attacking us in Jordan through this programme presented by a Syrian saturated with the political propositions of his leaders on the one hand and Zionist propaganda on the other.
>
> Abu-Shrek, *Shaihan* (7 November 1998)

Malangatana, Mozambique
***War Account*, acrylic on canvas, 1992**

'Malangatana was raised amid the myths and realities of Mozambique, as the assistant to a healer when his mother was beset by a mental illness. He became a servant and tennis ball boy, struggling to earn a living ...' In 1959, a Portuguese architect gave Malangatana a studio and an income. His paintings were an inspiration for the Mozambique independence movement. Exhibitions followed but political activity and imprisonment delayed his return to the arts until 1981. His works 'denounce social injustice ... establish communication and thus help to change reality.' In 1997, Malangatana received a Prince Claus Award.
(Paulo Soares, *'Art on the Move'*, *Art from the Frontline: Contemporary Art from Southern Africa*, Frontline States Ltd/Kariia Press, 1990, p. 122) Courtesy of the artist

Cildo Meireles, Brazil
Incerções circuitos ideologicos: Projecto Coca-Cola**, Coca Cola bottles, transferred text, unlimited samples, 1970**

Cildo Meireles 'has lived in several parts of Brazil from the central plateau, including the capital Brasilia, to the Amazon region and remote areas of Rio de Janeiro state. [His] artistic career was exposed to the military dictators and the problems it entailed: repression, censorship and more. He was obliged to resort to guerrilla tactics, namely the creation of new political metaphors, deploying counter-information and using the element of surprise ... even showing his work outside the ordinary art circuits'. In 1999, Meireles received a Prince Claus Award. (Frederico Morais, 'Nowhere is My Home', *1999 Prince Claus Awards*, The Hague: Prince Claus Fund, p. 54)
Photo: Collection New Museum of Contemporary Art © Phaidon Press

> Al-Jazeera does everything except TV and journalism. This thing that is called Al-Jazeera is a non-identified visual idiot, a total incarnation of anti-television and bluffing.
>
> Mohamed El-Gahs, *Libération* (22 April 1999)

> I reject the present orientation of Al-Jazeera. It provoked our Arab brothers whom we won through Qatari diplomacy. Everything we gained can be lost in a few minutes because of Al-Jazeera's approach.
>
> Mohamed Youssef, *Al-Raya* (6 July 1998)

> Al-Jazeera adopts a scandalous attitude based towards Saddam Hussein against the UN.
>
> Abdel-Aziz Al-Khamees, *Al-Jadeeda* (4 March 1998)

Al-Jazeera's main weapon of defence is its viewers, millions of them, who appreciate its service and find themselves reflected in its broadcasts. In populist terms, Al-Jazeera is stronger than its adversaries. But this should not prejudice the more serious criticisms levelled against the channel or, even more importantly, the need to acknowledge the limitations and drawbacks of its structure and service.

Al-Jazeera is a 'free' news channel, but, paradoxically, it is also state-funded (like the BBC) – a dependent relationship that probably makes it vulnerable to censorship or self-censorship in the interests of national security. There is nothing to guarantee the continuing coincidence of interest between Al-Jazeera and the Qatari state, which has gained tremendous prestige through its hosting of the channel. Al-Jazeera is a contemporary version of the Medici style of renaissance, enlightenment and modernisation: the subsidising family remains in control until the subsidised agent gains full autonomy over a long historical process, with compromise and constraints imposed or self-imposed along the way.

Al-Jazeera's pluralism leaves it in a vulnerable position in the Middle East. Large Arab states such as Egypt, Iraq and Syria have all threatened to ban the channel. After 11 September 2001, the U.S. examined ways of blocking satellite reception of Al-Jazeera for its citizens, but they found the technology too complex and too diffuse to obstruct. Smaller countries too have the means to hit back at the channel: Kuwait mobilised its press and Tunisia its diplomatic apparatus.

What Al-Ali referred to as 'difficulties' are more a matter of pressure than actual crises. Al-Jazeera has deftly narrowed the range of items which might alienate certain Arab governments, including Jordan, where the channel's office has been closed. It is an ongoing game which requires, at the very least, mitigating the language of criticism from time to time.[9] More importantly, Al-Jazeera, for all its journalistic objectivity, does not cover the corruption of the ruling élites of Arab states. While criticism of Arab regimes is allowed, the mentioning of leaders by name is avoided.

In particular, sensitivities surrounding religious issues impose a priori calculations of reactions on the part of the channel. This was explained by Maher Abdalla, the presenter of *Sharia and Life*, Al-Jazeera's only talk show on religious issues, where the one guest taking questions from viewers is an authority on religious matters.

> My conviction is that there are no administrative restrictions on discussing religious issues but there are cultural restrictions. However, I do not hesitate to tread onto some sensitive terrain, like inviting a Shi'ite sheikh in a predominantly Sunni society. To some people this is [dangerous ground]. Nevertheless, I tell my critics it is not wrong to invite a Shi'ite once a year – that is one-fifty-second of the space of our weekly programme.[10] The one aspect I have to take into account

> – willingly or not – is that this programme needs to be credible to its viewers. You are a journalist and showmaker and you cannot afford to lose your viewers. This is not to be opportunistic. But I must invite guests who have religious credibility to the man in the street. The latter sometimes asks simple questions, while we are discussing sophisticated issues. Also, many protest telephone calls come from the conservative environment of the Gulf. When a guest of the programme adopted the notion of citizenship, some viewers considered this yielding to western pressure. Some even think we have an agenda aiming at the destruction of Islam altogether.

Al-Jazeera lives with the contradiction of its dual discourse: sober language for the news and fiery language for the views. While it goes to lengths to use terminology which is not value-charged in its news bulletins (for example distinguishing between freedom fighters and terrorists), it lets the fires flame in its views programmes – even at the cost of being attacked by the press in certain countries or having its offices closed there.

The channel's sensational talk shows are often criticised for their abrasive language in which the outcome turns into 'a mere release of tensions that express themselves in talk rather than action'.[11] The bulk of the attacks are directed at Al-Jazeera's most sensational talk show, *The Opposite Direction*. This programme has infuriated every Arab government; some take action while others let it be known where they stand. Al-Ali admitted that, 'We have problems with governments. But some of them do not respond to our queries and everyone accuses us of bias. There is also a scarcity of speakers from certain Arab countries.'

For the presenter of *The Opposite Direction*, Faisal Al-Kassem, the programme's format and ratings are interconnected:

> The political programme … requires a theatrical touch. Why not? It must be exciting and there is no harm in some allurement and sensation. Political programmes in the Arab world usually attract only the élite. We aim at attracting a larger constituency that had hitherto no interest in politics. All strata watch our programme, including young people and housewives. This is an achievement in itself. We are criticised for having a show of 'cockfighting', and, truly, some episodes have been really hot. But if that were all, Arab governments would not have become that furious about it [twenty volumes of articles written against it in three years]. The programme deals with the most sensitive topics and has hosted persons no one had dared to invite before. In so doing we have been true to Al-Jazeera's slogan of 'The View … and the Other View'. The culture of dialogue is absent in the Arab media, where you have one opinion. Instead of settling differences by bullets and warfare, dialogue can be a safety valve for the Arabs.

The Opposite Direction, according to Al-Kassem, has had an impact. 'The fruit of our programme is raising awareness and motivating the mind in the long term. Years would prove it was not a mere release of tensions.' It remains to be seen whether Al-Jazeera's talk shows represent a flash of lightning that quickly extinguishes, or a radiation of enlightenment that will endure, reach maturity and become a part of culture.

Like any other channel, Al-Jazeera is faced with the subjectivity of its own broadcasters. This difficulty is more acutely felt than at other channels, since Al-Jazeera purports to be freer than most Arab channels where broadcasters are merely parrots echoing official pronouncements. Like its societal milieu, Al-Jazeera has its own Islamists, secularists and nationalists. Elements of in-house ideological disagreements, power struggles and professional jealousies are to be found within Al-Jazeera off-screen.

Nalini Malani, India
Remembering Toba Tek Singh, installation, 1998

For *Remembering Toba Tek Singh*, an installation by the Indian artist Nalini Malani, the viewer listens through headphones to the story by Sadat Hasan Manto, while entering a rectangular room, where images are projected on the walls. On the floor, television sets in crates show fragments from world newscasts of the religious conflicts in India and of forced migration during the 1947 Partition, when 500,000 people lost their lives and twelve to fourteen million were left homeless. Malani's work is a criticism of the present situation in divided India that culminated in the 1998 underground nuclear tests conducted by India and Pakistan. She also reflects on history, the consequences of colonialism and the macho behaviour of the powers-that-be. Photo: Gert Jan van Rooij, courtesy of the World Wide Video Festival, Amsterdam

Fernando Alvim, Angola
***War and Art of Elsewhere*, film, 2001**

This 'faction' film – part fiction, part documentary – made by Fernando Alvim with Valerie van Nitsen – reflects the artist's multimedia art intervention *Memorias Intimas Marcas* [Memory Intimacy Traces] based on the Angolan-South African war. Alvim and two other artists, Carlos Garaicoa from Cuba and Gavin Younge from South Africa, were dropped at the Cuito Cuanavale military airstrip. 'During their twelve-day visit ... they found themselves marked, yet again, by a trauma repeating itself well after the impression of its demise: on the fourth day, their Angolan guide was mutilated by a landmine.' Both the film and exhibition engage in 'the psychic trauma of war, the wounding of social memory, and the meaning of African identity'.
(Brenda Atkinson, 'The Intimate Marks of War', Za@play, www.mg.co.za/mg/art/fineart/9804/980423-memorias.html, 23 April 1998) Film still courtesy of the artist

The style of presentation of each individual broadcaster adds another dimension which amplifies the differences. Al-Jazeera's off-screen mélange is concrete proof of its belief in and practice of pluralism, although it takes considerable executive ability to manage the differences.

Al-Jazeera is also faced with the subjectivity of its viewing constituency. It takes pride in having reached millions of viewers inside and outside the Arab world. Yet, every group of viewers appears to have a stake in the channel, as well as something to hate about it: Islamists vs. secularists, traditionalists vs. modernists, pro-Iraqis vs. anti-Iraqis, pro-reconciliation vs. pro-confrontation over the Middle East conflict, even pro-Kosovans vs. anti-NATO. 'My viewers are split in their opinions and I have to present both views,' insisted Al-Ali.

Pluralism is the mother of ambivalence. Everyone wishes to make a space for her or his own freedom, be it individually or collectively. To instil a universal belief in freedom on the part of its viewers would be an impossible mission for Al-Jazeera. Instead, the channel tries to promote freedom in a real way. According to Abdalla from *Sharia and Life*, 'To us, the problem of freedom is connected to other social and cultural dimensions. It is not a question of abstract priority. But the fact that we generally speak up and deviate somewhat from convention means that we are not identifying with freedom just as a slogan. On the contrary, we are practising it as a form of behaviour.'

Conclusion

Within the context of Arab media, it is no small credit to both its news objectivity and its liberty of views that Al-Jazeera has succeeded over a short span of time in attracting such a large audience; in linking, on subjects of common interest, Arabs from the interior and from the outside; in allowing viewers from the silent majority to speak up; in giving visibility to the ignored members of the disenchanted élite; in making a place for professional standards in Middle Eastern news broadcast; in sowing the seeds of uncensored debate and a culture of dialogue; in opening the critical eye of the viewers;[12] in accelerating competition for quality broadcasts from that part of the world (at least in the satellite sphere); in forcing 'freedom' as an issue for realisation, thus pushing the enemies of freedom into the defensive (creating space by default); and in sustaining the pressure for broader democratisation in the Arab world.

Al-Jazeera has achieved many of these Ten Commandments in the five years since its creation. Despite its problematic relationship with the west, it has successfully shifted the paradigm of mass communication in the Arab world and is building the dialogic framework that will eventually facilitate increased democratisation. Its integral coverage of the war on terrorism will be crucial in establishing Al-Jazeera as a major media player – a bridge to the west, and a liberator of the Arab nation.

Additional research by James Westcott

The editors took the liberty of changing the essay,
'The Arabic Satellite News Network: Al-Jazeera',
after the 11 September 2001 terrorist attacks in New York City.

1. Deans, Jason; 'UK TV to Show Bin Laden Footage', *The Guardian*, 11 October 2001
2. Faisal Al-Kassem, presenter of talk show *The Opposite Direction* has said: 'No matter how much I disagree with certain views, I still defend to death their right to be presented, as Voltaire said.'
3. Wells, Matt; 'How Smart Was This Bomb?', *The Guardian*, 19 November 2001
4. *The Guardian*, 17 October 2001
5. In presenting the 'other view' through his programme *No Frontiers*, the broadcaster, Ahmed Mansour, known to have a background of Islamic ideology, was accused, ironically, of being anti-Islamic. He had to remind his viewers that it was a prerequisite of his job to behave this way.
6. The Al-Jazeera broadcaster Faisal Al-Kassem explained: 'There is no contradiction between being professional and missionary at the same time. You cannot be purely neutral in the media. You have a mission to accomplish. We are good professionals because we present all views. But we have an emblem, and in one way or another we propagate freedom and we have a space for it more than others.' (Interview, 1 September 1999).
7. 'Since almost all hard news coming from the war zone comes from Al-Jazeera, its coverage is often cited, but generally with the proviso that this information "cannot be independently confirmed", as if there were any question about its credibility. There is more than a hint of racism in this double gesture of simultaneously relying on and undermining Al-Jazeera's reporting.

   'Among the pots calling the kettle black, *The New York Times* opined that Al-Jazeera "often slants its news with a vicious anti-Israel and anti-American bias" and "deeply irresponsible reporting [that] reinforces the region's anti-American views". Dan Rather questioned whether there was "any indication that Osama Bin Laden has helped finance this operation". Britain's *Daily Telegraph* called the station "Bin Laden TV," while NPR [National Public Radio in the U.S.] warned listeners that Al Jazeera's coverage should "come with a health warning".' Ibish, Hussein and Abunimah, Ali; 'The CNN of the Arab World Deserves Our Respect', *Los Angeles Times*, 22 October 2001
8. The JSC has been nicknamed the 'Jewish' Satellite Channel by some opponents.
9. As Faisal Al-Kassem, presenter of the most popular and also the most hated talk show *The Opposite Direction*, admitted: 'I do not succumb to intimidation. But when criticised, I try to redress the balance in a professional way.' (Interview, 1 September 1999)
10. The presenter of the programme was also preparing to invite a prominent Christian patriarch.
11. Salama, Ahmed; 'Cursing without Dialogue', *Al-Ahram*, (Egypt, 10 August 1999)
12. Also to Al-Jazeera's own weaknesses and shortcomings in form and content, for example being 'mild' on Qatar and other Gulf states or not putting on its screen a single news broadcaster from the largest Arab country, Egypt. Both the managing director of Al-Jazeera and the host of *The Opposite Direction* affirm that Qatar, too, was subject to scrutiny, for example in the editions of *The Opposite Direction* entitled 'Why is this Qatari rushing towards Israel?' and 'Is Qatar off-line in the Gulf Cooperation Council?' As Faisal Al-Kassem explained, 'Gulf states are five times more angry at us than other Arab governments.'

Yinka Shonibare, Nigeria / UK
***Vacation*, wax printed cotton textile, fiberglass, 2000**

The history of the textile used by Yinka Shonibare begins in Holland, where the batik print process obtained in Indonesia through colonialism made its way to Africa. Shonibare's outer space figures, above, turn this history upside down and question colonial patterns of trade and importance. His art 'signifies the inventive appropriation of [the material's] ideogrammatic character by Africans who now have found numerous ways to weave their own narratives, hence new ownership, into the surface of the cloth'. (Okwui Enwezor, 'Tricking the Mind', *Authentic Ex-Centric*, Ithaca: Forum for African Arts Inc.,/Prince Claus Fund Library, 2001, p. 214) Installation at Tate Britain, 2000, courtesy of the artist and the Stephen Friedman Gallery

António Ole, Angola
***Hidden pages, Stolen Bodies*, mixed media installation, 1996-2001**

The history of slavery was hidden not only in the west but also in Africa, where the role of Africans was never discussed. António Ole literally took documents out of the dust, by going into the archives of the city council of Benguela, Angola's national symbol of the slave trade. His placement of historical documents and old film footage in new settings has resulted in 'rewriting the history of slavery. The power of Ole's work derives from the poetic manner of his treatment of the appalling sufferings of earlier times. He does this in a way that transforms misery into beauty without becoming sentimental ... ' (Els van der Plas, 'António Ole', *19th World Wide Video Festival*, Amsterdam: Stichting World Wide Video Festival, p. 218) Photo courtesy of the artist

Contributing Authors

Ahmed Abdalla (1950, Cairo, Egypt) is a political scientist who received his PhD from Cambridge University in 1984. His main interests are in the field of human rights, child labour, democracy and freedom of expression. Among his publications in English are 'The Egyptian National Identity and Pan-Arabism', published in *Cosmopolitanism, Identity and Authenticity in the Middle East* (1999); 'Egypt's Islamists and the State', in *Middle East Report* (July-August 1993); and 'Human Rights and Elusive Democracy in the Middle East', in *Middle East Report* (January 1992).

Ahmed Al-Mukarram (Sudan) previously worked as a journalist for the *Al-Khartoum* newspaper in Cairo. He was an active member of the exiled Sudanese community in that city until he moved back to Khartoum in 2001, where he is the director of the Abd Al Ghani Merghani Cultural Centre. He is preparing a bibliography of Sudanese literature in the twentieth century.

Arif Azad (1964, Pakistan; based in the UK) is a researcher and journalist. He is a regular contributor to the *Economic and Political Weekly* in Bombay, India, and he monitors the South Asian region for *Index on Censorship* in London. He was a reporter for the weekly *Viewpoint* and for the daily *Frontier Post* (both Lahore-based; 1989-1992). He is the coordinator of *Aaj Kay Naam* [In the Name of Today], a campaign organisation for social justice, human rights, democracy and freedom of expression in his country of origin. *Aaj Kay Naam* runs a website at www.solidarity.freeserve.co.uk which is devoted to raising awareness about the effects of militarisation on civil society in Pakistan.

Carmen Boullosa (1954, Mexico City) is a poet and a dramatist, and has published nine novels. She is a scholarship holder from the John Simon Guggenheim Foundation, a resident writer of the City of Berlin, a literary laureate of the City of Frankfurt and a recipient of the Xavier Villaurrutie award in Mexico and of the Anna Seghers Award. Since 1994, she has been a member of the *Sistema Nacional de Creadores* [National System for Creativity]. She teaches at Georgetown University in Washington D.C. and at the State University of San Diego in California. She is also a member of the International Parliament of Writers and founder of the Citlaltépetl house, a safe house in Mexico City for dissident writers.

Duong Thu Huong (1947, Thai Binh, Vietnam) is the author of such bestsellers as *Les paradis aveugles* [Paradise of the Blind] (originally published in Vietnamese in 1988), *Au-delà des illusions* [Beyond Illusions] (1985) and *Roman sans titre* [Novel without a Name] (1991). She has also published plays and has produced a documentary entitled *The Sanctuary of Despair* (1986). All of her work displays a clear political and social engagement. Because of her critical analyses and her call for reforms and freedom, she has been subject to censure and imprisonment, but also international recognition and respect.

Richard Eisendorf is the director of Search for Common Ground's Middle East Media Working Group and is the founding editor of the *Bulletin of Regional Cooperation in the Middle East*. He has facilitated and participated in numerous international meetings in Europe and the Middle East, and has monitored elections in both northern Iraq and Cambodia. His publications include: *Vision 2020: Middle Eastern Outlooks on the Future of the Region* (Common Ground Publications, 2000) and 'Media and Peace-building' published in *Palestine-Israel Journal* (Winter 1998-99).

Mohamed Fellag (1950, Azeffoun, Algeria) is a comedian. He studied theatre at the Institute National d'Art Dramatique et Choréographique in Borj el Hiffan, near Algiers. He has worked in Canada, the U.S., France and Algeria. From 1992-1993 he was the director of the Théatre Régional de Bougie (Algeria). He emigrated to France in 1995, where he has continued his career as a performer. His theatre shows include 'Les fils de l'Amertume' (1996) and 'Djurdjurassique Bled' (1996 in Arabic and Kabyle; 1997-1999 in French).

Laura Graziela Gomes (1951, Rio de Janeiro) earned a bachelor degree in Social Sciences at Universidade Federal Fluminense, an MA in Social Anthropology at Museu Nacional/Universidade Federal do Rio de Janeiro and a doctorate in Social Anthropology at Universidade de São Paulo. Presently, she teaches social anthropology in the Department of Anthropology at Universidade Federal Fluminense in Niterói. She is also a Conselho Nacional de Pesquisa researcher specialising in cultural studies, urban anthropology, anthropology of consumption and visual anthropology.

Malu Halasa (Norman, Oklahoma, U.S.) is the daughter of Arab and Filipino immigrants. She is the features editor of *Tank*, a visually-led bimonthly, and of *Mined*, a biannual of new ideas. Both publications are published in London. She has written for the *Guardian, Index on Censorship, New Statesman, The Sunday Times* and *Rolling Stone.* She recently started www.fidela.com, an independent record label in the UK.

Ernesto Ortiz Hernández (1969, Pinar del Río, Cuba) is a physicist (University of Havana), a poet and a writer. He is an editor of *Vitral* magazine and director of the literary magazine *deLiras* published by Ediciones Vitral (Pinar del Río). He has had several articles published in magazines such as *Extramuros* (Spain) and *Cauce* (Cuba). His collections of poetry include *Noche Interior Noche Ciudad* (1998), *Fragmentos del Ojo* (1998) and *Obelisco del Hereje* (1996). In 1999, he published an anthology of Cuban poetry from 1980 to 1998.

Kiran Karnik (India) recently retired as the managing director of Discovery Communications in India, a post he held since 1995. He was involved in the India-U.S. Satellite Instructional TV Experiment (1975-1976), the first-ever large-scale use of satellite direct-broadcasting to take education and development to remote rural areas in India through TV programmes – a project that was awarded the first UNESCO-IPDC Prize for Rural Communication. Karnik has worked with the UN as special assistant to the Secretary General of UNISPACE 82, and has consulted on communications planning for UNESCO in Afghanistan. He has also consulted for the WHO, the World Bank and the Ford Foundation. An expert for a study conducted by the UN Institute for Disarmament Research on Dual-Use Space Systems, he has been involved with a number of educational institutions in the areas of environment and science popularisation.

Edmundo Paz-Soldán (Colombia) is a novelist and an assistant professor of Hispanic Literatures at the Department of Romance Studies, Cornell University, in Ithaca, New York. He has co-edited a volume on the relationship between Latin American literature and mass media (Garland, 2000). His other research interests include contemporary Latin American narrative and Andean literature. He has also published four novels and three volumes of short-stories. He won the prestigious Juan Rulfo Award for the short story in Paris in 1997. His novel *Río fugitivo* has been translated into Danish and Finnish.

Exhibition: *Zhongguo Xiandai Yishu Dazhan*, PRC, 1989

In February 1989, the first nationwide avant-garde exhibition *Zhongguo Xiandai Yishu Dazhan* [China Avant-garde] was held in the National Art Gallery in Beijing. Curated by a group of critics including Gao Minglu, Li Xianting, Zhou Yan, Fei Dawei, Kong Chang'an and Hou Hanru, among others, it was at once a retrospective of the last decade of the Chinese avant-garde movement as well as its manifestation.

Signs for the exhibition outside the National Art Gallery

>>

Exhibition: *Zhongguo Xiandai Yishu Dazhan*, PRC, 1989
Xu Bin, installation

More than 300 works by over 200 artists from different parts of the country were exhibited in four sections ranging from conceptual experiments, searching for new humanity, re-exploration of traditional languages and 'pure linguistic experiments'. It provided the first spectacular and vital space for China's contemporary artists to express their innovative ideas and practices in an art establishment. It was also a challenging experience for the public.

>>

Jens Robinson (1961, U.S.) is vice-president and editor of the Cartoonists & Writers Syndicate (CWS), which syndicates, exhibits and publishes the work of over 550 leading cartoonists from over 50 countries. He developed the Cartoon Archive, the CWS cartoon and graphics database which serves the print and electronic media with cartoons, caricatures and graphics on thousands of topics. He has coordinated the weekly selection of cartoons and graphics in CWS, internationally-syndicated features, created the series of focused features by region and subject and also developed the CWS' online presence, the Cartoon Web at www.cartoonweb.com. CWS exhibitions and publications have been co-produced by the UN, the U.S. Information Agency, the Freedom Forum and Amnesty International.

Albie Sachs (1935, Johannesburg, South Africa) is a justice at the South African Constitutional Court. He was professor of law at the Eduardo Mondlane University in Maputo, Mozambique (from 1977), at Columbia University in New York City (from 1989), and at the Universities of the Western Cape (1992) and of Cape Town in South Africa. He took an active part in the negotiations for a new constitution as a member of the Constitutional Committee of the ANC and of the ANC National Executive. He has written extensively on human rights, culture, gender rights and the environment. Among his publications are: *The Jail Diary of Albie Sachs* (1966) and *The Soft Vengeance of a Freedom Fighter* (1990).

Wole Soyinka (1934, Abeokuta, Nigeria) took his doctorate at the University of Leeds in the UK, in 1973. He worked as a dramaturgist in the UK and was a professor of drama and of literature at the universities of Lagos and Ife, Nigeria. During the civil war in his country he appealed for ceasefire. As a result, he was arrested and imprisoned for 22 months and released in 1969. He has published over twenty works: novels, poetry and drama. His novel *Season of Anomy* (1973) is based on his thoughts during his imprisonment. Purely autobiographical are *The Man Died: Prison Notes* (1972) and the account of his childhood *Aké* (1981). In 1986, Soyinka was awarded the Nobel Prize for Literature.

Els van der Plas (1960, Netherlands) is the director of the Prince Claus Fund. An art historian, art critic and curator, she was the founder and director (1987-1997) of the Gate Foundation in Amsterdam, an organisation for the intercultural exchange of contemporary art. She co-edited *The Art of African Fashion,* published by the Prince Claus Fund. She writes for several magazines and lectures at different universities worldwide. She curated, among others, the following shows, *Het Klimaat* (Netherlands, 1991), *Indonesian Modern Art* (Indonesia / Netherlands, 1993), *Orientation* (Indonesia / Netherlands, 1996) and *Secrets* (Netherlands, 1996).

Marlous Willemsen (1969, Netherlands) is a policy officer for the Prince Claus Fund. She studied Arabic language and culture at Utrecht University (1988-1994), and Islamic art at Otto Friedrich University in Bamberg, Germany (1991-1992). She is a member of the board of the Centre of Islamic Art and Culture, Rotterdam, which she managed (1994-1997) before joining the Prince Claus Fund in 1997. In this centre she ran partnerships with cultural organisations in the Middle East and North Africa and set up intellectual projects in the Netherlands.

Acknowledgements

Turaj Atabaki, Assistant Professor of Persian, Utrecht University, the Netherlands
Geert A. Banck, CEDLA, Amsterdam, the Netherlands
Mohammed Bennouna, Justice, ICTY, The Hague, the Netherlands
Djamel Benramdane, editor, Algeria Interface, Paris, France Gene Bird, INIVA, London, UK
Geraldo Casé, Globo TV, Rio de Janeiro, Brazil
Al Creighton, literary critic, Kingston, Jamaica
Roberto A. DaMatta, University of Notre Dame, Brazil / U.S.
Jeroen de Kloet, Sinologist, Amsterdam, the Netherlands
Mieke de Vos, Amsterdam, the Netherlands
Wieland Eggermont, RASA, Utrecht, the Netherlands
Basma El Husseiny, Ford Foundation, Cairo, Egypt
Farhad Golyardi, De Balie, Amsterdam, the Netherlands
Ni Haifeng, artist, Amsterdam, the Netherlands
Mohamed Handaine, historian, Universìté d'Eté, Agadir, Morocco
Hou Hanru, art critic, Paris, France
Salah Hassan, Africana Studies Center, Cornell University, Ithaca, U.S.
Jay Hess, designer, London, UK
Ineke Holtwijk, correspondent for *De Volkskrant* in Brazil
Joke Huurman, Nederlands Comité Nederland-Vietnam, Amsterdam, the Netherlands
Rohan Jayasekera, web editor, *Index on Censorship*, London, UK
William Kentridge, artist, Johannesburg, South Africa
Jeannette Kruseman, NCRV, Hilversum, the Netherlands
Jennifer Law, anthropologist and critic, London, UK
Khaled Mahrez, IFJ Algerie, Algeria
Nalini Malani, artist, India
Anne McIlleron, William Kentridge's office, Johannesburg, South Africa
Mohamed Mehdi, journalist, *Libre Algérie*, Algeria
Anja Meulenbelt, writer, Amsterdam, the Netherlands
Erena and Gerardo Mosquera, Havana, Cuba
Joost Nijssen, Podium Editors, Amsterdam, the Netherlands
Niyi Osundare, author, University of New Orleans, U.S.
Tahar Ouattar, *Al-Jahidhiya*, Algiers, Algeria
Ursula Owen, editor-in-chief, *Index on Censorship*, London, UK
Gordan Paunovic, New Media Editor, FreeB92
Pim Petersen, World Wide Video Festival, Amsterdam, the Netherlands
Flavio Pons, artist, Amsterdam, the Netherlands
Ashish Rajadhyaksha, film critic, India
Lazhari Rihani, *Al-Jahidhiya*, Algiers, Algeria
Claire Robertson, photographer, London, UK
Hazim Saghie, journalist and Currents editor, *Al-Hayat*, London, UK
Harry Stroomer, Leiden University, the Netherlands
Ravi Sundaram, New Delhi, India
Maghiel van Crevel, Sinologist, Leiden University, the Netherlands
Dominique van der Elst, University of Amsterdam, the Netherlands
Tom van Vliet, director, World Wide Video Festival, Amsterdam, the Netherlands
Julius Vermeulen, Amsterdam, the Netherlands
Judith Vidal-Hall, editor, *Index on Censorship*, London, UK
Sandra Werneck, filmmaker, Rio de Janeiro, Brazil
Li Xianting, art critic, Beijing, PRC

Exhibition: *Zhongguo Xiandai Yishu Dazhan*, PRC, 1989
Wei Guanqing, performance

The first exhibition of its kind, it immediately became 'explosive' national and international news, especially when some events were turned into 'outrageous scandals'. Wang Deren handed out condoms in the gallery, Wu Shanzhuan sold fresh seafood, Li Shan washed people's feet, Zheng Nian bred eggs, to name a few events.

>>

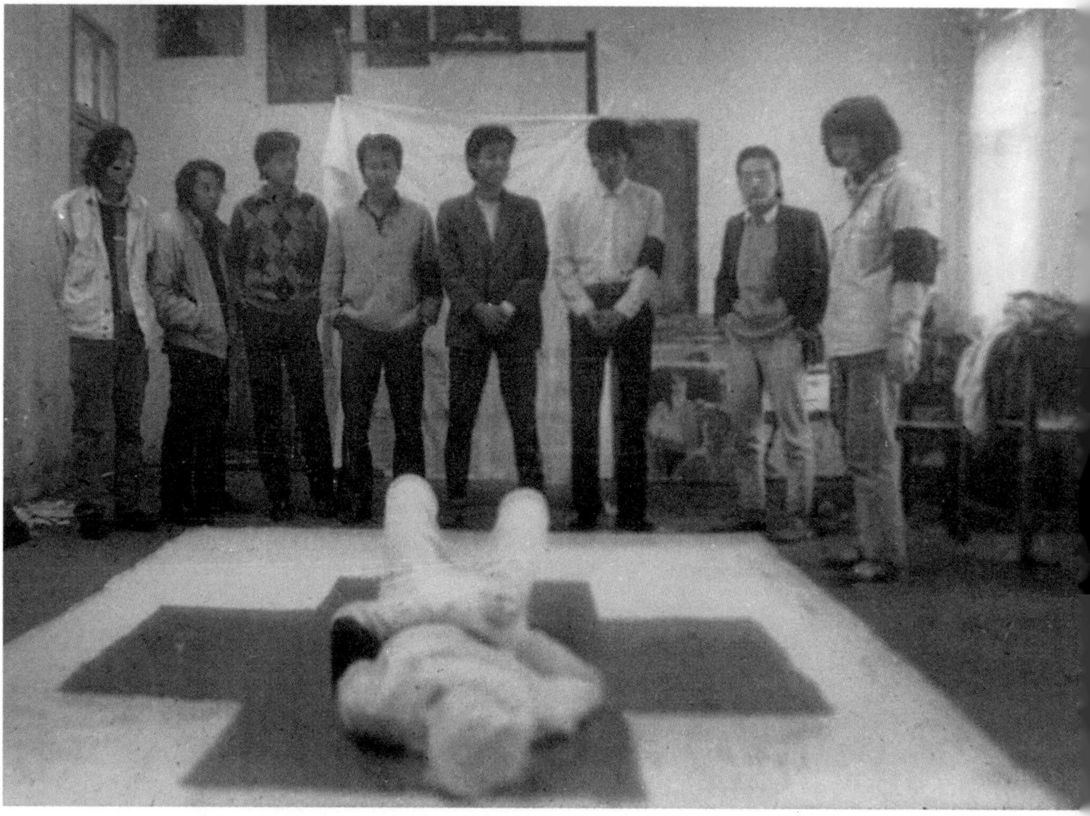

Exhibition: ***Zhongguo Xiandai Yishu Dazhan*****, PRC, 1989**
Huang Yong Ping, performance

The most aggressive and spectacular performance was that of Xiao Lu and Tang Song, who fired shots at Xiao Lu's installation *Dialogue*, and consequently, were arrested. Being the children of high officials and having used an army officer's pistol, they were soon released. Their art happening was reviewed by some critics, such as Li Xianting, as a test of the tolerance and limitations of the Chinese legal system. Others even considered it a presage of the democratic movement of the coming spring. The 1989 China Avant-garde exhibition is a historic milestone. It has not only presented a panorama of the first decade of contemporary art experiments in China but also predicted a much more diverse development of Chinese art in the coming decade. (Hou Hanru) Photos courtesy of the Gate Foundation, Amsterdam